Dear Dave + Kell

You came from hardwo
give up heritage ... an
+ dad tell me business ownny
is your dream. Go for it.

PEACE
by
Piece

Kathi Hyde

PEACE
by
Piece

A Practical Guide to Stepping Up or Starting Over in Business and in Life

Kathi Hyde

Published by Quickfox Publishing
on behalf of Building Best Business
PO Box 50660, West Beach, 7449
Cape Town, South Africa
www.quickfox.co.za | info@quickfox.co.za

PEACE by Piece: A Practical Guide to Stepping Up or Starting Over in Business and in Life
ISBN Print: 978-0-639-73133-9
ISBN Kindle: 978-0-639-73134-6
ISBN ePub: 978-0-639-73135-3
ISBN Audiobook: 978-0-639-73136-0

First edition 2023

Disclaimer: Some names have been changed to protect the privacy of those depicted.

And to those who have done life with me and made this possible …

My Bookends in Life – Mum and Bryony Clarke
My Big Hand of God – ably assisted by Rob Steiner
My Besties – Ali Beere and Les Kriel
My Bloke – Neil Hyde
My Biz Coach – Michael Cody
And Small Business Owners – all of you, everywhere.

Table of Contents

Introduction

I stood there numbly in my mum's garage, like a shell-shocked soldier unable to get to grips with what was happening to me. This was not the script I'd chosen for my life. My little daughter was saying something, but I couldn't respond. I was struggling to simply breathe. I'd just carried the last box from the removal van and dropped it with the rest of my worldly belongings in my mum's garage. For weeks I'd been getting stuff done, packing, organising the move and then, standing there looking at those boxes, all I could do was ask myself how, how, how had I got here? This was not how it was supposed to be. This was not how it was meant to work out!

And yet there I was … forty-one years old, moving back into my mum's house with my six-year-old daughter. My marriage was over. I had no job and no money. I felt like a total failure. Surely, I should have had my sh*t together by now!

But life doesn't always go according to plan, does it?

I was born and grew up in Zimbabwe when it was still called Rhodesia. My dad was an expat from Northern England who came to Africa with the RAF. He met my mum at a 'drinks do' when she was on a working adventure from South Africa. When I think of my childhood, it's sky blue. The weather was beautiful, my parents, brother and I lived in middle-class suburbia. There was so much open space, and we were happy. It was a great life … until it wasn't.

Things changed when I was 15 years old. I arrived home from school one day and as soon as I approached the house, I felt like I'd hit an invisible wall. I was literally stopped in my tracks, and I knew something was wrong. I walked into the house, and I could see that dad had been crying. Turns out he'd been diagnosed with cancer, and we all had to pack up and leave Zimbabwe to go to South Africa so that he could get treatment.

That was my first experience of upheaval, but it wouldn't be my last.

In what felt like a whirlwind of a few short days, with just what we could fit into the combi, we set off with our bags on the long, sad drive south. And I hated it. I hated that dad was ill, I hated leaving my school, my friends and my boyfriend. Plus, when we got to this new country I immediately felt like an outsider. And to make everything 100 times worse, Dad died just a few months later – he was only 58 years old.

He'd been my hero, an airforce captain with two great loves – flying and his family. He'd always been the strong, thorough, uniformed, impressive and present father. He was always 'there' and then suddenly he wasn't. I'd watched him fade away as cancer took hold and while people would say things like, "At least you could be prepared"; one never is.

Until you've been through it yourself, you just can't fully appreciate how life as you know it disintegrates when someone you love becomes terminally ill. This journey to certain death for one person is a seismic dislocation that cuts everyone else around them off at the knees. For me, it also brought a deep-seated anger at the injustice, prematurity and finality of it all. I was broken by the grief and unspeakable unfairness of all the combined losses piling up for me at a time when other teens were enjoying life, worrying about spots on their faces and what to wear for their school-leaving dance. That's a lot to process at 16 years old.

What followed was hard. We stayed in South Africa because Mum had family there and moved into a small house that felt like it was at the wrong end of town. Mum worked two jobs to support us. My brother did the garden and DIY, while I was the self-appointed 'cook and bottlewasher'. Life as a teenager certainly wasn't what I'd hoped it would be. Plus, we were all trying to wrestle with our grief in our own way. I'd always planned on going to university, but now it felt more important than ever. In Zimbabwe, I'd been on track for a good school result, but in South Africa I needed to pass 'Immigrant Afrikaans' to get my school-leaving certificate, otherwise there'd be no university for me. Luckily, I have a good memory, so I was able to scrape through. But inside, I was miserable, and in that misery, I comforted myself with food. The new school only added to my feelings of disconnection, as I struggled to make any true friends, which wasn't helped by being the sad, chubby girl. So, when it came time to choose my university, I decided to go to whatever university no one else from my school was going to. I think even then I'd been hoping for a fresh start.

What followed were some fun times, but mainly a series of adventures and experiences where I found myself in the wrong place with the wrong people doing the wrong thing – nothing bad or criminal, I just didn't feel like I really belonged. Everywhere I went I felt like a fish out of water, wanting to but never quite fitting in. I did however graduate with an Industrial Psychology Masters. By the time I was 28, I'd had some solid work experience behind me, I'd had a mixture of great and unpleasant experiences, and I'd managed to make some decent money. I'd also managed to take a few more significant wrong turns in life. I just couldn't find my place. My solution: I decided to travel. No one belongs anywhere when they're travelling – that's the whole point! And although I had some means, I wasn't rolling in cash, so I decided to travel on the cheap by backpacking. Once again, I packed the bare minimum, this time into a rucksack, and off I went. Over the next few years, I travelled by myself right across Africa. I started in Cape Town and travelled up through Zimbabwe, Zambia, Malawi, Mozambique, Kenya, Uganda, Tanzania, Ethiopia, the DRC and the Republic of Congo. I loved travelling. I loved the freedom. I loved meeting new people and the magic and synchronicity that springs up on the open road. I can't tell you how many awesome, funny, wonderful experiences I had, all the incredible people I met, the gorgeous places I visited and the many times where I felt truly guided or supported by some invisible force. I came to call that invisible force God and, over time, that relationship has become settled, sweet and secure.

But I had shrugged off His influence in my youth. I was too busy living the adventure. Once I'd ticked off most of the eastern side of Africa, I swapped continents and started travelling through Europe. This time, I started in Istanbul and travelled through Germany, Spain, Austria, France, UK, the Netherlands, Belgium, Monaco, Italy, Greece, Cyprus, Portugal, Turkey and the Czech Republic. Packing only what I needed, each new place was a fabulous new start. I got very good at new starts. When I finally stopped, I went back to Uganda to be with a man I'd met while travelling

14

and for many years we were really happy together. We got married, had our daughter and life was good … until it wasn't.

When my marriage ended, I also lost most of my friendships and my home too, which made it especially difficult and lonely. I found out that pretty much everyone in our social circle was using and/or was okay with recreational drugs. Right from the start I'd been very vocal and clear about being anti-drugs so, apparently, when parties had been thrown there had been an unspoken 'rule' of waiting for me to go to bed so that the 'real party' could start. I felt completely betrayed, especially as I'd explained to everyone before my then-husband and I had even got together, that drug-taking was a red line for me. I thought I'd been heard and that everyone had understood and respected my heartfelt beliefs. But I was wrong. I'd seen what I wanted to see and heard what I'd hoped to hear – as one does in the honeymoon stage of anything. And in this, I'd done both of us a disservice.

When I found out the truth, I was shellshocked. I also felt naïve and more than a little stupid. I'm a smart woman – how could I not have seen that? It did, however, help to explain much of what had confused and upset me for years. If I'd known the truth earlier, I certainly could have saved myself much futile introspection, self-criticism and personal second-guessing. But I was still appalled that much of what I had been living was based on what was, to me, such a central lie. I wanted to curl up into a ball and die.

Don't get me wrong. Everyone is entitled to live their life as they see fit, but I didn't want that life and had been very honest about that right up front. And I knew I certainly did not want to raise our daughter in an environment in which drugs were considered acceptable. As a psychologist I'd seen their toxic impact on lives, had spent years counselling against their use and was an outspoken evangelist for abstinence.

And yet there I was, unheard, divorced, homeless, jobless, friendless and pretty broke, back with my mum. As I stood looking at those boxes, I couldn't believe I was going to have to start again – AGAIN! Only it was a lot scarier this time. My soon-to-be ex hadn't been able to get new work in East Africa. He'd had to start his 'own thing' and we'd had to rely on my expat contract, so to add insult to injury, the split left me with a precarious future indeed, financially. As a result, I needed to get back on my feet and this time I had an innocent little human being who needed me, and it changed everything. I had become very good at packing up and making fresh starts, but now it wasn't just me. Now I had the responsibility of a daughter, and I was absolutely determined that she would not pay the price for our divorce.

So, I made a pact with myself. I would do whatever it took to launch my daughter into her own life. I would do whatever it took to make sure she had the best education so that she could forge her own path. I would choose a new career that would gift me with the time and the resources to be the best mum I could be. And I absolutely would not be the crazy cat lady in an emerald-green velvet shawl (an image that had stayed with me from a horrible documentary I'd seen about pensioners living below the breadline) living with her mum and eating cat food because it was cheap and nutritionally balanced. No. Absolutely not. I had no idea *how* or *what* or *where*, but I had my *why*.

I was a single mum now, so I had to find a way to make money that didn't involve me getting a 9-to-5 job. I needed flexibility so that I could take care of my daughter. And that's exactly what I did. It didn't happen overnight and there were twists and turns and umpteen setbacks, but I started my own business as a business coach, and I became my own first client. Everything you will read in this book, I have done myself and used to create my own business and help thousands of clients create, build, scale or rescue theirs.

Today, I am an international business growth expert, providing industrial psychology and business know-how to businesses – large and small. I've built an extremely profitable, lucrative business and investment portfolio that can fund my life, including four houses – all from a business run out of my home between 9:30 am and 3:30 pm because the rest of the time I needed to be a mum. My daughter was able to attend private school and she graduated from university in 2022. I work with clients in various parts of the world, and I currently live in the UK. I've won loads of coaching awards and been a consistent high performer in the industry because I get results. And I get results because I know that everything I teach works – because it's what got me to where I am now.

Bottom line: everyone's life is a sh*tshow from time to time. There is no insulator from the challenging cards we get dealt and have to live with. These periods of turmoil are unavoidable, and they happen to everyone regardless of gender, ethnicity, background, wealth, position, education or geography. No one is immune. If we are lucky, the wheels will fall off only a couple of times in our lifetime. For most of us, we will experience significant upheaval and heartache more than once – possibly several times. That upheaval may be caused by the end of a marriage, an unexpected redundancy, money problems, runaway business growth, inheriting a windfall, health problems or something else. It's life. It happens.

The only thing that matters is what we do about it.

Time for Action

This book is a kick-start guide for when you know in your heart that the life you are living is not the life you want, need or deserve and you have 'crossed the Rubicon', at more than just an emotional level. The phrase comes from when Julius Caesar crossed the Rubicon River in 49BC. The river was the border between Cisalpine Gaul and Italy and armies led by generals were forbidden by law to traverse it. When Caesar crossed it, he is said to have uttered the phrase *alea iacta est* – the die is cast. Meaning, he knew he was passing a point of no return.

In life, we all face such moments – a last straw that makes the current reality untenable. A situation where we flip from enduring things as they are to a settled sense that seismic change for the better is needed in our business and/or life. A left turn made where we are suddenly resolute that we must exchange a dead-end job or a failed relationship or success that's costing us too much personally or causing poor health, for something better. Something clicks inside us, and we know that the situation has gone beyond talk and intention. The die is cast.

For this book to work, you must have crossed your own Rubicon and got to the point of being prepared to do whatever it's going to take to carve out something different, something better. And something better almost always needs to be funded. The temptation is to immediately focus on how to fund that new life, but there is work to be done before we even consider that question.

The first part of this book is therefore an honest and pragmatic review of YOU so that you can get to the start line. You are your greatest asset. You are the only person you really have dominion over. Everything starts with you.

My work is about change. Most people who hire a business coach are looking for help to change something about their business, or to grow it, or they are looking to create a business to fund a new life. And yet without fail, there is always another root consideration to the reality they are facing – good or bad. This root is usually a flashing neon sign that they've chosen to ignore and have done so for years.

We naively think that our business or work life is separate from our home life, or that our health or finances are separate from our relationship with our family. It's almost as if we have convinced ourselves that the various roles and parts of our life sit in neat little boxes that never come into contact with one another. But, reality check time: we don't live our life in silos.

You must get this: EVERY aspect of your life is intimately interwoven with all the other aspects.

This means that before we can even think of attempting any type of change on a business front, we need to get our own personal house in order.

> **We don't live our life in silos – EVERY aspect is intimately interwoven with all the other aspects.**

Sorry – that may not be what you were hoping for, but it's the inescapable truth. We are always 'ground zero' for our greatest victories and our troubles and disasters. We may not be able to take all the credit or be to blame, but we are always responsible.

That means that before we can change anything 'out there', we have to have a very honest and robust look at what's 'in here'. If we don't commit to a rigorous self-assessment, then none of the external change will hold any sway because we will just find new and novel ways to self-sabotage and revert to old, automated patterns that will render our change temporary.

This book is called *PEACE by Piece* because when life deals us a poor hand, or we become swamped by the daily stresses of our lives, we have to first find some measure of peace in the chaos. We need to take stock of our role in that chaos and then rebuild our life a little piece at a time. PEACE in this context is an acronym covering the important considerations that we need to address to get us to the start line. When covered and considered fully, PEACE then supports successful change.

- **P = Purpose** – What is your 'why' that's going to sustain you as you rebuild or recalibrate your life?
- **E = Energy** – How are you going to access the resources or fuel you will need?
- **A = Aspirations** – When all is said and done, what is it you really want to have, own, create; what is 'success' for you?
- **C = Connection** – Who is in your network that can help you achieve your aspirations and support you in your endeavours, and what personal wells do you need to dig?
- **E = Environment** – Where are you going and where do you 'need' to be, clearly defined and publically stated so that no one (including you) is confused or unclear?

Part One can be tough, because it demands clear-headed objectivity and facing some hard truths. Do your best to park your emotions. Emotions matter, but facts – usually brutal ones that you've been trying to ignore – are the key to your liberation. Emotions are a bit like children – they're awesome to have around, but don't put them in charge!

Part Two is all about creating a livelihood. A business can be a great vehicle for the life you want to live, but you need to engage with business from a position of reality and readiness. That's why Part One is so important – it gives you the clarity to reassess your current personal position in relation to your business aspirations.

When we are desperate or stressed or damaged in some way, it's virtually impossible to create anything new or successful. First, we need to heal a little, or find some measure of closure or peace around the situation we find ourselves in. Only then can we create the right vehicle. We are then strong enough to take on the challenge and work hard for what we want without having our 'issues' pull us off course.

This process also gives us much needed perspective. One of the most important lessons I've learned on my journey is that while business can be exciting, compelling and consuming, it is just and should never be more than a vehicle to life. Money is not the prize or the thing we must endlessly chase; it's just what makes the wheels of life turn. It is very hard to have a good life without enough money – period. We don't need buckets of the stuff, but we need enough for whatever type of life we have decided we want to live. And a business is a brilliant way to create that money – on your terms.

So, let's get started.

PART ONE

Getting YOU to the Start Line

CHAPTER 1

P = Purpose

> "The two most important days in your life are the day you are born and the day you find out why."
>
> – Mark Twain

Purpose may sound a little lofty, especially if we are up to our neck in crisis or overly busy, but that's exactly when we need it most. Purpose is a big part of the content of our True North, and it doesn't have to be a bumper sticker or motivational poster that speaks of world peace or curing cancer. It's usually much more powerful when it's personal, simple and meaningful to us.

Perhaps your purpose is to pay next month's mortgage or making sure your kids are okay through the change. I worked with a bloke once who overheard his father-in-law say that his daughter 'could have done better'. His purpose suddenly became crystal clear – he wanted to be successful enough to buy a BMW Seven Series so that he could drive past his father-in-law's house and quietly give him the middle finger – out of view of course. It may sound petty, but his determination to prove his father-in-law wrong was enough to bring out his 'inner cheetah'. Every time things got tough, he thought about that comment, and it spurred him into action. And it worked.

Ultimately, purpose is about finding something that excites our passions, where we can make a contribution to something or someone we value or believe in while using our skills and strengths.

Although there are many ways to help us find our purpose, it is incredibly easy to get lost in the self-help labyrinth. So much so that we can get stuck in inertia or indecision about what's the best way to discover our purpose. So, let's focus on practical, workable to-dos that ordinary people like you and I can use without necessarily having any special talent, money or resources. Certainly, when I was in the middle of my crisis, I wanted simple, practical uncomplicated ways to get back on track. I was still having to eat on a budget, bring up my child and engage with other people while I was feeling like a bit of a failure, so 'doable' was essential. Here are some simple to-dos that worked for me and have universally worked for my clients:

- Resolve your Spirituality
- Find your Why 101
- Explore your Beliefs.

Resolve Your Spirituality

Sometimes life gets too big for us, and we're faced with a struggle that makes us question our ability to cope. In those moments, it's more than physical, mental or emotional. It becomes spiritual – a matter for the soul. This spiritual work doesn't necessarily mean resolving a relationship with God, although it did for me and many I have worked with. I am also acutely aware that God may be called by different names in different cultures and that sometimes people are referring to some type of Universal Force. I don't want to get hung up here on terminology, or get into a debate on whether there is a God or which God is the 'right' God, but rather to say that human beings are made up of mind, body and soul. We all have a soul, even if we choose to ignore it. And making peace with our soul, especially after a life-shattering experience, usually involves an internal wrestle where we reach out or up to someone or something bigger than ourselves. When we do, we can often find a place to ask the hard questions, live through our rage or despair and find a measure of inner peace amongst the hard, big, personal stuff we may be facing. Help from an expert may also have its place here.

My experience, irrespective of culture, has been that purpose is found in the realm of the soul. Deep-seated values and beliefs that we live or die by, also seem to reside in this soul-space. So, when we experience change and upheaval that pull the rug from under us, part of learning to cope is by making peace with hard, not-always-answered whys and becoming able to live with that which remains in our hearts and souls. There are very deep, personal waters that we have to navigate when faced with questions like:

- Whose hand can we hold when the hands we normally hold are no longer there?
- Who or what can help us make sense of the big life questions that have no easy answers so that we can find a reason to keep going through the chaos?
- How do we forgive the seemingly unforgivable?

These and even harder questions are sometimes in our path and finding some level of acceptance of them is part of what we have to do when connecting with our spirituality.

I remember meeting Maddie (not her real name) at church. She was such a wonderful, warm, open woman. As I got to know her, I discovered that she was the daughter of a minister and, up until the age of 19, her father had raped her regularly. I remember my stunned disbelief as she told me this. And the disbelief was twofold. First, how could anyone have had to deal with, let alone recover from, that? And second, I couldn't square her past with who she was in the present. It seemed utterly unbelievable to me that she could have gone on, never mind forgiven her father, and become the happy and contented human being she was. She'd even invited her father to her wedding, and he'd walked her down the aisle.

Now that's 'next level' forgiveness!

And I'm certainly not saying you should aim for such lofty heights, but Maddie not only survived her trauma, she went on to thrive because she was able to resolve in her soul what she still believed to be true about herself and her world and find something – in her case, someone – bigger to hold on to in her protracted storm.

What Maddie discovered was one of the greatest powers given to us as human beings – the power to decide what things mean to us.

Picture me on stage. I hold up a glass coffee mug, and I ask the room how many people feel deeply emotionally attached to this coffee mug. Obviously, no one does. Then I say, "If I dropped and broke this mug, you might think I'm all thumbs and a bit haphazard, but you wouldn't be emotionally devastated." At this point, everyone can agree. Then I say, "But what if this mug belonged to your mum or dad, and they used to drink their coffee from this mug every day of your life growing up. On their deathbed, they gave you this mug and said, "Whenever you drink from this mug, know that I am smiling down on you from Heaven," and then I grab it and smash it on the ground. How many would be crushed by this situation? Almost everyone can agree that we all would. What's the difference? It's the same mug. The same molecules, the same glass, but now you've decided that it means something.

> One of the greatest powers given to us is the power to decide what things mean to us.

Maddie took control of what things meant to her and defined them in such an empowering way that she was even able to restore her father to an honour no one in their right mind would think to ask of her. She was able to do it because she wasn't serving her history; her history was serving her. When she redefined what it meant in a way that empowered her life, she moved from being victimised to being empowered. This is a critical concept to overcoming or rebuilding anything in business or in life and, in most cases, it is a matter of the intersect between choosing to rethink, determining to do things differently, and then engaging in some deeply personal soul work.

To me this soul work embraces connecting with something bigger, because the issues at play are often 'beyond us'. I call that something bigger, God. But you may call it Fate or the Universe or God by some other name. But this essential soul work needs to culminate in you finding your centre and identity – who you are in relation to something or someone bigger. It needs to help you connect with a hope and purpose that's not derailed by life's crap.

This soul work has to enable you to find and collate your values and your 'forever trues' so that you can be clear on what you stand for, what matters to you and what you will be willing to do to get through whatever challenges you currently face. And this is much more easily said than done if you've had your trust betrayed or a huge and sudden loss to process. These mega things in life cause us to question our very existence and the fairness of the universe. Restoring an internal measure of peace when you've just buried your child or are now confined to a wheelchair or been the last to know your spouse was cheating on you, is about finding some sort of resolution to unanswerable whys. And it is possible.

My unanswerable why was how could God have taken my dad when we needed him so badly? I was only 16. And probably the most helpful commentary was from a little, elderly, Roman Catholic priest who reminded me that we mourn the life we roll out for our loved one, which is not necessarily the life that was theirs to live. Our version of their life in our mind's eye is always filled with the sweet anniversaries and occasions that would have marked the way most gloriously – making a wonderful speech at my 21st, walking me down the aisle as a proud dad or clapping at my graduation in the weird, loud way he had. But what if my dad's life included bitter unknowns – depression at being laid off from flying due to a market downturn when he turned 60 or an accident that paralysed him at 59? Here I was mourning the loss of an idea or vision – which, don't get me wrong, is not nothing. But that priest gave me pause and allowed me to move to acceptance that the timing I was resenting may well have had an importance beyond what I was able and willing to grasp or appreciate and I could choose, in faith, to allow this new appreciation to refine my sense of loss. I could choose to believe that the timing, while challenging for me, was best for dad because it circumvented something in his life that my 'puppies, candies and unicorns' version could not know and chose to ignore.

> Restoring an internal measure of peace is about finding resolution to unanswerable whys.

This soul work is about ensuring we have the resources and coping skills we need so that we don't have to endure an empty echo to the question, "How, in God's name, could this have happened?" It's about finding narratives, personal examples, tools, meditational realities and inspiration to make sense of the impossible and still re-believe in hope, happiness, a future and a purpose when something essential and core has been stripped away irrevocably.

This soul work also has to be about finding a safe place where you can call for help. A place that allows you to recreate real and resilient meaning, to pick yourself up and to try again. A settled sense that even amongst the chaos, something bigger matters; you matter. A place where you can find a way to go on, in spite of what may remain.

It's how clients have coped with death, divorce, betrayal, financial ruin, broken promises, partnerships that went belly up, families who let them down, civil war, breathtaking loss, abuse, unfairness of the highest order and legal crap. It's how Maddie moved on, past unforgiveness to a restored relationship and a sweet rather than bitter life. That's spirituality, for me and for those I coach.

Done well, resolving our spirituality is about reconnecting 'inside' and allowing this to recalibrate what we hold on to as truth about ourselves despite what's going on around us. And this is foundational to us finding a higher purpose that can shift our mindset and support us as we move through the challenges we face.

Now, not everyone relates to the idea of spirituality and the soul easily because they think it automatically means God. And not everyone is comfortable with God. Personally, I have a warm and nurturing relationship with Him and have found Him to be hugely comforting in my darkest moments. And while I know this is not true for everyone, I have found, as a psychologist, that everyone can still find this sense of something bigger and an internal sense of peace that can help make sense of disappointment, hurt and sorrow. It's the solid ground onto which we scramble that doesn't collapse or shift.

Whatever the chosen 'Source', this is what matters because this soul work seems to be the place in which purpose resides. And when a measure of internal peace is found, purpose often emerges. This intersection of having lived through the 'dark night of the soul' and wrestled conclusively; things we find we are still passionate about and care about; things we are able to do because of our circumstances, our skillset and very often all that we have been through; and what we can or may be able to make money from, becomes clearer. Purpose is what calls to us and inspires us to take action.

In his amazing TEDtalk, Jocko Willink, ex US Navy Seal, author and podcaster talks about purpose being linked to a sense of extreme ownership. When a country goes to war, there are never days where the soldier wakes up and thinks, "Oh, I don't feel like it today. I'm tired – get someone else." That never happens – everyone just shows up, willing, ready and prepared for action. Day in, day out. And life can be a bit like that, where we are called to be a warrior on a battlefield for something bigger than ourselves. Instead of resenting the war, we just need the self-discipline to take up our sword and shield every day – regardless of whether we feel like it or not. Our quest awaits – like Frodo in *Lord of the Rings*. Nobody asked Frodo to destroy the ring in the fires of Mordor. But he knew it was his purpose. The task chose him.

Although never quite as spectacular as fighting Orcs, this is how life often unfolds for us. Life happens. There are elements that we love and parts we resent. Parts we don't like and wish we could escape, but we know we can't and probably shouldn't. These are the things that matter because when we look back, they've been the making of us or some form of essential springboard. The only way out is *through*. This is our quest. We have to go through the difficulties and when we do, a new version of ourselves emerges, a little stronger and wiser from the challenge.

> Nobody asked Frodo to destroy the ring in the fires of Mordor – the task chose him.

With this foundational piece in place, you'll have more success at finding your deeper purpose. You'll get a glimpse of who you really are and who you're called to be. And importantly, you'll be more able to tap into your 'why power' which always trumps willpower when it comes to taking self-disciplined action. Determined intention or motivation is never enough. When we access this something bigger, nothing is changed but everything is different. Life may still be hard, but we tap into a more settled sense that it will be okay and we feel that, yes, we CAN.

It's the foundation from which we can then refuse to constantly relive the bad/sad/mad times or argue about them or rail against them or feel sorry for ourselves. By standing on it, we will find ourselves better able to pick up the broken pieces of our life and make a mosaic out of them – something new. We will find it easier to dust ourselves off and, as Israeli-American violinist Itzhak Perlman so beautifully said, "Learn to make music from that which remains."

Find your Why

For me, as I sought a new hand to hold through the chaos, wrestled with and found my peace with God, what became clear to me was that my daughter and helping others were my purpose. I was in a pickle, but I knew I would do whatever it took to ensure that she didn't pay the price for our divorce. And I also knew that there were literally hundreds of thousands of parents just like me, wondering how they were going to restart and get through. Every time I thought of her and others like us, I could feel my inner cheetah stir.

> Life is often about having to "learn to make music from that which remains".

In truth, our purpose evolves as we get more of a handle on the situation we are currently grappling with. So, if you are in crisis then consider what – or more often, who – you are willing to go the extra mile for. As you take charge of your life PEACE by Piece, you may be inspired to reconsider your purpose from a broader, more expansive perspective.

The Four Ingredients of Purpose

The Japanese have a beautiful concept known as 'Ikigai' (pronounced ick-ee-guy), which translates into 'a reason for being'. The model sees the intersection of four critical components in determining purpose:

- What you love
- What the world needs
- What you can be paid for, and
- What you are good at.

The interconnecting circles create territories which display certain characteristics, and right in the centre is your purpose – an optimal mix of all four components (see Figure 1.1)

29

Figure 1.1 *The Four Ingredients of 'Why'*

It's a useful model to consider when thinking about what business to create. If you've already got a business but it's not going well, it can also help to focus in on the things that align with your purpose so you can re-shape that business in a way that reignites your mojo.

For now, just use it as a guide as you consider your purpose. What is going to unleash your inner cheetah? Purpose is crucial, because it gives you a meaningful reason to get into action to solve the current crisis. It's the fuel that drives the effort. It's the fuel that keeps the tank full, even when you feel exhausted. It's different to the energy you get from food; it's the fire that lights up within you and powers you forward to a better life. It's at the heart of what makes you do the hard yards.

The mistake many people make is to jump straight into action. They aren't clear about what their purpose is and have shied away from doing the thinking work because it takes too long or isn't tangible. And instead, they dive headfirst into action mode. It's like the marksman firing the gun because he thinks he'll get a better result faster, instead of taking the time to aim before taking the shot.

This is why purpose, and the rest of Part One for that matter, is so important. It's the 'ready and aim' before firing that creates a solid platform. Without it, the action you take and work so hard at sustaining is unlikely to work, let alone work long-term or well. Any gains are vulnerable to being too easily undone by wallowing in self-pity, rehearsing the wrongs and wasting precious mental and emotional resources on unresolved emotional baggage, inconsistent execution or giving up too quickly.

People who succeed and live meaningful lives know their purpose. They still have to put in the hard work to achieve success and happiness, but the effort has a deeper meaning, which makes it possible to keep going when the going gets tough. You may wonder how some people always seem driven and full of energy while others struggle to stay motivated. But the truth is, nobody is always driven and full of energy. We are all human and we have our good days and bad days. But those who drive forward most of the time are fuelled by a clear purpose – their inner cheetah has locked on to its prey. It is a sustaining force that makes things just that bit easier to do.

Explore your Beliefs

So often when things go badly – a business meltdown, the end of a marriage or financial challenges – people feel trapped. They can't see a way out or through. They are stuck in some sort of self-made prison. As a business coach specialising in make-or-break personal and professional transformation, I can't tell you how often I've watched someone cycle through the Kubler-Ross grief curve (Figure 1.2), often right before my eyes and sometimes in a single session!

This now-famous model by Swiss-American psychiatrist, Elisabeth Kübler-Ross,[1] originally described how people react to a diagnosis of terminal illness, but it is now acknowledged to be the journey many of us travel when experiencing any type of change – especially unwelcome change.

When the sh*t hits the fan, the change is *always* unwelcomed.

First, it's denial. "Look, it's not really that bad; I'm pretty sure it will come right if I just give it a bit more time", followed, often quite swiftly, by anger. "This is just so unfair; why should I have to be the one to change? This is too hard – I'm just not doing it". Once they run out of rage and colourful

When the sh*t hits the fan, the change is always unwelcomed.

expletives, there is a swift and sudden drop into depression. This is when the overwhelm and helplessness emerge. "It's useless, it won't work anyway." With some prompting, they can be nudged into bargaining: "Maybe if I just change this little thing over here, then the big flashing neon issue over there will disappear."

Figure 1.2 *Kübler-Ross Grief Curve*

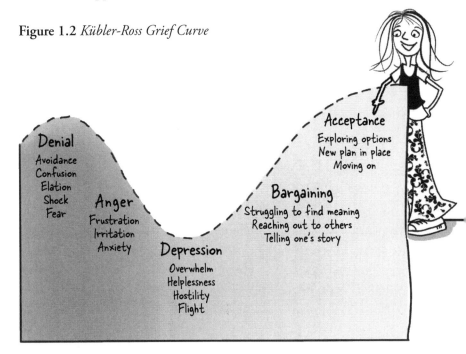

I don't see the point of business coaching if it doesn't create positive change and that calls for some hard truths on occasion. As a truth-teller it's my job to ask the questions, hold up the mirror, underline the price tags, provide the sanity-checks, bust the myths and spell out the things that are 'also true', so they can get out of this denial-anger-depression-bargaining cycle as soon as possible, and over the hump into acceptance and action.

All your justifications for being angry or depressed may be true. But they are not necessarily *the truth*. There are other things that are 'also true'. And together what's true and what's also true make up the truth. It's hard – whatever you are facing. I get it. You don't like or aren't comfortable with it and never have been because it's just 'not you'. Possibly so. It's tough and it's unfair and you may have every right to be angry and depressed, but none of these reactions is terribly helpful, especially if you start dwelling on them or set up camp there.

As we travel through the change curve, we have to purposefully separate what we feel about our situation, and what we've unconsciously made those events or situations mean for us and our future, from the facts about those situations. The two are never the same.

The work of Viktor Frankl and Albert Ellis has been instrumental in our understanding of the ups and downs of life, our creation of 'meaning' and how those meanings then affect us.

During WWII, Austrian psychiatrist and philosopher Viktor Frankl and his wife were transported to Auschwitz. He had written his life's work and, in an attempt to save it, he'd sewn it into his coat lining. Unfortunately, it was discovered and even though he pleaded with the guards, they destroyed it. But before the war was over, he would lose much, much more. Of his wife, parents, brother and sister, only his sister survived the Holocaust. And yet, amid the horror, Frankl realised something profound. Despite taking everything he loved and valued, the Nazis could not take his mind or his ability to choose a higher purpose or meaning for himself. Frankl went on to write one of the most influential books of all time, *Man's Search for Meaning*,[2] to remind us that, "Between stimulus and response, there is a space. In that space is our power to choose our response. In our response lies our growth and our freedom." Remember Maddie and the choice she made? Recall how that wee, elderly priest enabled me to make sense of my dad's premature death as a blessing that circumvented possible tragedy and difficulty in his life should he have lived longer?

In truth, these types of ideas have been around a long time. Building on ancient philosophical traditions including the Stoics, Marcus Aurelius and Epictetus, Albert Ellis created rational emotive behaviour therapy (REBT). It is based on the idea that people are rarely emotionally affected by external events but, rather, by their thinking about those events. As Epictetus once said, "Men are disturbed not by things, but by the views which they take of them." Shakespeare wrote something similar in Hamlet: "There's nothing good or bad but thinking makes it so."

Human beings are meaning makers and it is often the meaning we attach to events or situations that cause us the angst and upset rather than the

We are meaning makers, and it's often this rather than the event itself which causes angst and upset.

event or situation itself. When things go wrong or fall apart, we tend to dig into a whole raft of beliefs that keep us stuck. REBT suggests that people have erroneous beliefs about situations they are involved in, and that these beliefs cause disturbance, but they can also be disputed and therefore changed.

When life takes a wrong turn, it is very easy and, in some ways, natural for us to attach our bad fortune to some 'fact' about ourselves and our world. This creates a cause-and-effect relationship that may not actually exist, but which then alters what we believe about ourselves, what we attract into our lives and what we are capable of.

When we look at exceptional people through history, most of them prevailed despite something. The majority of them found a way through impossible circumstances and massive constraints. They chose to explore the often-brutal truth of their situation, get real about it and choose something else in pursuit of what they wanted to achieve. And then they did the hard yards to get there.

> "If you don't like something, change it. If you can't change it, change your attitude."
>
> – Maya Angelou

Questions to consider …

1. What do you believe about your current situation and what have you made that mean for you? Have you found yourself beating yourself up internally, or berating yourself for something you did or didn't do or say?

2. What do you believe that may be untrue?

3. What is 'also true' about the situation? Bring to mind at least two or three examples where you were not the 'belief' you have attached to this situation. For example, if you have made the situation you are facing mean that you are 'always unlucky in love' or 'always saying the wrong

thing', then bring to mind examples from your past of any loving relationships. Just one is enough to mean you are clearly *not* always unlucky in love. Bring to mind just one time where you said exactly the right thing to help a friend. If you can think of that instance, then you don't always say the wrong thing. Pay attention and seek out the 'also trues' to get to the whole truth.

We always have a choice.

Things can go wrong – even really badly wrong – and we can be as upset about it as we want, but we always retain the sole right over how we respond to what's happened. We can choose not to hate. We can choose to find a higher purpose. We can choose to let go and move on. We can choose to accept. We can choose to see the misunderstood mercy in disappointment.

We Get What We Focus On

One of the most important things that we need to learn as human beings, which is not taught well enough in school or post-school, in my opinion, is that we get what we expect. We grow and enlarge what we focus on. And we attract and invite into our world what preoccupies us mentally. And this is not just new-ageism; it's a biological and neurological reality.

According to Hungarian-American psychologist Mihaly Csikszentmihalyi,[3] our nervous system is capable of processing about 126 bits of information per second and yet we are privy to significantly more than that. We are literally being bombarded by information through our five senses every second of every day. The way the brain deals with this is to become a deletion machine, based on our chosen focus. As a result, we stop seeing what's right in front of us.

This was brilliantly demonstrated in a study by Daniel Simons of the University of Illinois and Christopher Chabris of Harvard and later published in the book, *The Invisible Gorilla*,[4] in which they asked volunteers to watch a video of people playing basketball. The volunteers were told to focus on how many passes one of the teams made during the game and to report anything else they noticed.

About halfway through the game, someone dressed up in a gorilla suit walked onto the court, mingled with the players for nine seconds, turned to the camera and beat its chest, then walked off. About half the participants didn't see the gorilla because they were so focused on counting the passes.

You've probably experienced this same phenomenon at some point in your life. Maybe you've decided to buy a new Mini and, as soon as you switch your focus to that car, you see them everywhere. The only difference between the point where you didn't see many on the road and every second car now being a Mini is your focus.

> Paying attention to what we pay attention to helps shape our reality.

We have to pay attention to what we are paying attention to, because that focus is helping to create our reality. Just imagine what we may be missing if we are constantly focused on how angry we are or how unfair the situation is. And what we may be inviting into our orbit by mentally dwelling on negatives like 'not having enough', 'dissatisfied clients', 'a cheating world' or 'how everything sucks'?

The story goes that, just before 8 am on Friday, 12th January 2007, a young man walked into a Washington DC subway station and took a position against a wall. He opened his violin case and started to play. During the 40 minutes that he played, 1097 people passed him, most focused on getting to work. The man played six pieces by Bach, 27 people made a donation and he collected $32.17.

Once he finished, there was no applause. He packed up his violin and left. That man was Joshua Bell, one of the greatest violinists in the world. One of the pieces he played was one of the most intricate pieces of music ever written. His violin was a Stradivarius worth $3.5 million dollars. Three days earlier, Joshua Bell had played to a sell-out audience at Boston's Symphony Hall. Those watching paid a minimum of $100 a ticket and yet only seven people stopped to listen when he played in the subway because they hadn't put two and two together and appreciated or even noticed who the busker actually was.

What might you be missing when you are focused only on the chaos or crisis you may be in right now? You are more than your crisis. And there is still goodness all around you – you just have to look.

The Laconic Cowboy

When we are thinking about how to be happy or contented in spite of the drama, it's worth remembering the lesson of the laconic cowboy.

During the Wild West in America, there was a laconic cowboy who ran a ranch. One morning, while breaking in wild horses his son fell off and broke his leg. The horse jumped the fence and disappeared into the hills. Word of the injury spread, and the cowboy's neighbour arrived at his door to offer his condolences. "I'm so sorry to hear about your son's accident, that's terrible news" said the neighbour, to which the cowboy replied, "Thank you, but we don't know if it's good news or bad news." The neighbour was confused, "Of course, its bad news, he's broken his leg; who is going to help you around the ranch?" The cowboy just smiled and said, "We'll see."

A couple of days later, a scout for the military arrived at the ranch and informed the cowboy that all able-bodied men were being called to war. He was too old, but his son was not. However, his son had a broken leg, so he couldn't go. The same neighbour heard about what had happened and visited the cowboy again. "That's amazing! You said you didn't know if it was good news or bad news that your son had broken his leg, and now it turns out that it was good news after all."

The cowboy thought for a moment and replied, "I can appreciate your thinking, but we don't know yet if that's good news or bad news." Again, the neighbour was confused. "What do you mean? Of course, it's good news; your son could be killed if he goes to war. His injury has probably saved his life." The cowboy smiled and said, "We'll see."

Six months later, when the war was over, all the able-bodied men still alive returned home with the spoils of war. Money and land were shared out equally amongst all the men who had fought. Of course, the cowboy's son hadn't fought because of his broken leg, so he hadn't received anything. On hearing this news, the neighbour returned to the cowboy. "Wow, you were right again. That's really bad news that your son didn't go to war because he missed out on the reward."

Once again, the cowboy said, "We don't know if it is good news or bad news yet." Suffice to say that the cowboy and his neighbour went on having this same discussion for years.

The point, of course, is that in the moment, even in the thick of a crisis, we can't ever really know how things will work out. A curse today may end up being a blessing tomorrow or vice versa.

One of the worst times in my life, following the end of my marriage, was when I finally found my first paid gig. It was a Christian school that needed to fix its falling occupancy rate. My job was to revamp the marketing to increase the number of pupils attending the school. My daughter was a pupil at that school, and we had moved out of my mum's house into a little house on the school site. Everything was ticking along nicely until one day a member of management cornered me physically, fumbling at my fly and pressing himself up against me. I was pretty shocked – not least because he was married and purported to be a 'principled Christian'. I couldn't quite believe what had just happened but rather than saying anything I carried on as though it had been nothing and moved quickly but definitely out the way. He blustered some lame excuse that my fly had been undone, which was ridiculous. I was shaken but I thought that was the end of it. Sadly, no. The next week I was summoned to a disciplinary meeting where I was accused of fraud I hadn't committed. I was suspended without pay, even though the admission numbers for the school had reached an all-time high. What followed was a concerted effort to get me out that went on for months. I was harassed and bullied, the police were sent to my mum's house, my colleagues were told I was a criminal, and my ex-husband was even contacted in an effort to garner support against me – it was awful.

But I was adamant that I would fight the accusations. There was no way I was going quietly into the night in the face of such blatant lies. So, I refused to leave the house and got a lawyer. Everyone on the campus, apart from two people, was against me. Five months later, the case went to court.

The day of the court case, I was really worried but also weirdly calm. I'd reached up for my when-life-gets-too-big-for-you hand and felt God there. I'd been reading the biblical account of Daniel in the lion's den, surviving the fiery furnace, false accusations, high drama and political intrigue and eventually emerging triumphant. I felt very much like Daniel and the story gave me huge comfort. I would be hard pressed to explain the logic, but I just knew that it was all going to be okay. Besides, I knew I hadn't done what I was being accused of.

Unfortunately, the other side had done a pretty thorough job of shredding my reputation. They had three attorneys, and I was acutely aware that the law is not always logical, just or true. We sat down in court and the judge started the proceedings. I was told later that my case had been the 41st occurrence associated with my actual accuser. One of the attorneys had been trying to settle with mine the day before court because he'd been privy to the background facts, but the school and his client had refused. By the time we were in court, the judge had been made aware of all this and asked me what I wanted.

I wanted my name cleared and a certificate of service reflecting the truth so that I could move on. After this had been explained to the judge, she then asked, "And the money?" I said I didn't care about the money, but she was pretty insistent that there should also be some form of compensation if I was proven innocent. I replied, "Whatever you see fit." At that point, the other side was livid and started shouting, to the point where the attorneys asked for a 'caucus', which is apparently legal speak for, 'We've got a problem and need to talk to you, Judge.' So, my attorney and I were sent into the corridor while more shouting took place inside.

About twenty minutes later, we were both asked to go back in and sign an agreement. Not a file had been opened, not a single question asked, and no evidence shown. My name was cleared just like that, never to be associated with fraud or dismissal again, as the Court cautioned. I would get my certificate of service and also receive a lump sum in compensation. And that lump sum enabled me to buy an international coaching franchise that kicked off my coaching career.

The truth is that even when things are really sh*t, we don't know the full picture yet. Being falsely accused of fraud because of how I reacted to what was essentially sexual harassment, was really horrible and insanely stressful. At the time it just felt like another kick in the guts, and it definitely qualified as 'bad news'. And yet, it turned out to be a blessing and set me off on my true path and purpose.

CHAPTER 2

E = Energy

> "The idea of overcoming is always fascinating to me, because few of us realise how much energy we have expended just to be here today."
>
> – Maya Angelou

At its core, energy is that combination of resources that enable us to be happy or contented in spite of the problems or challenges we may be facing right now. No one else is responsible for our happiness – just us. No one is going to ride in on a white stead to save the day. We must find ways to grab moments of happiness in the midst of ordinary life. And this is true regardless of what we face. If we don't prioritise our happiness, it will elude us even when things are good!

And when things are dire, and we can't see the light at the end of the tunnel, finding those moments of happiness becomes even more important – like little life rafts in the storm. Besides, even in chaos, we still need to live. We can't wait for our circumstances to get better before we feel happy or allow ourselves to feel okay. That may not be happening tomorrow. There may be quite some way to go before what we are dealing with right now is in the rearview mirror.

We can't wait to be happy at some point in the future. Instead, we must focus on finding happy moments and a measure of internal peace and contentment while we're still in the thick of things. So how do we do that when everything's a sh*t show?

Again, the best way to learn how to be happy or contented in spite of the difficulties is different for everyone but there are common principles that work consistently well:

- Practicalities and Little Wins
- Improve your Health
- The E-Motion Myth and Gratitude.

Practicalities and Little Wins

Think about what happens when you have things that you need to do but you keep putting them off? Maybe at work you have experienced the cost of procrastination. The outcome is always the same – the energy you expend avoiding doing something ends up being significantly bigger than the energy you would have expended if you had just done the thing you were avoiding. Kicking the issues down the road doesn't solve them. All it does is allow the issues to gather weight and momentum, which suck in even more energy. Over time, this reality dims our verve as it contributes to an unnecessary burden on our shoulders.

If you want to reclaim some of that energy so that you have more reserves to deal with other big issues, then deal with your immediate practicalities now and don't wait. For example, if you have money problems then you need to get brutal about how to solve them. If that means that you take a second job or do some overtime – then do it. If that means that you sell something – sell it. If that means heating only one room in your house – do it. You've got to re-cut your cloth if the money is tight.

So, what are your 'elephants in the room'? What are the things that you are trying to ignore? What are the issues you keep putting off for another day?

You've got to resolve these practicalities. That doesn't mean you have to solve all your issues right now. It means you have to pick your battles, be honest with yourself and work out what challenges you are ignoring and brushing to one side so that you can start tackling them once and for all. You have to get on the scale and see for yourself the unfettered view of the state of play! As former US President, Calvin Coolidge, once said, "Do what you can. With what you have. Where you are". It doesn't have to be perfect, but do something, not nothing – and do it now.

I see this so often in the coaching work I do. My clients will say they want to achieve something, and they are often really clear about what that is. They may even have a tactical path worked out towards its achievement. And yet, in the room with them is this elephant sitting in the corner – sometimes in a bright pink tutu. Everyone else can see it except my client, who tiptoes around it and pretends it's not there. But it is there. And ignoring it doesn't make it go away. These 'elephants' are a bit like vomiting – it rarely gets better if you just wait it out. Sometimes, it's just easier to head to the loo and get it over and done with. Deal with it now and you will immediately feel better.

In order to get to the start line, you have to deal with the big energy robbers and obstacles, otherwise you'll never get out of the blocks and engage successfully in the full-contact sport of building a business or a life. Sometimes that elephant isn't even a specific problem; it's a mindset. Again, I've seen this so often where someone is haemorrhaging their personal resources and energy banks on feeling bitter or upset at someone or something else. And whilst this may be understandable, it's completely useless and keeps them stuck, miles away from that start line. Get real about wasted emotion. If you are upset, great, feel it and then put it in a box and park it. If you are angry, great, feel it and even get help with it, but then put it in a box and park it. Or even better, try a spot of transmutation and use it. If you are angry, use that anger to get to the start line.

Back in 1943, American psychologist and philosopher Abraham Maslow proposed the hierarchy of human needs (Figure 2.1).

According to Maslow, we are motivated to tackle things in order of priority from survival up to self-actualisation.[5] You can much more safely and easily have a good cry and an emotional meltdown when you have yourself on solid ground with four walls to protect and stabilise you. You can't worry about self-actualisation and finding your purpose when there are real live bullets flying over your head and survival isn't guaranteed as you flee a war zone.

It explains why we are able to go through the motions and logistics of burying a loved one with surreal calm and efficiency and only then, once it's all over, do we suddenly feel and experience the full extent of the grief and sadness. It's how we're able to prioritise under pressure and do what's needed to get through civil unrest and havoc and then, only afterwards, worry about how we'll find work or where to live.

And in this our brain is a friend. The amygdala is designed to get you into action when crisis hits rather than allow you to slip into reflective contemplation of your navel, which may feel nice but solves little in the heat of the moment. Survival at a physiological level, our personal safety and security, then our basic social needs and need for love, and finally our sense that we have significance, are what have to precede whether we are fulfilled or in purposeful work, or not.

Figure 2.1 *Maslow's Hierarchy of Needs*

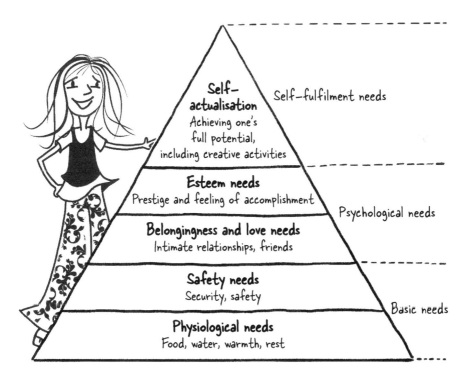

> We get what we expect. We get what we focus on. And nothing ever really has any meaning beyond the meaning we give it.

Go back and read about beliefs and expectations from the previous chapter. We get what we expect. We get what we focus on. And nothing ever really has any meaning beyond the meaning we give it. Give your anger or upset a new meaning. Make it energise you instead of defeat you. It may feel a little odd to start with, but stick with it. No one has control over your mind but you – use it to help you, not hinder you. Remember the bloke who heard his father-in-law say his daughter could have done better? He was angry at that and had every right to be, but instead of dwelling on it in a negative way, he used that anger to fuel his purpose and successfully prove his father-in-law wrong.

You definitely need to deal with the practicalities of your life right now. Often those things have been repeatedly kicked down the road and not dealing with them has already robbed you of too much energy. Get them sorted out.

As you are dealing with the practicalities, you can also focus on the little wins. Go back to the purpose chart in the previous chapter and really stop to think about what you love to do. These things don't have to be epic or important; just hone in on what makes you happy. For example, I have a friend who loves listening to music. It lifts her spirits and soothes her soul in the hustle and bustle of daily life. Or perhaps you love going to a coffee shop and reading a book, an old-school printed book. Or maybe you love having a bath or going for a walk on the beach or cold-water swimming. Retrace the steps of your life and seek to re-identify those small and ordinary things that make you happy – even for a few glorious minutes. Grab hold of those things and do more of them and relish the little bursts of joy they deliver. Or find something new that makes you happy. Take up yoga or painting – whatever. It doesn't matter. The key is to take a little bit of time amongst the chaos just for you and for something that puts a smile on your face.

When I was living back home with my mum and daughter at 46 years old, life was not great. I was massively thankful to be there and so warmly welcome by my wonderful mum, but I was definitely wrestling with my reduced station in life. There were honest moments when I didn't have a clue how I was going to get through it all, but I found a little piece of doable happiness – bright red toenails! When I was down and out, I got tremendous satisfaction from having a pedicure. No one else might ever see them, particularly in winter, but I knew and it put a smile on my face every time I thought of them.

Think of these little wins as tools in your kit bag. They need to be simple, easy to use and accessible.

My kit bag has always included:

- Good food in the fridge instead of crap snacks in the cupboard. (What we eat impacts how we feel – period! Sh*t food makes us feel sh*t.)
- A jug of cold water. If you want to mix it up a bit, add some freshly squeezed lemon, mint and cucumber.
- A 'Little Wins Playlist' on your phone of all your favourite upbeat tracks. Play it whenever you need a little hit of positive energy. Try listening to Elvis Blue's *Shine* without feeling your spirit lift!
- A mini trampoline. You can pick one up pretty cheaply and they are great for detoxing the body. The rebounding helps to stimulate the lymphatic and immune systems and even three minutes a couple of times a day can give a mental health boost.
- Schedule a call with someone you love every week.
- A favourite walk, ideally in natural places of beauty within commuting distance that makes your heart glad.
- Hug your pet … or someone else's.

Start there if you have no idea and then add your own happiness triggers to your kit bag as you get more familiar with the idea.

When I suggest this to people, they will often say, "A holiday would make me happy, but I can't afford one." OK, go on the red bus around your city then. Have a date in a nice restaurant. Start with small, relatively inexpensive things, but don't do nothing because we behave our way into right feeling. Remember, we've got to get ourselves to the start line. And to get there we have to get ourselves feeling okayish. We've got to be ready – mentally, physically and emotionally.

It's truly amazing what these small shifts can do over time.

I had a client whose business-building was being hampered by what he saw as a terribly unhappy marriage. As his truth-teller, we resolved in coaching that he had three choices: to stay and accept things as they were; to end the marriage, which he wasn't quite ready to do, or to fix things (although he didn't know how). As there was no infidelity, abuse or neglect going on, we agreed that he would do one very simple thing, starting immediately. He was to buy a journal and every day for the next eight months until his wife's birthday, he'd make an intentional note of *one thing* that she did or said that day that he was able to admire or appreciate. Then, on her birthday, he was to give her the journal as his gift.

Right behaviour can lead to right feelings, which can change everything.

Well, even I underestimated the result. His wife was stupefied – in a good way! And he was a changed man. He said he'd never forget her face and the tears as she read page after page of small things he'd observed and noticed her doing – positive, ordinary things. And concentrating daily on just one positive thing had changed his mindset towards his wife and allowed him to see her through a different lens. Noting what he saw in her each day and committing this to paper caused both of them to see the relationship differently. This simple exercise saved their marriage.

Right behaviour can lead to right feelings, which can change everything.

Deal with the practical issues so you can liberate the energy that is wasted ignoring them. Ignoring a problem doesn't make it go away; it usually just makes it bigger so that you need to waste even more energy ignoring it in the future. Deal with it. Then convert that liberated energy into finding things that make you happy – do more of those. Get your kit bag ready so that you have a bunch of supportive, easy-to-access actions or ideas that can immediately help you to get into a more positive state of mind so that you can behave your way into feeling better.

Improve your Health

I know! How can you possibly improve your health when you are already struggling to get through each day – right? It's pretty tough to adopt the warrior mindset and get to that start line when all we really want to do is stay under the covers all day with tissues and a box of chocolates. But that won't help.

We need energy. We need to recoup energy and replenish our stores and we just can't do that without making some improvements to our health. One of the most effective ways to kickstart our journey towards our best self is exercise. Now don't panic – I'm not going to ask you to run a marathon or do three hours of Bikram yoga, but you do need to get off your backside if you want to build the bigger, better, functioning you. And that functioning you is absolutely essential before you even think about building a better relationship, business or life.

As human beings, we can use our mind and our body to impact our emotional state. If our mind is already foggy, then the body may be the easier option to start with.

Even mild exercise, such as a walk around a local park or by the sea, will change the internal chemistry of our body. When the wheels come off in our life in any way, it creates a spike in our stress response which means that our body is literally flooded with cortisol. Cortisol creates a negative feedback loop, which means that the more cortisol that's created, the worse we feel, which creates even more cortisol, which makes us feel even worse – hence the tissues and chocolate. It's incredibly hard to break free from that cortisol trap using just positive thoughts and determination.

But we can break cortisol's negative spell by moving our body. Put your favourite music on really loud and dance around the living room for 20 minutes. No love ballads – just upbeat power anthems, dance music, disco or grand classical greats (my favourite). If you can, without upsetting the neighbours, sing your heart out to your favourite tunes while you dance. The physical activity of moving your body will alter your internal physiology and help to break the negative feedback loop caused by excess cortisol. And you'll immediately feel better.

We all feel rubbish from time to time – that's life, but we need to have a set of bog standard, largely free, anybody-can-use-them tools and tricks at the ready to make sure we don't set up camp in those negative emotional states. That's what the kit bag is all about.

This connection between what our body does and our internal chemistry was brilliantly demonstrated by social psychologist Amy Cuddy and her colleague Dana Carney. Originally, they were interested in whether it was possible to 'fake it until you make it'. In other words, can we pretend to feel happy, confident and positive and end up feeling those feelings? It turns out that the answer is yes.[6]

First, Cuddy and Carney took baseline saliva tests from volunteers that checked for levels of testosterone (the confidence hormone) and cortisol (the stress hormone). The group was then divided in two and each set was asked to engage in various poses for two minutes. One group did 'high power' poses, and the other did 'low power' poses, but neither group was told which was which.

The high-power poses were any stance or movement that increased or expanded the physical space that the person occupied – the best-known being the superman pose: stand like a superhero, legs hip-distance apart, hands on hips. Draw up to your full height, back straight, and breathe deeply as though you've just arrived to save the planet.

The low-power poses do the opposite by shrinking the space the body takes up in the environment. They include hunching our shoulders, looking down, and basically anything that makes the physical space we occupy smaller.

After just two minutes, everyone's saliva was tested again. Incredibly, everyone's internal chemistry or physiology had changed. Those who had engaged in the high-power poses experienced a 20% increase in testosterone and a 25% reduction in cortisol, whereas the low-power-pose group experienced a 10% reduction in the confidence hormone and a 15% increase in the cortisol.

Considering that many of us spend a lot longer than two minutes in low-power poses commuting to work or hunched over our phones, is it little wonder that we don't feel primed and ready to take on the world? Far better to incorporate a spot of superman posing into our daily life. Maybe in the shower in the morning!

As an absolute minimum, pay attention to these power poses, but ideally take your health seriously. Get into nature, go for a run, go to the gym, invest in a mini trampoline, clean out and restock the fridge with 'good food', drink plenty of water, play a sport you used to enjoy. Whatever you do – fuel a bit better and move. It will make you feel better and put you in a better place mentally, emotionally and physically to deal with what's ahead.

If you're serious about creating your business as a vehicle for life, you are your own business card.

Plus, if you are serious about creating or using your business as a vehicle for your life, you are your own business card. We can argue about whether that is fair or right, but it remains a fact. I had a client who had a wellness business that had plateaued. She thought it was an issue of marketing. She was right, but not in the way she assumed. She was noticeably overweight, and this created an incongruency that people just didn't trust. This is not rocket science. She thought I was being unfair and that her weight was just something she struggled with, but why would anyone have been willing to take wellness advice from her when she hadn't been able to get such a fundamental aspect of wellness under control herself?

While thin doesn't always equal healthy and overweight doesn't mean you can't be healthy, extra weight puts extra strain on your body. Strong may be the new skinny, but taking our weight and health seriously is essential.

When I moved to the UK, I put on weight and knew that I had to get it off. Bottomline: people are less likely to listen to my business advice if I can't get my own health house in order.

It's really important for all of us to take our health seriously. Good health is a business tool that all entrepreneurs can benefit from and an oxygen mask that becomes critical when we are in crisis. Think of when you last took a flight – the cabin crew would have told you that an oxygen mask would drop from the ceiling in the case of an emergency and that you were to fit your own before trying to help anyone else. Our personal physical health is that oxygen mask and we absolutely need to attend to it before we help anyone else or consider starting or fixing a business!

Our personal health is an oxygen mask we need to attend to before starting or fixing a business.

The E-Motion Myth and Gratitude

As adults, we usually pride ourselves on our ability to make rational decisions, see what's going on and work out a plan of action. But this can be elusive, especially when we are stressed.

Remember that pesky cortisol? As well as creating a negative feedback loop that perpetuates the stress and negativity, it also facilitates a Do-It-Yourself (DIY) lobotomy. Have you ever had that experience where you were under pressure or stressed and someone asked you a question, and you knew the answer, but would just stare at them like a deer in the headlights? Your fight/flight or freeze mechanism had been triggered and you no longer had access to your best thinking.

And most of us don't even realise that this is what is happening when it happens. What and how well we think can be massively impacted by what we feel and the emotions that are swimming around inside us. But e-motion is largely energy in motion – the biological physical signals and processes that make up our physiology at any given moment. Feelings are the names we give those emotions. This is why the idea that we are rational is a tad mythical – or more specifically, e-mythical – because of how our emotions and feelings influence our actions, behaviour and decisions. Under pressure, we often can't even access our executive function!

Emotions are a bit like children – they're awesome to have around but you wouldn't put them in charge!

Of course, emotions are part of being human. We can no more escape them than we can decide to stop breathing, but we really need to recognise their hold over us and start to use them as a force for good, rather than let them derail our best intentions. Again, emotions are a bit like children – they're awesome to have around but you wouldn't put them in charge!

When we learn to recognise and actively manage our emotions by using the tools in our kit bag, the results are improved health and sanity. We are also able to develop greater emotional range and flexibility. This, in turn, allows us to unlock greater intellectual capacity so that we can maintain a connection to our best thinking. This emotional self-management also positively impacts our energy reserves and ensures that we are not haemorrhaging energy through unhelpful emotional reactions.

As well as the tools we've discussed already, practising the art of gratitude is another really useful way to recalibrate your emotions on a daily basis.

> "Piglet noticed that even though he had a
> Very Small Heart, it could hold a rather large
> amount of Gratitude."
>
> – A.A. Milne, *Winnie-the-Pooh*

Practising more gratitude is something we should all do a lot more of, regardless of whether we are in the middle of a crisis or not. It's simple, free and easy to do. It's also especially crucial when life is hard. Being happy or contented despite our problems demands that we pay attention to the things that are still good and working, to the people we love, to the people who love us, and for all the things that remain. We all have some good things – even one or two – and that is enough for us to make music and start a habit of expressing regular heartfelt appreciation.

Make it part of your daily ritual to take a few minutes to call to mind three things that you're grateful for. Don't just note them like items on a shopping list but really engage with them, feel the gratitude and appreciation for that person or experience or skill set. Say them out loud or write them down to anchor this practice into your brain architecture. Remember what a profound impact my client experienced when he journaled about the things he was grateful for and appreciated about his wife? Not only did this gratitude practice save his marriage, but it also created the foundation on which he was able to build a thriving business.

Psychologist Sonja Lyubomirsky, from the University of California, found that when we take the time to consciously count our blessings and take note of what we are grateful for, even once a week, we become happier and more satisfied.[7] Her colleague, Robert Emmons, also found that gratitude improves physical health, gives us more energy and helps to combat pain and fatigue. He noted that, "The ones who benefited most tended to elaborate more and have a wider span of things they're grateful for."[8]

Taking the time daily to bring to mind something we are grateful for, helps to trigger a human quirk known as the 'peak end rule'. According to Nobel Prize-winning psychologists, Daniel Kahneman and Amos Tversky,[9] our appreciation of an experience is dependent on the most extreme point in the experience (either good or bad) and the end of the experience. In other words, we take snapshots of the high (or low) and the end of something and draw conclusions from those two specific moments.

So, when we end our day by calling to mind all the things we are happy or grateful for despite the chaos, we help to trigger the peak end rule. It's like a band saving their best song for the end of a show so that everyone leaves the concert on a high. We can mimic the same result by ending our day on a high, via a few minutes of gratitude and appreciation.

CHAPTER 3

A = Aspiration

"Our aspirations are our possibilities."

— Robert Browning

The next ingredient for PEACE is A for Aspiration. What do you really want? Who do you want to be? What is your definition of success? It's easy, in the thick of battle, to get lost in the moment-to-moment chaos or to chase some fantasy ideal of what we hoped our life would be. Or worse, feel obligated to march to someone else's tune of what our life should look like. All of it is pointless until we stabilise the situation through purpose and energy. Purpose reconnects us to our True North and energy makes sure we can function through the challenges with some measure of happiness or contentment on the way. This True North also gives us the courage to own our definition of success despite what others say or want, which, in turn, allows us to say a clear and confident "no" to anything that takes us off course. It becomes our guiding light. It's time to prioritise what we are saying to us about ourselves instead of what others think we are capable of and should be chasing.

Once you have your own personal purpose and energy, then you can dare to dream again. You can indulge yourself with thinking about the twin forces of pleasure and pain. Both are motivational to us in varying degrees when it comes to us dreaming our dreams. Some of us are more motivated to get away from pain; this is called 'away from' motivation. Others are more motivated to move toward something they want, which is known as 'toward motivation'. We are all inspired by a combination of both. Purpose and energy provide us with a new perspective and access to new energy reserves so that we can live with the difficulties we face without allowing them to overwhelm us and we enjoy a measure of hope for what lies ahead.

Aspiration is when we look at the pleasure side of the coin. What exciting new future might you create? What do you really want? It's impossible to even contemplate these questions before we have come to terms with our reality and learned some measure of acceptance and contentment amidst the chaos. And yet working out what you want and aspire to is – while undeniably helpful – often harder than you may imagine.

We are conditioned by the society we live in, the media, culture, religion and our parents and siblings into believing certain things about who we are and what we are capable of. Working out what we really want is only possible if we become ruthlessly honest with ourselves. We must let go of what other people would like for us and focus, instead, on what it is that we enjoy and feel passionate about. All those other people can't possibly know what we want the way that we can. A doctor parent may hope that their child follows in their footsteps, but there is no guarantee that they will. We must find and follow our own path. Getting clear on our aspirations is about ensuring that we march to our own drum, rather than to a definition of success or borrowed destination from someone else.

It's very hard to recognise your purpose or what you love when you are used to settling for what you can get. Also, forget about the whims and trends that may capture your imagination for a day or so. If it doesn't last, then it's probably not something you really want.

So, what do you really want?

What is Also True?

You may have found that last question tough. When we are in a crisis, often all we really want is for the crisis to be over. Our dream muscle is damaged or sorely underused.

One of the things that I found helpful was to focus on what was also true. For me, I was divorced and my life as it was had ended, including the connection with my friends and support network. I also have a secret to share – this was my second divorce. I felt even more of a failure because of that. I wasn't in a great place in my early twenties and so I ended up marrying the first man who asked, who then promptly disappeared a few years in. He was never home, was always 'working', and then one day he just stopped coming home altogether. That marriage came to an inevitable end. So, when my 'proper grown-up forever' marriage ended, I was devastated. Loads of people get divorced once – but twice?

In the thick of this, I deliberately hunted for the things that were 'also true'. OK, it was true that I was a divorcee – twice – but it was also true that I had a loving family and a mum who was my biggest fan. I had friends and peers who still saw value in me even though I was dented, flawed and cracked. I found that I still had an ability – unbelievably – to inspire others.

I relied on good books, loving family, remaining friends who mattered, a small group at my church and the Bible to find these 'also trues' for myself and I 'took' them as medicine three times a day. I used these 'also trues' to neutralise the other mental narratives that were negative or unhelpful, as I dealt with the daily struggles of my not-so-lovely circumstances.

I made Post-its of positive affirmations and rehearsed them out loud. Things like:

- "I can do all things through my God who strengthens me."
- "I am a much-loved daughter to a mum who is my greatest fan."
- "None of this took my God by surprise." (I liked that one because it reminded me that I was where I was supposed to be, and it would work out.)
- "It'll be okay in the end and if it's not okay, it's not the end." (A quote from *The Best Exotic Marigold Hotel*.)
- And my all-time favourite was Perlman's, "My life's ambition is to make music from that which remains." And he, after all, is a violin virtuoso.

Start with the End in Mind

Stephen Covey talked about this in his book, *The 7 Habits of Highly Effective People.*[10] Very often, what lies in front of us is new territory. That's why change is so daunting. We don't know what to do, and we may not be sure how to do it or when or where to access the information we need in order to feel more confident in our ability to cope. So, instead, we approach life from where we are. We tackle it from where we stand, which is usually from a position of insufficient experience. This is normal and understandable, but it isn't an optimal way to set our brain in motion.

Starting with the end in mind is the solution.

When JFK announced that the US would put a man on the moon and bring him safely back to earth, that was a very clear goal to achieve something that had never been done before. Apparently, when the President came out of congress where he'd made his public announcement to the American people, he is said to have turned to the bloke who would become the head of NASA and apologised for not telling him beforehand. The story goes that the bloke said it was OK: "I know where the earth is, I know where the moon is, I know what you want, and I know by when. I will do everything I can to deliver that."

And of course, they did. On the 20th July 1969, Apollo 11 touched down on the moon and Neil Armstrong and Buzz Aldrin arrived back safely four days later.

Why? Because everyone started with the end in mind.

One of the best movies to explain this is *The Martian* with Matt Damon. Within the first five minutes of the movie, he discovers that he's been left behind on Mars. Clearly, this is a bit of a problem. But he starts with the end in mind. He decides that his end will not be death but that he is going home to his family, and from that end point he works backwards to figure out how to make that possible. First, he needs to work out how to stay alive and then he needs to find out how to tell other people that he's still there and still alive so that they can launch a rescue mission. And that's exactly what he does. Right at the end of the movie he says to us, his audience: "If you can hold something that matters to you in front of you and solve enough problems, you get to go home."

This is why I think Stephen Covey's book still endures some 30 years after it was published – it speaks to the psychological reality that if we have something to aim for that we've articulated and that matters, and we work logically back from there, we will find a way. Starting with the end in mind allows us to identify problems. We come to appreciate what we don't know, and our brain starts to work on the seemingly impossible or unsolvable.

It's the same process that athletes use to visualise success. They haven't won the gold medal yet, but they start with the end in mind (the gold medal) and they identify and solve problems over and over again until they've achieved their goal mentally. And all along the way they keep seeing themselves on the podium. They taste the metal in their teeth as they bite the medal for photographers, they hear the applause ringing in their ears. Then they go on to achieve it practically.

In a now-famous study, four groups of world-class athletes of similar ability were put through their paces in a rigorous training regime although the training programme differed slightly between each group:

- Group I – 100% physical training
- Group II – 75% physical training and 25% mental training
- Group III – 50% physical training and 50% mental training
- Group IV – 25% physical training and 75% mental training

When the four groups were assessed prior to their departure for the upcoming Olympics, Group IV showed the greatest improvement, followed by Group III, Group II and finally Group I. The exact opposite of what most of us would have thought. Why? Because the act of visualising their own improvement and seeing the future they aspired to in their mind created greater actual improvement than physical training alone! In his book *Peak Performance*, Charles Garfield, former NASA researcher and peak performance guru, tells of this study and also of his own experience of the mind's ability to improve performance.[11] Under the instruction of a coach who advocated this approach, Garfield was hooked up to a portable EEG machine to measure his brainwaves, an ECG to measure his cardiac activity and an EMG to measure his muscular activity. Many years before, Garfield had bench pressed 365 pounds – once. In recent times, he hadn't managed over 280 pounds. He was then taken through a relaxation process and asked to visualise bench pressing 365 pounds again. After 40 minutes of guided imagery where he was asked to step into that chosen future where he could bench press 365 pounds, he approached the bench. In his book Garfield wrote, "*The imagery now imprinted in my mind began to guide my physical movements. Slowly and patiently their voices, sure yet gentle, led me through the lift. I became convinced I could do it. The world around me seemed to fade, giving way to self-confidence, belief in myself, and then to deliberate action. I lifted the weight! I was absolutely astounded.*"

Everything in life is created twice. From the book you are reading to the chair you are sitting on to the train or the car you commute to work in. First, it emerged as an idea inside someone's imagination. Then, as they started with the end in mind, they worked back to find out how to make it a reality on the outside through planning and action. Working back from the 'end' helps to convert the idea into something real and will help you to make your chosen future a reality. This is why taking time to really drill into your aspirations is so crucial. You have to uncover an aspirational future you want badly enough to keep you going through all the wins, losses and surprises on the way.

> Everything in life is created twice – first as an idea in someone's imagination and then through planning and action as a reality.

The journey ahead will not be easy, but it's also worth pointing out that in his book *Flow: The Psychology of Happiness: The Classic Work on How to Achieve Happiness*, the late Hungarian psychologist Mihaly Csikszentmihalyi reminded us that, "*Contrary to what we usually believe, the best moments in our lives, are not the passive, receptive, relaxing times – although such experiences can also be enjoyable, if we have worked hard to attain them. The best moments usually occur when a person's body or mind are stretched to its limits in a voluntary effort to accomplish something difficult and worthwhile. Optimal experience is thus something that we make happen …*

Such experiences are not necessarily pleasant at the time they occur … Getting control of life is never easy, and sometimes it can be definitely painful. But in the long run optimal experience adds up to a sense of mastery – or perhaps better, a sense of participation in determining the content of life – that comes as close to what is usually meant by happiness as anything else we can conceivably imagine."[12]

You may feel that you have a mountain to climb, but the climb may be the making of you. It may be your finest hour, your peak experience and something that you look back on for many years and smile – especially if the view from the top or the destination proves to you that it was worth it.

Cost Your Aspirations

Once you have figured out what you want to achieve and what's important to you, it's also worth spending some time costing those aspirations.

I've lost count of the people I've worked with who have announced that they wanted to double the turnover in their business. And yet when I ask why that number, or what it will be for, they can't tell me.

We are so deeply conditioned into feeling that we should want more money or to live some particular lifestyle that signals to the world that we are successful. But why?

Firstly, the assumption is that more money will buy more happiness, but social science has already proven that to be false. Researchers from Princeton University studied Gallup data for almost half a million Americans and found that there is actually a cut-off point equivalent to US$75,000, after which no extra happiness can be squeezed from money.[13] In another experiment, Elizabeth Dunn and Michael Norton did something similar by taking a national sample of Americans who earned around US$25,000 and compared them to people who made US$55,000. Those in the first group believed that they would be twice as happy as they currently were if they could double their income, and yet the people in the second group were only 9% happier than the first group.[14]

So, if you've decided that you will need millions to be happy and achieve your aspirations, you may be wrong. You are almost certainly wrong on the happiness front.

And the second is the reality that life – any life – costs. It needs fuel to run on and that fuel is money. It's all very well to sketch out your dreams and what you want, but all dreams need a reality check to work out what they will cost. Everything needs to be paid for. How much will it cost to travel the world? How much will I need to buy the house of my dreams,

Life and dreams cost – and costing them helps test your resolve around them.

or raise a family comfortably? What will I need to retire safely? How much will my philanthropy cost? Even ballpark figures can be helpful to shaping and contextualising what you need to build, how big and with what return.

Costing your aspirations will also help you to test your resolve around them. When you see a number against your aspirations, does that reality drive you on, or make you question the aspiration? Costing your dreams is a powerful experience.

CHAPTER 4

C = Connections

> "When we have done our very best, Papa, and that is
> not enough, then I think the right time must have
> come for asking help of others."
>
> – Charles Dickens, *The Magic Fishbone*[15]

Every cloud has a silver lining and the silver lining that Covid delivered to the world was a forced reset and a recalibration around what was really important. We collectively got off the hedonistic treadmill and, in so doing, millions of people all over the world realised that they didn't really want or need to spend money they didn't necessarily have in order to be happy. Just hanging out with friends and spending time with loved ones was what they really missed. It was the connection, not the stuff, that mattered.

Social science has also proven this to be true. According to Martin Seligman, the father of positive psychology, what really matters for happiness is satisfying work, avoiding negative events as much as possible, being in a healthy intimate relationship, and having strong social networks.[16]

These findings around the importance of connection have also been borne out by one of the longest-running life studies ever conducted.[17] Since 1938, The Harvard Study of Adult Development has followed the lives of 724 men from all walks of life. Each year, the men have been interviewed about their work, home lives and health, and their health would be tested. The results are conclusive: what makes a good life is not money, fame, a swanky car or even good health – it's the quality of our connections. Good relationships keep us healthier and happier, and yet this critical component of life is often sidelined in the clamour for 'success'.[18]

Good relationships and strong connections are key for us as human beings. And yet in our daily life it can be very easy to forget that, and even more so when we are in crisis. When things are bad, we often shrink away from others. In many ways this is natural, and often encouraged by social conditioning, which can help compound a nightmare as society seeks to encourage us to present a positive face, hide weakness and not ask for help.

But no one is an island. You can't do everything yourself. Getting help isn't weak – it's sensible and practical. We can't know everything; the world is too complex. Putting up our hands and 'being teachable' is a mark of maturity, wisdom and sound thinking. Think of the sporting world – even those with real talent, drive and promise invest in help, and they are at the top of their game!

What do you need help with? Who will you ask? We need to keep our connections open and healthy, especially when we are going through tough times. And that takes work and effort. Below are a few suggestions that I've found useful.

- Learn to Dig Your Own Well
- Read More Books
- Watch Your Social Media Diet.

Learn to Dig Your Own Well

When I moved to the UK, I didn't know anyone, so I had to dig my own well. No one was lining up in my area and saying, "Oh, look, there's a new person in town; let's go and say hello." That doesn't happen. Not in the UK or anywhere else in the world. People are busy with their own lives. Whether we like it or not, it's up to us as the outsider to get out there, be a friend and make the effort. And, who knows, perhaps the next time we encounter outsiders as the insider, we'll treat them with a little more compassion.

Here's what I tried as the newcomer. Give these a go or think about what you could add:

- Make a regular commitment to talk to your friends – wherever they are.
- Join the local gym or a group that appeals. I joined the cold-water swimmers.
- Sign up at the local library. A book can be a diverting friend and the staff are friendly.
- Make a point of learning the names of ordinary folk in your sphere of influence – the bank teller, shop assistant and bus driver, and engage with them intentionally when your paths cross.
- Join local online community groups and contribute wisely. Stick to positive engagement and support.
- Visit the local theatre and learn to go to movies alone.
- Ride local transport and see the area.
- Frequent local delis/eateries/bistros for a weekend brunch and converse with the staff and other patrons.
- Stroll around local markets and engage the stall holders in conversation like, "How's business going?"

And hey, I know only too well that this stuff is not always easy. But it is simple and therefore doable.

Thanks to Covid and the resulting schizophrenic social situation it created, even after being in the UK for two years, I could go days without real human contact. I remember one day I had a wobble at the enormity of so much aloneness and ended up calling my mum and brother for a pep talk. We are social animals and I was missing other human beings. I had edged near the negative mental pit that we can all fall into if we aren't careful. That place that can leach our positivity, cause our self-discipline to stutter and damage our self-belief in what we are doing and building. The next day, I was determined to feel less sorry for myself. There was bright sunshine and the temperature was 16.5°C. I got up and 'dug my own well' by going to the hairdresser for a treat; doing brekkie at the gym next to, if not with, others; and then took a book with me on the 300-yard stroll down the river to my local beach – alone yes, but not lonely – to enjoy some peaceful, beautiful, sunny solitude that many would give their eye teeth for.

And I realised again that while feelings can be so present and compelling, it is possible to choose to behave oneself into a positive frame of mind where the blessings loom larger than the challenges. It is possible to decide not to feel blue and 'without' and instead choose to focus on and add up 'what is'. Peace is priceless, beautiful nature on my doorstep is a balm and 'enough' financially creates liberating options. After some sun, sea air and a lovely cup of tea, I felt better about things, life and myself. It just took a few small shifts and better, more constructive choices.

It's always easier to dig a new personal well before you need it.

These efforts to connect to more people wherever we are, means we tent peg ourselves in because we can never know, until we try, how or who will respond or when we will need someone or something. These efforts also sharpen our habits and competence in being a connector and starting the process of making us visible in our new world. And visibility is the first rule of any marketing!

It's always easier to dig that well before you need it. We all need community and connections. Sometimes, we just need others to give us a sanity check and help support us through the most challenging times. Sometimes, when we don't have everything within us to fix ourselves, we need that support network. And finding our place in community opens up so much opportunity for alliance, doing business together and exchanging competencies. For example, you may exchange your bookkeeping expertise for social media marketing insight.

Start digging your well now.

Read More Books

Another great way to access other people and new ideas is to fall in love with reading, especially books, e-books or audio books. Maybe even combine digging your own well with reading and start a local book club or an online book club with your friends. Read a chapter a week and discuss the findings over a coffee or a beer.

Although books are only one-way traffic – the authors insights on a particular topic – they can be a great source of comfort and inspiration. They can absorb and divert us, they make terrific company to stave off loneliness, and they can be a natural 'sleeping pill' when we wake up in the early hours of the morning. Try it.

I'm a huge fan of books and I encourage all my clients to read:

- *Good to Great* by Jim Collins
- *Getting Things Done* by Dave Allen
- *The E-Myth Revisited* by Michael Gerber
- *The Compound Effect* by Darryn Hardy
- Just about anything that Jim Rohn has written or published
- *Mastering the Rockerfeller Habits* by Verne Harnish.

And before you shout at me that these books are OLD HAT and have been around for so long and you've never heard of some of the authors because they died before you were born – try them. They are enduring, magical texts with logical, common-sense stuff that is STILL relevant, useful, impactful, and works.

Social Media Diet

There is now a significant body of knowledge to indicate that too much time spent on social media is detrimental to our mental health.[19] Hours spent 'doom scrolling' through Facebook, Twitter, or Instagram feeds may pass the time, but it is also making us more anxious. And it can feel a hundred times worse if you are in a crisis and all you are seeing are other people having a great time on holiday or at a fabulous restaurant in their new car. Equally, it can make us feel even worse to hear about all the stuff that's going on globally – little of it good or positive, so it seems – so why do that?

Of course, bad news sells and those other people with a 'great life' are also only displaying their 'show reel' and will definitely have their own dramas going on, but still, it can add up to making you feel crap. Do yourself a favour and turn off all your notifications on your phone, except the important ones. Just in case you are unsure which ones are important, Facebook, Twitter and Instagram are not important. Phone and WhatsApp, where you are communicating one to one with someone you care about, are important.

Who we hang around with also has an impact on how we feel about ourselves; what we prioritise; our thoughts, feelings and actions; and, ultimately, who we become. And while 'hanging around' used to mean being with our friends and peer group, today it includes the online sites, podcasts, YouTube's, Ted Talks and influencers that we give our time and ears to.

We need to be judicious and vigilant about what is serving and helping us, and what is not, so that we ruthlessly chop and prune back until we surround ourselves with enough challenge, vision and accountability to avoid being blindsided, while ensuring plenty of affirmation to remain hopeful, inspired and positive.

And this dance is an elegant and ongoing one that we need to regularly review and recalibrate.

CHAPTER 5

E = Environment

> "Be sure to put your feet in the right place,
> then stand firm."
>
> – Abraham Lincoln

Environment really comes down largely to physical location, but also involves purpose as we apply what we have discovered through our PEACE journey to determine 'what next'.

Let's start with where you are, right now.

Most of us don't consider where we live as a question. Albert Einstein once said "we are boxed in by the boundary conditions of our thinking". Where we live tends to be one of those boundary conditions. We are born in an area, we grow up in that area, make friends in that area and our family and support network is in that geographic location – so we stay. This formula works for billions of people, but when it stops working for whatever reason, we rarely stop to consider that moving location may open new doors.

Of course, our 'where' is going to be influenced by our purpose, energy, aspirations and connections, and it's also going to be an important consideration when we get into Part Two that deals with how to improve your business or create a new one.

What you want to achieve or create is clearly linked to where you need to be or live. If you decide that you want to open a scuba diving school, then your 'where' needs to support that aspiration. There is no point setting up in a town that's 100 kilometres from the ocean – even if that's your much-loved hometown. If you want to open a café selling artisan coffee and amazing cakes but you live in a place with no passing traffic and diabetic locals, then you may have a problem. Your 'where' doesn't match your 'what'.

Sooner or later, we all need to stop and consider if where we are is the best place for what we want to achieve. And remember, you're not a tree. It's not like we get planted in the soil when we are born and just have to endure whatever comes our way. You may be angry that you even have to consider moving to solve a problem and you may be able to come up with all sorts of valid reasons as to why that is unfair or why you don't want to do it. And all of those reasons may be true. But it's not necessarily the truth. There are other things that are 'also true'. And remember, what's true and what's also true, is what makes up the truth.

What's true and what's also true, make up the truth.

For example, it may be true that you have lived in your hometown or city all your life. It may be true that a lot of your friends and family live close by. It may also be true that you don't really want to move, but is it not also true that thousands of people up sticks and change their geography or location every year and find the happiness and success they desire? The truth is always more expansive than we may initially imagine or hope it is.

The reality is that we lug around baggage about who we are in relation to where we live when, in reality, where we are is just a location. There is often very little stopping us from moving to a new place beyond our own entrenched beliefs, attitudes and values.

The Tale of Two Clients

I had two clients, both South African, both working in a similar industry, who are a stark reminder of the importance of environment.

One has built a world-class service to the architecture and design industry that is used by property developers to market to would-be buyers what their home or building will look like, inside and out, after it's built. The image quality is so good that people are constantly surprised that the building doesn't yet exist in the real world. The images look like photographs.

The product offering is fantastic, but the market for it is limited in South Africa. Globally the markets that emerged for him as potential winners were Europe, the Middle East and the US, where this type of high-quality visualisation is deemed essential for getting a development over the line with investors or for selling property 'off plan' to customers, rather than a grudging addition to marketing expenses.

Since 2014, I worked with him to improve and grow his business. He went from a one-man band to an international team by recruiting the right people, right. Everyone who now works there is doing world-class work; the systems to run the business are in place; the monthly order book is healthy; the website and marketing/sales process works; and on a personal note, he became a happy family man.

But the market pressures remained a brutal truth. To get traction and increase his profit margins, he needed a much bigger percentage of overseas work, which his test and measure showed conclusively needed to be signed up for in person. His overseas prospects just weren't willing to sign on the dotted line without a regular, trusted, face-to-face relationship. In short, to create the business he wanted to create, he needed to move overseas. It was increasingly non-negotiable.

But moving overseas for any family is not easy. We can see the merits, but it's hard, and it may mean uprooting the family and saying goodbye – even temporarily – to an unmatchable lifestyle. It will definitely mean additional expense, real cash flow pressure and dealing with the genuine fear around whether it will work. So, like my client, we may recognise that we want and may even need a global business necessitating a move, but at what expense? If we love where we are and what we currently have, and have successfully scaled up and now turn over in a month what we used to turn in a year, it's so easy to settle for making frequent trips to these other markets, and not emigrate. It's so easy to justify staying and then look for other possibly 'also true' reasons to explain why margins stay frustratingly slim.

High-end product offerings have high-end purchasers, and high-end purchasers of anything expect the personal touch. We may try employing agents, forging alliances and hiring salespeople to avoid having to relocate ourselves to service high-end clients, but if and when none of those things works in the long run, we may have to just accept that speaking passionately or eloquently about what we do is our job, and thus resign ourselves to going.

You may be thinking at this point, "Yeah, but people can't just up and leave and go and live in whatever country they fancy." True. But what is also true? It could be that a family member is already a citizen of where you need to be, so you could trade on that? Or perhaps the kids are still young enough to see this as an adventure that doesn't have to be permanent, so why not go now? Moves also don't have to be permanent – it could be a case of just for two or three years or maybe even an international house/life swop? The bottom line is that building a business base, establishing a sales presence and momentum, strengthening an essential network and securing market visibility is a full-contact sport that can seldom happen at arms-length. Embrace the necessity and make the move. You can always come back later.

But what you dare not do is ignore the reality that it's usually the business that is funding your lifestyle and if the business needs it, then it has to take priority over everything else, at least for now.

If the business funding our life needs it, then it has to take priority at least for now.

Now let's look at Mark. When I met him, Mark was, and still is, a talented, ambitious and successful landscape architect. He was based in Cape Town, South Africa, and found that when he wanted and needed to scale the business, most homeowners, commercial builders and property developers that he was dealing with were obligated to nickel-and-dime landscape architecture. He soon discovered that priorities in South Africa weren't what they were elsewhere in the world – regardless of why – and most developers begrudged extending the budget to include the critical work Mark and professionals like him do. As a result, too many projects Mark worked on were fraught with budget constraints, price wars and cost cutting. It was a great business, but there seemed to be increasingly limited scope to really scale it, pay attractive salaries to substantial professional team members and make the sort of money Mark had decided he wanted to make.

Together, we leaned into this idea of his environment. Where should he be? In exploring that question, Mark shared that his mum lived in Sydney and Australia's relationship to landscape architecture is completely different, so much so that the outside space is often designed ahead of the building architecture. People in Australia take what Mark does very seriously and with existing ties to the country through his mum, he was able to move there. The only catch was that he needed to do so before he was 40 years old and that was mere months away.

With the clock ticking, Mark made some fast, hard and big decisions and jumped on a plane. It was scary and, by his own admission, he wasn't ready or prepared. But the cut-off date gave him that extra impetus to go for it.

> "Leap, and the net will appear."
>
> – John Burroughs

For Mark, his why was also really clear to him and he could see that what he wanted to achieve was almost impossible if he stayed where he was. It wasn't easy, but he moved to a new geography, initially moving back in to live with his mum at 40 years old, before eventually moving into a tiny flat in Sydney that cost the earth. However, just a year later he was on the radar of all the right people there. He had numerous project opportunities cross his desk, landed some big projects spanning three to five years, and he and his company had won a bunch of international awards. He subsequently picked up some big projects further afield, moved into Sydney-based offices and has now grown international talent – all because he'd had the courage to ask, "Am I in the right place?"

Look, I get it. Moving to a new place is hard and it's daunting. But it's always an option. And I've done it myself many times, so I know how both challenging and liberating it can be. My latest move to the UK was prompted by my daughter. For most of her life, my priority has been about launching her and creating 'enough' financially. But as she graduated from school, she started asking me about my 'what next'? And they were good questions. For the past decade or so, my focus had been on being a mum and building my business so I wouldn't be that mad cat lady. But then what? I have a coach too and we would discuss this question a lot. And what I really wanted was personal, not business – it was to find a partner again. Someone with whom I could share this adventure called life – someone with means and motivation who'd pick me and take my hand. I started Internet dating in South Africa, but let's just kindly and shortly say it didn't go well.

> Moving to a new place may be hard and daunting – but it's an option.

I spoke to my coach – was it me? But my coach was pretty sure it was just a side effect of strong woman syndrome – something they'd seen often. My coach's advice: "Swim in a bigger pond and attract men who need neither a fan nor staff." In other words, I needed to revisit where I was ... again!

And hey, if I can't keep taking my own advice then what kind of coach am I – right? So, I set out on another adventure. I started off trekking in Peru (there's nothing quite like the vista of the Andes to ponder life's big questions) and then I delivered some global training for new coaches in Las Vegas (a great pacey, punchy place to spark new business thoughts and ideas) and then finally I touched down in chilly Scotland. I'd been to Scotland before and really loved it. I also had romantic notions of sitting in cosy cafes writing this book, just like JK Rowling! I did kiss the odd frog in the UK too, but my intuition, practised ability to confront brutal truth and start afresh, and my well-established financial cushion came to my rescue. I was able to make personal choices, say no thank you to what did not serve me well, up sticks, dig a new well, invest in new roots and fund a new start that included a cute 'home' that could be locked up to go and new interests like cold water swimming and proper cycling. And I have met someone lovely – in fact, at the time of writing this book, we got engaged and are now happily married.

Sometimes, we just have to find the courage to change the geography.

Questions to consider …

1. Do you have to move? Is there something about your current situation that makes it impossible to stay where you are? Get real about the situation.

2. What do you believe about where you currently live and what it means for your life? Get real about the unconscious beliefs you may have about where you are now and what it means to you. Are those things true? Are there other things you have not considered that may also be true?

3. Is where you are supporting you? Does it make you happy and allow you to do what you need/want to achieve? Or is it just safe and comfortable?

4. What's the real cost of staying where you are and not moving?

Making the choice to leave your current location is rarely an easy option. But change of any type often isn't. It may be hard to go, but it can also be hard to stay. Which hard do you want? It's hard to go on a diet and get fitter, but it's also hard to stay overweight and unhealthy with its medical complications and social stigma. They are just different types of hard. It's hard to start a business or to fix a business, but it's also hard to be an employee or to be unemployed. Just different hard. It's hard to get divorced, but it's also hard to stay in something genuinely untenable.

You can look at where you are now, your experiences, who you are, and how and where you've been brought up. And while those things may help explain your current situation, none of them need define you going forward unless you let them.

So where could you be?

Take a moment to consider the cost of doing nothing and staying versus what you will or may gain if you take action and move location.

Cost of Doing Nothing	Reward of Taking Action

Revisiting Purpose

At the start of Part One, we looked at purpose mainly from the perspective of finding a reason that would unleash your inner cheetah – something meaningful that could inspire you to find solutions to whatever situation you found yourself in. And here's why it matters so much.

One of the things I have found over and over again while coaching people who are in crisis or stuck in some way, is that as soon as they get a couple of these YOU pieces sorted out or addressed, it begins to establish a sense of something solid – some sort of foundation. This stability is often enough to reignite hope and start the move out of panic, even if they know that everything isn't fixed yet. It's comforting and it's why the central tenant of this book is to get results *PEACE by Piece*. As Lao Tzu said, "The journey of a thousand miles begins with the first step." These YOU pieces, like finding a renewed sense of purpose, are a great, solid and comforting first step.

Invest the time to find your personal True North.

As we move into Part Two, it's worth pondering what those first steps might be. By now, you should be clearer on your purpose and you have learned to manage, preserve, reclaim and create personal 'fuel' for the journey. You've invested effort in finding your personal True North and thought more deeply about what you want vehicle-wise that can help you fund life. You've fostered your connections, thought about your environment, arrived at some manageable level of inner peace and started a habit of making music from that which remains.

Congratulations, you are at the start line.

But what race do you want to run?

Revisiting purpose helps you take everything you've learned about yourself and apply it to the business you already have to make it better and more fulfilling for you, or apply it to the business you might like to start.

What You Love

Take some time out to really think about your life. Buy a new journal and dedicate it to your explorations throughout this book. Think about the following questions and seek to answer them honestly:

- As a child what did you spend most of the day doing? When you were not at school where were you? What were you doing? Were you alone or with others? Were you inside or outside?
- What makes you happy? What delights you?
- What events, situations or circumstances have you thoroughly enjoyed?
- What makes you feel alive?
- When do you lose track of time? Is there any situation where you are busy with a task and minutes turn into hours without any loss of concentration or focus? What are you doing?
- What do you do on a Saturday morning or when your time is truly your own?
- If you already had all the money you needed, what would you still do?
- If you knew you could not fail, what would you do?

Think about the things you've identified and dig deeper into the memory and experience. Consider what it was specifically that you found so appealing. Was it the people, the environment, the fun, the conversation, the challenge or the adventure of it? What is it that makes that memory or situation stand out? Are there any similarities between the things that you love? Thinking back, do you realise that you love being with people, or can you see how much you enjoy your own company? Think about the environment in these situations. What was similar about the environment that might shed some more light on the things you love?

When considering these questions, we often search for specific events or tasks that we love. But actually, the way we operate and interact with others can give us more clues. For example, there are people who love the outdoors and others who would rather do just about anything than go on a hike. These differences indicate a direction of joy. Think of yourself as a detective and look back on your life to find the clues. Investigate yourself. We spend far too much time paying attention to others. Make a note of as much detail as you can so you can narrow the field of interest. These areas of interest will almost certainly be influenced by your values, which show up in your behaviour, by what takes priority on your calendar and what influences your world view.

Often, we have simply not been exposed to enough things in life for us to know if we love something or not. It may be that you love painting, but if you've never picked up a paint brush how can you possibly know? One of the drawbacks of modern schooling is that we are pushed through a set curriculum that covers maths, language and science, with little time for much else. How can we know if we would love building things if we've never even seen the tools we need, never mind learned to use them? How can we know if we would love football if we've never had the opportunity to kick a ball around?

 HELPFUL TOOLS
Values in Action (VIA) Character Strengths Survey

If you are unsure of what you value, then you might want to take the free survey at: **https://www.viacharacter.org**
In the early 2000s, the VIA Institute supported pivotal work on the nature of values and positive character. A three-year, 55-scientist study led by Christopher Peterson and Martin Seligman culminated in a book and the creation of measurement tools. The survey takes about 15 minutes to complete and may help you to better understand what you value the most, or what are showing up as your existing character strengths which, in turn, may help you appreciate what you love. Values tend to influence our actions and behaviour and can help us understand ourselves more. There are also additional in-depth reports that you can buy if you want to. These insights may also be really helpful once you get into Part Two.

Exercise #1 Make a list of five things that you love

If you're struggling, consider opening yourself up to new experiences. Find out what floats your boat and experiment with something new every couple of weeks. Or try some activities that may use different abilities. There are lots of low-cost night classes or after-work talks that allow people to try things out. There are also online courses on platforms such as Udemy.com or FutureLearn.com where you can sign up for an online course for less than the price of a decent pizza. I know of someone who slogged his way through a four-year university degree in engineering, only to get a job in computer coding based on a course in Python that he bought for less than £15 on Udemy. Obviously, he started building programmes and his engineering background would have helped, but he got the job of his dreams because of a diversion he took in his spare time.

And I have a client who decided she'd love to learn the harp at age 28 and in a few short years worked her way up from scratch to Grade 8 performance level. She started playing at weddings and events and now uses her skill and passion in a profitable six-figure business teaching clients (mainly in the USA) the harp. She employs 10 people (including her two sisters) who work from three different continents and together they bring everyone who knows them delight and joy. She regularly meets fellow musicians who are quick to tell her, "It's so hard to make money as a musician!" And she smiles!

You just never know.

What the World Needs

The next ingredient of your purpose is working out whether what you love is something that the world needs. Of course, the world needs a lot of things: more kindness, better green energy options, a way to assess immediately if something is fake news the list is endless.

Take some time to consider what you think the world needs right now – without censor – and write it down.

Exercise #2 What do you think the world needs?

What springs to mind often indicates what feels natural and meaningful to you and usually resonates with your values. Someone who suggests that the world needs a faster car is likely to have a quite different purpose to someone who thinks the world needs more ways to recycle plastic. Talk to people. Do some research. Read the paper. What are the big problems that people are wrestling with? What are the small problems? Think locally and globally.

What You can be Paid for

This is the issue most people get stuck with, immediately questioning whether it's possible to make money from whatever it is they love. But, before you fall into that trap, just consider the ways people make a living today that never even existed five years ago.

Who would have thought that it was possible to make money dressing your dog up in Star Wars outfits and posting them online or teaching people how to put make-up on? And yet there are now vloggers who are doing just that. There are people making money walking other people's dogs; you can even rent a dog. Social media marketing never existed ten years ago and now it's big business. Busy lives and technology are creating all sorts of new opportunities all the time.

Exercise #3 Can you get paid for doing what you love?

Do your research. Is anyone making money doing what you love? Because if they are, then it's possible for you too. And even if it hasn't been done so far, there is nothing to stop you being a pioneer. Never forget the power of your uniqueness. Your time will come, if you commit to your purpose.

At this stage, don't rule anything out because you're worried about the money. Let the thinking percolate and remember that we urgently need to shift away from the mentality that being wealthy is the only way to be successful. It absolutely is not. We definitely need money to live in the world, but satisfaction and fulfilment are just as important. We may have to earn a crust doing one thing and do something outside work that ticks our 'happy and fulfilled' boxes. And just because it can't make money now, doesn't rule out the fact that the world is changing all the time. You may be able to find a novel way to monetise it in the near future – remember my harp-playing client.

What You are Good at

We tend to enjoy what we are good at. This just makes sense.

According to Geoff Colvin, author of *Talent is Overrated*,[20] the last 40 years have seen an increase in research on whether innate ability is real or not and, more importantly, whether it's enough to guarantee success. Having looked into top-level performance in management, chess, swimming, surgery, fighter pilot flying, violin playing, sales, novel writing and many others, the overwhelming conclusion was that there is actually no such thing as natural talent. What separated the very good from the rest was their willingness to invest thousands of hours practising and honing their skills. It's the 10,000 hours theory made famous by Malcom Gladwell in his book *Outliers*.[21]

The research behind this figure came from psychologist K Anders Ericsson and his team at Berlin's elite Academy of Music.[22] They found there was no such thing as a 'natural' – someone who just picked up an instrument and could play or someone who had a gift for football that showed up in that person almost fully formed. There wasn't a single student who floated effortlessly to the top while practising a fraction of the time their peers did. What's also fascinating is that they didn't find any evidence of the opposite either. There were no 'grinds' – people who worked harder than everyone else, yet just didn't have what it takes to break the top ranks. Hence the importance of finding your WHY. It's the combination of initial interest, ability or love of something, together with hard work and dedicated effort, that creates what we commonly refer to as talent. Hard work alone won't work and natural ability alone won't work. We need both.

Science suggests that we need at least 10,000 hours of deliberate, consistent practise to get really brilliant at anything. Neurologist Daniel Levitin confirms this, adding, "In study after study, this number comes up again and again … No one has yet found a case in which true world-class expertise was accomplished in less time. It seems that it takes the brain this long to assimilate all that it needs to know to achieve true mastery."[23]

Too often, the existence of talent is used as a convenient excuse to justify lack of ambition or effort. People believe that if they are gifted, they don't need to work. But it just doesn't work that way. The opposite is also true. There are those who point to their lack of talent as an excuse to give up before they've even begun. But it doesn't work that way either. What we consider natural talent is not the result of some cosmic lottery – much is within the reach of all of us if we are prepared to think deeply about what we love and what we may be good at and combine that with the hard work necessary to allow it to blossom.

The personal development industry loves to tell us that we can do anything we want to if we are just prepared to work hard enough. And the majority of the time this is true. There are obviously exceptions, like when trying for the national basketball team if you're only 5-foot tall. Chances are, all the drive and talent may not be enough. But these are the exceptions and should not become our excuses. I've seen a blind person overcome and achieve things many sighted people couldn't, and a stutterer become a gifted minister. I've seen a quadriplegic learn to fly their plane again, and a chronically shy introvert transform into a presenting giant. Both men and women are breaking previously immovable limits and moving into areas unimaginable just 20 years ago.

In the main, we are all unique individuals who do come with pre-loaded skills and abilities that provide clues to our purpose. But unless we are lucky enough to stumble upon a situation that uses these skills, we may never know they are there. We have to be proactive and go looking ourselves. Investigate, think, ask questions.

And once we've found our 'thing', we need to put in the effort and practise long enough to rack up the 10,000 hours needed to achieve mastery. And the reality is that unless you enjoy it, are reasonably good at it to start with or display a natural aptitude for it, then you won't do the practise necessary to create the talent. You may start off with great intentions, but if you don't enjoy it or make little to no progress, you'll probably give up after 100 hours, never mind 10,000 hours! Human beings are human beings, not machines, so eventually willpower will not be enough to sustain the slog.

Natural ability may be God-given, but talent is man-made.

Exercise #4 Are you good at what you love?

Chances are if you love it, you'll be good at it unless it's something you've newly identified. So, a practical way to tackle what you're genuinely good at is to forget for a moment whether you love it, or the world needs it, or you can get paid for it and consider:

- Back when you were a child, what did you want to be when you grew up? Try to name as many things as you can remember. If you can't remember, ask your parents or siblings what they remember about your early aspirations? They may point in the direction of what you are good at.
- What are you better at than most people?
- What do you do effortlessly that other people seem to find hard?
- What are you doing when people compliment your effort or ability?
- Where do you add value?

 **HELPFUL TOOLS**
CliftonStrengths

CliftonStrengths is based on the life's work of Donald O. Clifton, considered to be the 'father' of strengths-based psychology. Prior to the 1990s, especially in business, it was considered a smart career move to find out what your weaknesses were and fix them. In the late 1990s, Clifton up-ended that theory when he and a team of Gallup scientists shifted the focus to strengths. Working to fix weaknesses is soul-destroying work and a weakness will never become a strength, regardless of how much you work on it. The best you can hope for is to neutralise any negative impact and certainly learning to tone down your most destructive tendencies is still useful. But the real advantage comes from uncovering your natural skills and innate abilities. Based on a 40-year Gallup study of human strengths, Clifton identified 34 of the most common talents and developed an assessment tool to help people discover and understand those talents so they were better able to find their WHY. Once known, they could then focus their hard work and effort on those things.
To discover your own talents and strengths, simply complete an online questionnaire and, depending on what you want to pay, you will be sent your top five strengths, together with an explanation, or a full list of where you rank for the 34. **https://store.gallup.com/c/en-us/assessments**

Consider, too, what others have complimented you on. Statements like, "You're so good with people; I could never do what you do" can help us not to wrongly assume that the things we do well and easily are just skills or abilities that everyone has. Taking the time to discover our purpose allows us to regain access to our innate abilities, to value them as special and unique, and not discount them as something everyone can do.

What's in Your Hand?

We are all blessed with gifts or natural abilities that, if known, lend themselves to particular professions, ways of working or lifestyles, and provide a foundation for building talent and earning a livelihood. What fires our passion, is easy to love, brings us joy, and will enthral and capture us if we take the time to uncover it? Aligning our love-to-dos with what we think the world needs and will pay us for, are essential mercenary considerations that we have to arrive at – with help, if necessary.

But this sort of deliberation takes time, needs at least some measure of an intact dream muscle to be in place, and may require resources that we don't yet have! If life has worn us down, or time is of the essence, or we're cash-strapped, a practical audit of what's in our hand is a great place to start. We all have experiences, skills, connections, talents, training and affinity for something. What is it? What are we good at and what do we absolutely hate? What have we engaged with and gained competence in already? What have we tried before with some success and what do those around us say is special, different and better about us?

When it comes to saving money and time, talking with 'another' can be very helpful in getting to grips with what's going on inside our heads. So, what resources and infrastructure, connections, and opportunities for trade exchanges with friends and family do we have in our immediate spheres of influence? What is available locally in spaces like community services or a church that will provide us with helpful, cost-effective or free resources? Which laymen, wise family members or people in the community can we connect with? What books can we read and what admirable or inspiring muses can we research online? This can all be free and quite simple. It's definitely more productive and mentally stimulating than engaging in the endless 'doom scroll' of social media or going it alone.

And then, of course, there is the willingness to put up our hands and get some paid-for help from experts. Coaches like myself can be effective sounding boards and hold you accountable to answering some of these 'me' questions, and finding out what to aim for. We can help you structure a business so that you can pay for it. This is expertise that is available, if you need it. Sure, it will cost money, but with so much depending on it, it's actually an investment. Don't nickel and dime your own future.

But remember, we can all start here with what's in our hand and what's around us to get to some settled sense of what we are willing and able to do. What will we throw our effort and hard work into? It's a challenge, takes time and may be pretty scary at times, but if we can hit a spot that resonates and gives us traction to get started in a meaningful way, it can also be fun. And we may find that we have to do a couple of turns around the block or settle on a foothill before the actual

When it finally allows us to fulfil our potential, what used to feel hard just isn't anymore.

mountain. That's okay. We may also find that this process takes longer than we'd hoped or wanted – and that too is okay. Don't shortchange or rush this process – it matters. And when it finally allows us to fulfil our potential, what used to feel hard just isn't anymore!

So, who can you engage with? A counsellor, friend, minister, community worker, coach or professional? Who can help you question and answer your way to the needed clarity that will get you to the start line?

PART TWO

Getting YOU to the Winning Post

Introduction

Now that you've established some peace, got yourself to the start line and are prepared for what's ahead, Part Two outlines the puzzle pieces that you will need to implement to create, fix or grow a business that will become the vehicle for your life.

These puzzle pieces, based on 30 years of hands-on experience, represent tangible deliverables that are present in successful businesses and missing in unsuccessful ones. They fall into a 5-stage business model that is widely used in the business-building game. These 5-stages articulate universal business 'best practice' principles.

The Universal 5-Stage Business Model

Operationally, the stages in this universal model are largely sequential. To get the best result, and particularly if you're building a business from scratch, start at the purpose-driven foundation and end at promotion. If you're already in business and need to fix or scale it, you can think of these stages as scaffolding and consider where you need to add additional support to stabilise, strengthen and support each level to make your current business even better. Ignore this sequencing at your peril. It is very hard to prospect well if your foundation is full of holes and your thinking is incomplete. It is equally hard to invest in processes that cost money if you don't have a consistent turnover. And you'll find it very difficult to get the most out of your team without processes and systems for them to stand on and drive forward with.

And while all the puzzle pieces that follow fit into and are essential ingredients to putting each stage of this model into use, they themselves are not necessarily sequential, so you may need to develop a number of different puzzle pieces at the same time or cycle back to certain puzzle pieces depending on your felt reality.

These 15 puzzle pieces, and their corresponding deliverables, fall neatly into the various stages of the business model. When we analyse the cracks running through organisations in trouble, the problem almost always relates back to missing puzzle pieces at the different stages of business growth and development or, if they are there, they are not being used or implemented properly. Think of the deliverables as the building blocks of your business. They are what you need to implement on the ground, in order to ensure that any specific piece of the puzzle is in place and working towards business success.

Figure 5.1 *The 5-Stage Business Model*

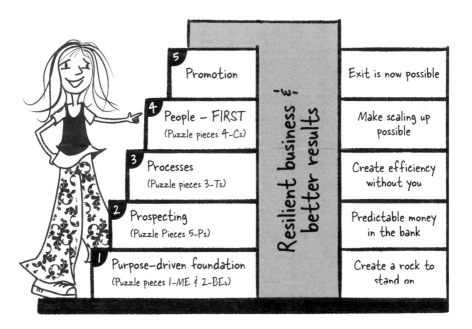

CHAPTER 6

1-ME

The first puzzle piece towards applying what you learned in Part One to a business you want to create or improve, is the 1-ME piece and the deliverable is a Dream Chart. This puzzle piece is foundational and so falls into the first stage of the 5-stage model. A Dream Chart helps to connect the aspirations you were toying with in Part One to a business outcome and articulates that dream in a way that firmly imprints it on your subconscious mind.

The Surprising Power of a Dream Chart

Almost without exception, when I tell my clients that they are going to create a Dream Chart they think I'm joking. Especially when I explain that it won't be a high-tech virtual one on Pinterest or some other visual platform, but an old-school one where we are going to cut out pictures from magazines and stick them onto a big piece of coloured card. It just seems juvenile or pointless to them, and this is especially true the more senior they are or the bigger the issue they are seeking to resolve. CEO types often dislike dream-charting as a matter of principle! And if the business is weeks away from a cash crisis, I can fully appreciate their reticence, but I've been doing industrial psychology work for over three decades now and I've seen results from this cost-effective exercise that are nothing short of magical. So, why not?

Let me tell you three true stories to give you an idea of the potency of this technique.

The Miraculous Chateau

I had a client who ran a travel agency and had come out of a bad divorce long before she began her coaching journey with me. It had been bruising to say the least, so when I encouraged her to do her Dream Chart her dream muscle was almost non-existent. But she really loved her daughter so could rally around that truth. Her daughter lived a two hour flight away from her and worked in an art gallery representing European artists. What they both really wanted was to have a long overdue European vacation together. Even as my client was cutting and sticking magazine images on her chart, she was muttering about how impossible it was because money was tight following the divorce and the legal costs that went with that! I told her to keep creating anyway, reminding her that she owned a travel agency – maybe she could get free tickets. "Oh right, yeah," she replied.

Anyway, she did her Dream Chart. In the left-hand corner was a rather lovely French Chateau that she had pulled out of a magazine. It represented her impression of what a holiday in France with her daughter would be like. She had the chart laminated and put it up on the back of the bathroom door so that she would see it every day. And then sort of forgot about it.

A few months later, I was talking to her and asking her how the dream was coming along, and she told me that she had managed to sort out free tickets from the airline thanks to a travel company she works with and was just waiting to hear what airport her daughter wanted them to fly into in France. Her daughter was sorting out the accommodation and they were both really excited about the trip. A month or so after that, around Christmas time, her daughter visited. Caught short by the trip, she rushed upstairs to the loo and shortly afterwards screamed blue murder. My client nearly had a heart attack and rushed up to see what was wrong. When she got there, she found her daughter pointing at the Chateau on the Dream Chart and asking, "How did you know about this, Mum?" Turns out, the

Chateau on the Dream Chart was the *exact* Chateau owned by an artist couple she represented, and they were going to be staying in it during their European adventure! Her daughter just hadn't had an opportunity to share the good news with her mum yet! What are the chances of that happening?

Paris Jolly

The second story is also about France. I had another client who imported a product line from China, packaged it and sold it locally and profitably. Her husband was terminally ill and her daughter had married a Frenchman and moved to France permanently. Because of her husband's diagnosis, my client needed to relocate the business so that she could manage it and look after him at the same time. Unfortunately, when she investigated the relocation costs, she discovered just how expensive it would be.

We needed a novel solution and, in the course of the business coaching, we identified a local 'funding corridor' that would work for the relocation, and which would also make the business eligible for Department of Trade and Industry (DTI) financial assistance. In many countries, there is often government-related funding available if a business is relocated to certain areas where employment opportunities are needed. My client received a good chunk in support for the new factory, which was a huge win in very difficult circumstances.

As part of the DTI deal she was expected to do some PR for them, which was fair enough considering the amount of money they had invested in her business. The first thing she had to do was host an incoming trade mission for European delegates. She wasn't very enthusiastic about this because, at the time, she was importing from China and wasn't looking to do business in Europe. My response was simple, "They gave you millions, smile and wave!" So, she did.

In one of our coaching sessions just prior to the trade delegation, she'd been in tears with the stress of everything, not least with the prospect of losing her husband, and she also felt like she was losing her daughter. So, I suggested that she put seeing her daughter on her Dream Chart, which she did, albeit a little reluctantly. Her exact words were, "Well, that's bullsh*t, isn't it?"

A couple of months passed and because she had handled the trade mission so flawlessly, the DTI asked her to be part of a delegation to go to Europe. Again, she wasn't keen. But I encouraged her to smile and wave again. They were paying for everything and, regardless of her situation, she still had some obligations to fulfil. Reluctantly, she agreed.

In the next coaching session, she was beside herself with excitement because she had just found out that of all the places that they could have been visiting in Europe, the delegation was headed for Paris. Her daughter lived in Paris. She was going to be seeing her daughter after all, all paid for by the DTI. And none of this made sense. She didn't import or export into Europe and yet she miraculously found herself in a delegation that allowed her to fulfil her dearest dream – to see her daughter.

She was a convert of the Dream Chart after that!

Sceptical CEO

The last true story is about the CEO of a successful wealth-planning company. As a chartered accountant (CA), I suspect he viewed Dream Charts as a waste of time because he was, let's say, lukewarm about the idea. But I made him do it anyway, along with his fellow business owners and their wives. They tackled it in the evening after work and had wine, which certainly helped.

Once completed, the CEO put his work of art behind his home office filing cabinet and didn't look at it again. About a year later, two younger colleagues, who'd come up through the ranks and bought into the business as minority shareholders, were involved in a quarterly strategic planning session in which we were doing dream charting. As the head honcho, the CEO was there to encourage everyone else to participate and then, as we got to the dream charting bit, promptly excused himself because he'd done his.

When I was doing the rounds of the workshop attendees to see who needed help, his two colleagues and I joked that they had pulled the 'short straw' to be stuck there cutting and sticking pictures onto cardboard – not the usual activities for qualified CAs! They obviously also knew what their CEO thought of dream charting. But then one of them added, "Yeah, but what's really interesting is the outcome of his dream charting." I was intrigued to know more.

Over the previous six months, we had worked hard to restructure the business to take some of the operational pressure off the CEO. To test the efficacy of the new organisational structure, I'd convinced him that he needed to take long leave from the business for three months, to which he'd replied, "But what the hell am I going to do for three months?"

I'd suggested that he do some of the things he had been putting off, like spending some overdue quality time with his family and friends and having a few adventures. Anyway, he'd duly taken the time off and the business had worked really well without him. The new structure had passed the test. What I hadn't known until this workshop was that, on his return, in preparation for the day, he'd photographed his behind-the-cabinet Dream Chart to give his colleagues a heads-up on what I would be asking them to do. It was only at the event, when one of them pointed it out to him, that he realised that everything he'd been so enthusiastic about on his three-month sabbatical and what he'd talked about constantly on his return, was illustrated on his Dream Chart – every single thing on it! He'd ticked off each item and had done so without having even realised it.

I'll hazard a guess he's more of a Dream Chart believer now!

What a Dream Chart does, whether we are aware of it or not, is capture something about our aspirations that are beyond the rational or verbal. By identifying powerful visual images that catch our attention and stir the soul, we fire up our neural pathways and switch on our all-important focus. Remember the audiences who didn't see the gorilla on the basketball court? They didn't see it because they were focused on something else – counting passes. We need to turn our focus on so that our brain knows what to pay attention to, what to look out for, what to watch for and what to aim for.

We need to complete our Dream Chart because it's a practical, affordable, easy way to activate Michael Losier's Law of Attraction[24] – that strange, but true and sometimes inexplicable, science that causes us to be in receipt of the resources, opportunities, encounters and chance encounters that we need to birth the things we put on our Dream Chart into reality.

In his book, *The Scottish Himalayan Expedition*, explorer W.H. Murray writes, "*The moment one definitely commits oneself, then Providence moves too. All sorts of things occur to help one that would never otherwise have occurred. A whole stream of events issue from the decision, raising in one's favour all manner of unforeseen incidents and meetings and material assistance, which no man could have dreamed would have come his way.*"[25]

> That is the power of a Dream Chart – it is a visual commitment anyone can afford to do which helps move Providence in ways that can be nothing short of miraculous.

We don't need to understand why. As William Arthur Ward said: "If you can imagine it, you can achieve it. If you can dream it, you can become it."

That is the power of the Dream Chart – it is a visual commitment that anyone can afford to do, which helps to move Providence in ways that can be nothing short of miraculous.

How to Create a Dream Chart

By now, I hope you are sold on this idea. And look, even if you are not, what do you have to lose? Worst case, you get to forget about your problems for a pleasurable hour or two of child-like escapism. Best case, you get to look back on that chart and be astonished at how much of it came true.

You can create your own Dream Chart or run through the process with others like your spouse, business partners or team. Each person does their own Dream Chart – this is personal.

It's time to exercise that dream muscle and regress a little to those uncomplicated pre-school days of cutting, pasting and colouring in to your heart's content.

I must confess that I do think our loss of childlike wonder is a bit tragic. If you ask a group of four-year-olds what they dream of, you will see loads of little arms shoot to the ceiling and hear excited cries of "A princess", "A doctor", "A footballer" and "A fireman". There are no limits – just joyful expectation and exuberance. By the time that same group hits their teenage years, most of those hopes will have been crushed under parental or social expectations and some form of not-enough-ism: not smart enough, not pretty enough, not strong enough, not confident enough. Ask a grizzled 40-year-old CEO what they dream of, and the response is probably, "I trust you're joking!" Ask them to cut out pictures and stick them on card for two hours and you may hear a few more colourful expletives!

That's why the Dream Chart process is so useful. It's so far removed from what we as adults do in our day-to-day life. It's also free and doesn't take long, so most people agree to give it a go. There is almost always a journey to that acceptance from, "No, really, you can't be serious?" to "Pictures, coloured pens, glue? Really? Oh, okay then." It's almost as though the unexpected medium of images and colour (so outside the black, white and grey of traditional business) transports us back to that carefree enthusiasm of childhood and we can't help but agree to give it a go.

If you're one of those more particular sorts who'd like to see a few examples or a template, we have some you can download from the website www.buildingbestbusiness.com.

What You Will Need

- A timer
- A pad of paper
- A packet of coloured felt-tip pens
- A large collection of magazines – ideally at least 30 different ones
- A pair of scissors
- A tube of glue
- A large A1 piece of brightly coloured card – pick your favourite.

1. Carve out some time, at least 90 minutes, where you won't be disturbed. Even if you are doing the Dream Chart with someone, you need to go through the steps on your own. So, each person creates their own Dream Chart.

2. Pour yourself a glass of wine or grab a beer, relax. No TV in the background. You can have music playing if you want, but ideally music with no lyrics as they can be distracting.

3. Open your pad and put your coloured pens next to you.

4. Consider if money and time were no object, what would you do? If you knew you could not fail, what would you create? Where would you go? What would you see?

5. Pick up the first coloured pen, set the timer for 30 minutes and start writing. Freeform. Don't think about feasibility or edit in any way – just write. Time is of the essence. If you spend too much time overthinking something, you can end up paralysing the process. We are trying to bypass your rational mind to get to your subconscious, so just write.

6. Every time you find yourself stopping or running out of things to write, change pen colour and ask yourself the questions again. Keep going until the 30-minute buzzer sounds. The coloured pens act as a primary stimulus, which can re-energise your thought process. The colour also better connects us to our creativity and imagination, which are essential in this process, and is really useful for triggering and retaining memory (so remember that next time you're putting together a memorable business presentation or designing Ts & Cs!)

7. Once the 30 minutes are up, put down your pen and move to your stack of magazines. These need to be magazines of all types, not just 30 issues of one publication. Mix them up. And don't pinch them from your doctor's surgery! That's just rude.

8. Set the timer again for 20 minutes and start flicking through the magazines. If a page stops you, then rip it out and move on. Don't stop to read the articles; just keep flicking through and pull out any image, or colour or wording that grabs you. Again, don't edit or wonder why you're choosing something; if it has gotten your attention, just add it to the pile.

9. Once the 20 minutes are up, you will have a pile of resources of images, words and colours.

10. These two processes are connected, because the 30 minutes of writing will have acted as a primer around what you then pull out of your magazines.

11. Next, cut out the images that you pulled out of the magazines, arrange and stick them on the A1 card. This may take another 45 minutes. You can have music on, get another glass of wine or beer – enjoy the process and be creative; there are no rules.

12. Warning: do not use Pinterest or some other digital platform to create your Dream Chart. Something special happens neurologically in the physical or kinaesthetic act of cutting things out and sticking them on the card. This is lost in the digital realm.

13. By the time you have finished, you will have your base Dream Chart.

14. Spend the next 15 minutes personalising it in whatever way you want. So, for example, some people add pictures of their kids, photographs or some quotations that are meaningful to them. Also put today's date on it.

15. Get it laminated and put it up in a place where you will see it every day.

Even if you think this is nonsense – just do it.

It will galvanise your subconscious and initiate the Law of Attraction. It's cheap, cheerful, easy and the results may just surprise you. And all without any further conscious effort on your part.

CHAPTER 7

2-BEs

According to international business coach, author and public figure, Brad Sugars, the formula for success in life is BE × DO = HAVE.

This puzzle piece, the 2-BEs, relates to the BE × DO part of this equation. First, it's about who you need to be to create the success you want. And second, it's about making that happen. Being is only operational if it is multiplied by doing. Hence, two parts to being (2-BEs). One is the internal mental positioning, and the other is the external expression or action. Together, they reinforce each other. 'Being' without the corresponding 'doing' delivers nothing sustainable or resilient in the long term. And 'doing', without the mental positioning 'being' component, is not always useful or effective because we feel and experience the rub of not really believing in what we are doing. They work in tandem. The being is the 'Ready, Aim' and the doing is the 'Fire'. If you fire without aiming first – you'll never hit the right target. And if you 'ready and aim' forever – you'll never hit anything!

Who Do You Need to Be?

Part of getting into the right mindset is to really look at who you are now and who you are going to need to be to deliver on your aspirations. Aspirations are not just about the things you want to own or experience; perhaps what's even more important is who you want to be. What is your set of 'I AM' statements?

When I wrote mine, they weren't all yet true or real about my life.

- I AM the sort of mother to my daughter and daughter to my mum that they value and their friends envy.
- I AM an award-winning, internationally acclaimed business coach with a consistent, profitable business of my own.
- I AM settled in my faith, under spiritual direction and an enthusiastic member of my local faith community.
- I AM a healthy, fit, 65 kgs, with a regular activity plan.
- I AM an annual overseas traveller.
- I AM in a loving, long-term relationship with 'my special person'.
- I AM a published author.
- I AM a portfolio owner with 'enough' to stop working if I wish.
- I AM financially fit and able to afford my preferred lifestyle.
- I AM the sort of friend I value to five good friends in my life.

The last one to be achieved was 'I AM a published author' and if you are reading this, then that one's true now too. These 'I AM' statements help tell our brain what is important so it can alert us to information that may help in its achievement.

In order to create your I AM statements, either convert some of your aspirations to statements, writing or saying them in the Present Tense, or take a few minutes to think about all the things you want to achieve and be known for in your life. Think about your health, connections, finances, business success, friendships, family, hobbies – all the things that are important to you. Make those statements active, as if you've already achieved them. Aim for ten. Put them on a small piece of card the size of a credit card, laminate them and carry these 'I AMs' with you at all times. If you are in a queue or waiting for an Uber, take a moment to read them and really engage with how you will feel when you have achieved the outcomes of all those things on your list.

What Do You Need to Do?

Once you have a greater sense of who you need to be to make the changes, you also need to get pragmatic and practical about how to make your Dream Chart a reality. Sure, you can do nothing and rely on the Law of

Attraction alone, or you can give the Law of Attraction a little nudge to speed things along. Dreams without grit often remain just dreams. Good intentions go nowhere.

The only difference between those who are successful in life and those who are not is that those who are successful are willing to do what those who are not simply won't do.

I'm a huge fan of business books, as I mentioned in chapter four. I have found so much wisdom and solace in books. What I love about them, especially books like those written by Jim Rohn, Dave Allen, Darren Hardy and Michael Gerber, is that they are quick, easy reads that offer some immensely practical tips on getting things done. Now, again that caution: these may be 'old books' or authors who died before you were born, but the truth between these covers remains just awesome. I'd go so far as to call it 'timeless truth' because in just about every practical situation I've been in, with different clients in different sectors in different geographies, no matter in what decade, the content has resonated with and been useful to them as business owners. Read them and, by all means, supplement them afterwards with more recent authors or podcasts/online resources that resonate with you. Don't miss them out. Consider them core textbooks!

Unless stuff actually gets done, nothing will change and nothing new will materialise.

It's true that action starts with a clear vision of what needs to be true about your business vehicle if it is to fund your life. Next, it's about you exercising your dream muscle to get clear on what you really, really want and engaging in a brutal assessment of what you will need to do to get from where you are to where you want to be. But unless stuff actually gets done, nothing will change and nothing new will materialise. So, I thought it would be useful to you for me to list my top 25 Life Hacks on getting stuff done, drawn from a variety of wise sources, life in general, impressive business examples and my own personal business and life-building experiences.

Are you ready?

#1 | Aim then Fire

If you haven't visualised it, thought it through, appreciated why it's important and got clear on what outcome you want or need, don't leap into action. So many entrepreneurs fire and then wish they'd spent a little longer getting ready and aiming at the right target first. They waste resources and time leaping before they look. They short-change themselves on the preparation (the BE work, the WHY work and the visioning work), erroneously thinking that they are saving time. It never saves time. In most cases, it creates even more delays as they end up having to regroup and start again.

Before getting into action ask yourself the following questions:

- Are you sure you are aiming at the right target for you? Think back to your Dream Chart and aspirations ... make sure this is your true target and not some hand-me-down from a parent or based on peer pressure.
- Are you sure that this action is going to deliver the outcome you need?
- Is this action taking you closer to your agreed target? Do you know or do you just 'think so'?

#2 | Brain Dump

When we are at the start of any endeavour, we need to get a sense of what's ahead. Once you have a clear target, make a list of everything you can think of that will need to be done. Sometimes, especially when we are under pressure, holding all the stuff in our head that we need to do just adds unnecessary stress and pressure to our lives. So, get into the habit of brain dumping all the things that need to get done, in order to meet your objectives. Don't worry if the actions are right or complete or what order they are in – just make a record of as many as you can think of. Also, don't worry initially if you have missed any – you will have. As long as you capture most of it, you can keep adding new items as you remember or discover new tasks that need to be done.

Some of the items on your to-do list may be tasks like 'open a new bank account' and others may be appointments or projects such as 'get healthy', which will be executed over a much longer period of time. Getting healthy, for example, is the result of many to-dos like 'stock the pantry with healthy foods', 'schedule gym sessions twice a week' and 'join a cycling group'. So, my best advice is to have two main columns: 'To Dos' and 'Projects'. If any items are in the shorter term, itemise them in the former column and if they have a number of steps that will need to be completed over time, then list them in the latter.

You can use Post-its, a spreadsheet, phone notes or specific software like Asana or Trello to keep a record of stuff and move it around between the two lists.

This brain dumping process can be daunting but it's also liberating and will help you sleep more soundly, rather than sitting bolt upright at three in the morning because you've suddenly remembered a task that needs to be done. Get all those tasks and actions out of your head to free up space for planning and execution.

- Based on where you are now and where you want to be, what are all the tasks and activities that need to be done?
- What people do you need to speak to?
- What resources do you need to access?

#3 | Eat the Elephant in Small Pieces

Your To Do and Projects lists can quickly explode and become overwhelming. To avoid this, it is critical to remember that once you've brain dumped out of your head onto paper, you can go back through the two lists to break stuff down into manageable, bite-size chunks.

There is an adage about change being like eating an elephant; you have to start at the foot and don't look up! In other words, you need to tackle things in small, bite-size pieces, otherwise the task ahead will feel too hard.

Big things get done by doing them in small, consecutive steps (see Figure 7.1).

Figure 7.1 *The Importance of Smaller Steps*

If each task is too big, it's hard to even get started, never mind build momentum. Lots of little steps are better. They feel easier and will also give you a sense of fulfilment and satisfaction as you tick them off.

Can you break some of the tasks on your list down to bite-sized chunks?

#4 | Organise Tasks into Categories

By now, your two lists may be very long. To avoid the overwhelm and keep moving forward, it's important to organise the tasks into categories. There are only five categories:

- To Dos that can go immediately onto a calendar: Add all your appointments to your calendar or diary.
- To Dos that are not now but Next Actions: Cluster all the tasks that are not project specific together, those that can be done at a specific time and on a specific day, and add them to the diary.
- Projects: Any task that has more than one action is considered a project, so you need to record it on your Projects list and regularly break each one down into tasks that can go onto the calendar or the Next Actions as time passes, or it makes sense. That way, you can bite-size your way through and prioritise steps on the way to completing your projects,

scheduling the time to work on the tasks step by step. You can also keep track of the projects that won't be finished for a while, but need to be nibbled away at nonetheless (remember that elephant?) by keeping your Projects list current.

- Waiting For: These are all the delegated tasks that can't be moved forward because you need something from someone.
- Someday: This is where you gather together thoughts and ideas that may require more research or are future- or wish-oriented and don't warrant immediate action. They are just ideas or creative thoughts that may become relevant in the future.

Whatever methodology, tools or software you have used to record all your tasks on your To Do and Projects lists, keep them current. Cross tasks off as soon as they've been done and keep adding new tasks as they emerge. Review your lists daily, weekly and monthly. Review your calendar several times a day and check your To Dos at least once a day to select your next task.

This approach sets out a process for organising and systematically working through what has to get done in a manageable way, while also keeping an eye on delegated tasks and longer-term or more complex tasks that may become more important in the future.

#5 | Use a Calendar and Diary

Getting all the tasks out of your head onto either your To Do list or your Project list is great, but unless you put them in a diary, it's too easy to forget tasks or choose not to do stuff, especially as you get busier. Being busy can be a convenient excuse that we tell ourselves when we avoid certain tasks over and over again.

You need to schedule tasks using a calendar and diary to ensure that they get done – regardless of whether you feel like it or not. Whether you prefer old-fashioned pen and paper or digital isn't really the issue; just ensure that to-dos get onto something that blocks out actual time on a real day so that they get done.

You can also enter milestones and reminders along the way so that you aren't blindsided or overwhelmed by certain big tasks or Projects. If you aren't adding tasks to your day, week and month, then you are wasting time. Remember, time is money so find a scheduling system that you like and use it religiously to power through your To Do and Projects lists.

- Do you already have a calendar or diary system that works well? If so, just use that.
- If you don't use a calendar already, it's time to start.
- Maybe get a large wall calendar, as well as a diary, so you can immediately see the tasks that aren't going to hit you immediately, but which you need to keep in your line of sight.
- Remember, keep both current and regularly break down Projects into To Dos that can immediately go onto a calendar or diary as daily, specific things to action and complete.

#6 | Don't Dodge the Hard Stuff

Doing nothing or putting stuff off doesn't make the hard stuff go away or make it easier. It just creates more and different, even harder, stuff. All that happens is that you get to feel guilty for not doing it; it chews away at your head space and robs you of energy.

There's the hard of doing and the hard of not doing. Which hard do you want?

While building a business is simple, it is never easy. Nothing of value ever is. It takes effort, hard yards and doing stuff that we don't like. This is true of so many things in life, such as health and wellbeing, relationships and a resilient business. Not doing the hard yards when called for usually just puts additional pressure on those other valuable parts of life.

We have to appreciate that it is just part of the fabric of business building and life, so block out the time and get it done. Remember, it may be hard, but it will just get harder if you keep putting it off. There is always a steep price tag for not taking action and it's often steeper than the hard stuff you're trying to dodge.

- Have a look at your tasks and your calendar. Are there any tasks that seem to roll over week on week? If so, you are avoiding those tasks. Don't do anything else until you've done them – your frogs!
- Have a good, hard chat with yourself about the 'hard of doing' versus the 'hard of not doing' to get some perspective. Both are hard, but you will probably find that the 'hard of not doing' is worse! Be brutally honest.
- Have someone hold you to account. If you find yourself procrastinating or not getting traction, it's usually a signal that something's up. Get a coach who will hold you accountable to deliver on what you have committed to. Talk is cheap; consistent action is what's required.
- Do the hard stuff first.
- Use the two times of day you have best control over – these being the start of the day (it can always be 15 minutes earlier) and the end of the day (it can always be 15 minutes later) – to initiate a new, hard habit of action, like reading or writing that report or getting to what you keep putting off.

#7 | Learn to Train in the Rain

If you wait to feel like it, you may wait forever. I hate to have to break it to you, but you are not three years old. As adults, we all have to do stuff we don't like and not whine or whinge about it. We all have to train in the rain sometimes.

In fact, when we just suck it up and get on with it, we may not like or enjoy the task but our ability to get it done helps the next time. When we bitch and complain about it, we lay down negative neural pathways that make it harder next time. We have to be like the soldier on the battlefield where we show up for the fight whether we feel like it or not because that's what's needed, not because we want to. It's a matter of honour and integrity. And the interesting thing is that the more we train in the rain, the less we hate it. Until one day we suddenly find we've learned to like or even love it. There is something deeply rewarding about facing our own flaws and our own demons and learning to dance with them.

- To help you get started, come up with a little reward that you can give yourself once you've trained in the rain. Maybe you do 10 sales calls and then meet a friend for coffee. Or you spend 30 minutes reading your favourite book in the sun after you've written the report.
- Promise yourself that you'll keep at it for 90 days before you make a judgement call on whether you're enjoying this or not. Notice what happens.
- BIG up the rewards of your training in the rain results – on social media, to your friends and family, and out loud to yourself.

#8 | Revisit "Start with the End in Mind"

Steven Covey's "start with the end in mind" is not only useful when thinking about your aspirations, but it's also a great tool for ploughing through tasks.

If you're crystal clear about the outcome you want to achieve, the brain has a most remarkable ability to work back from there – consciously and subconsciously – to identify what the problems are and how to solve them. It's how the first man got to the moon.

The big error people make is that they start from what they know and work forward, whereas they should be starting from the desired outcome and work backwards. That way, you set your brain up for success by helping to initiate the Law of Attraction and doing what it does best – solving problems.

This is also a great tool for helping to identify 'missing tasks' on your lists. Once you've done your brain dump and are working through your tasks, flip your thinking and start with the end in mind and work backwards. It can help you to discover To Dos and Projects you need to add to your lists.

- If you are stuck with a problem, take a few minutes to think about the ideal outcome (the end) before you go to sleep. Tell yourself internally that you are handing the problem over to your subconscious while you sleep and park it. You may be surprised to wake up with new ideas or perspective in the morning.
- If you believe, pray.

- Use a journal to record thoughts and problems. It's quite extraordinary how, over time, we can look back and join the dots on knotty problems.

#9 | Set Clear Outcomes, Timelines and Rewards

Any worthwhile journey includes hard bits and easier bits. Unless you have a clear, compelling outcome with a deadline, you risk creating a fuzzy or moving target. "I want to lose weight" won't galvanise your focus and effort like, "I want to be 65 kgs by Christmas so I can wow my family who will be visiting from overseas." The idea of SMART goals may be an old technique, but it works.

Take a look at your aspirations and desired outcomes and make sure they are SMART – specific, measurable, achievable, results-orientated and time-bound.

Combine your SMART goals with a reward – the harder the goal or effort, the better the reward. I recall two business owners, both of whom had young families. Neither knew the other but, when thinking about a great reward for the effort that was going to be needed to pull off their objectives, both decided on taking their young family to Disneyland. Both were encouraged to spend money they didn't currently have and book tickets for a year's time and then go home and tell their kids, "We're going to Disneyland in 12 months' time; start counting." One bought the tickets and made the declaration to his family, and the other one didn't. The one that committed to that outcome, through word and deed, went to Disneyland with his family 12 months later and the other one didn't.

- What amazing reward could you give yourself and those you love when you meet your toughest objective?
- What action, as a statement of faith in yourself, can you take to make it concrete and cement your resolve because then there's no easy way back, like buying tickets in advance?
- Consider making a public declaration of what you've done to cross the Rubicon.

#10 | Capture Your Thoughts to Aid Sleep

As a business builder, getting enough sleep is essential. We cannot build anything on sleepless, anxiety-filled nights. Often, things buzz around and keep us awake for hours because, on some deep level, we're afraid we'll forget them if we go to sleep, and that important thought will be lost.

Keep a notepad and pen next to your bed and if something wakes you up in the middle of the night, take a moment to make a note of it and then go back to sleep. Often, just writing it down can release you from its immediate mental grip and allow you to rest, knowing that you can attend to it in the morning.

- If you don't want to wake anyone else, then consider keeping a little torch by your bedside too, so you can quickly capture the thought and get back to sleep.
- If you find it hard to resettle, remember there is probably nothing you can do about that thought right now anyway, so just rest. Drink chamomile tea and read a good book for a little while. Both can help you nod off. NB: Screen time won't!
- Buy a journal or use your smartphone for capturing thoughts throughout the day.

#11 | Do the Stuff you Don't Like First – Chores before Treats

I'm sure when you were young, your parents tried to bribe you, "If you eat your dinner, then you can have a sweetie?" How often did it work?

If you were anything like me, it always worked. Many a spear of broccoli has been eaten by children on the promise of a chocolate! Building treats into your work rhythms can help to make the medicine go down a little easier – especially around tasks that you don't naturally enjoy. That way, the reward acts as a pull to get you through the work. And it's funny how even a little pull can help. It's just basic psychology, so use it to help you.

No one enjoys that sick feeling of having to do something they don't like. Often, we think that the solution is to ignore it and hope that eventually it will miraculously go away. How many times has this approach ruined your evening or day? It almost never works. It's the same when we are physically nauseous. Sometimes, it's easier to get it over with and throw up, and enjoy the reward of feeling better almost immediately.

> No one enjoys that sick feeling of having to do something they don't like.

It's the same with workload. You can avoid something and hope it goes away or you can just get it done and out of the way first. So, at the start of each day look at what you have on your plate and get the stuff you don't like or don't really want to do over with first. And set yourself a little after-it's-done treat.

Procrastination is not a character flaw that some of us suffer from; it's usually our creative excuse for putting off what we don't want or know how to do. It's not a case of being wired that way; it's just that practically we don't have enough love, need, skill or information to execute a particular task, so we hesitate. Most people delay on taking action when they have a gap in their knowledge around how or why. Filling this gap can usually release the procrastination. If it persists, then revisit the vision and tune into the cost of not doing the hard work!

Remember, getting the tasks you don't like out of the way is also great for your energy levels because, once done, it will give you a boost of confidence. The reward is that the rest of the day can be spent on more enjoyable tasks.

- How can you use smaller treats and little rewards to help you get through the workload? Think of the big rewards as prizes for eventual success, whereas the treats are little rewards for milestones along the way.
- In what order do you routinely do things? Consider rearranging this, so that you do the stuff you normally avoid first. Then you are free to get on with the tasks you enjoy more. As author Brian Tracey suggests, "Eat the frog for breakfast, not lunch or dinner". It's why so many people exercise in the morning – it gets a necessary task out of the way early!
- Is your procrastination being caused by an information gap? If so, see tip #13.

#12 | Learn or Get Help

We can't all know everything about everything. It's just not possible. And there is certainly no shame in not knowing. The shame emerges when we refuse to acknowledge our shortcoming and bluster on anyway.

Swimmer Michael Phelps has an interesting podcast. In one of the episodes, he talks about why he's had the same coach for the last 20 years, beyond the fact that this coach has helped him to phenomenal success! Interestingly, his coach is neither the same league of swimmer as him nor someone who is particularly ripped physically. But nonetheless, his coach is vital for the days when Michael doesn't want to get out of bed or is struggling to maintain his success mentally. Michael Phelps may swim sublimely, but he gets help to be the best he can be because he knows that ongoing help and support is vital. All top sportspeople know this.

We cannot know everything or be our own cheerleader all the time. If we don't know how to do something, it's just common sense to get help from someone else who does know, or who can be that cheerleader we need.

- Is there something that you don't know that is holding you up from taking action? If so, identify what it is and source a solution. Look online; there's an astonishing amount of information on how to do things on YouTube alone.
- If you find you are getting stuck or sidetracked too often, consider hiring a business, sports or life coach to keep you focused and on task.
- Make a list of who can help and get in touch with them. Ask for help.

#13 | Don't be Rubbish

Work hard to be the best you can be when it comes to execution. This is especially important before you delegate a task to someone else. There is a theory that you should never ask someone else to do something that you can't or won't do – especially as a business builder. There is no way that you can be great at everything but do your best not to be rubbish either!

Being able to do something and show others how, is a powerful leadership tool that earns respect. It's not OK to be rubbish at selling or presentations or understanding the numbers of your business. You need to hold yourself to high standards of excellence and not be lazy.

- Are there any business skills that you don't believe you have? If so, hone them. Get some coaching, learn how to do them better and practise, or sign up to do a course. As a business leader, you are setting an example – make sure it's the right one.
- Where are you abdicating or delegating? Be alert and take back responsibility for doing the things that matter.
- Do your own performance appraisal. What score out of 10 would you award yourself for each element of your job as a business leader? Do you need a bonus or a written warning to shape up?

#14 | Interest or Enjoyment not Required

As a business owner, you are going to have to deal with a lot of stuff and have at least a basic handle on many areas in the business, from accounts to marketing to logistics – certainly in the early stages. That's just a reality of business building.

The other reality is that you will need to action stuff you are not interested in, enjoy or look forward to. No one wants to fire a non-performing team member or exit a business partnership that isn't working. No one. But stuff has to get done. If feelings are getting in the way, choose to consciously park them and crack on.

I'm not diminishing or downplaying emotions that gather around certain tasks or activities, but neither do I want to give those emotions more status or power than they deserve. We can behave in ways that are not supported by our feelings and hold that contradiction without any loss of integrity for a while, or at least until the task is done. In fact, it is absolutely essential as a business builder. You don't have the luxury to allow *blah* or *meh* attitudes or feelings to stop you from doing what you have to do. Actions are what create success, not feelings.

- Can you identify a negative feeling you have around certain tasks? If so, decide to mentally put it in a box and get on with the action. What's especially liberating is that when you do this, you'll usually find the negative feelings about that task evaporate or at least dissipate.
- What tasks excite negative feelings? Check how you've mentally labelled them and then relabel them positively. For example, "The language I hate and have to do," becomes "The subject that is the key to my A-class school pass".
- Picture how you'll feel once the tasks you're dreading have been well completed. Keep that end in mind.

#15 | Avoid Denial

Denial is NOT your friend and the ostrich thing of putting your head in the sand or your hands over your ears is not useful. You have to be willing to have a blunt look at your situation, come up with a strategy, and measure the outcome and whether things are working out as planned, or need tweaking.

Who you hang around with, and the books you read, can be real allies in keeping your perspective grounded and real. Also look at the facts. What do your results tell you about the activity you are engaged in? Don't just implement a strategy and leave it or rely on your feelings or gut instinct alone.

Pretending it's OK when the results say it's not, wastes valuable time and money.

Review it. Test and measure it. Is it doing what you expected it to, or not? Face the facts of the outcomes and avoid denial – it will just slow you down.

- Is there something about your business that you are not willing to accept?
- Are there people in your business who are not pulling their weight or delivering enough value?
- Have you doubled down on a strategy even though it's not really working?

If so, you need to embrace your denial and make some changes. Pretending it's OK when the results say it's not, wastes valuable time and money.

#16 | Stay Accountable

When you are fatigued, don't feel like it, want to dodge your workload or feel lazy, you have to find a way to stay accountable to your aspirations.

Having someone whom you respect in your corner, on your side and there to hold you to account rather than allow you to wallow in your misery, is crucial. This is also just psychology 101 – when someone else is watching you and is going to check in with you to make sure you've followed through on your commitments, you are much more likely to keep those commitments. When that accountability is no longer there, it's too easy for the fatigue or negative feelings to win.

- Consider hiring someone independent to keep you accountable. I'm a coach and I still have my own coach, even though I'm an expert at all of this. Everyone, from business leaders to Olympic athletes, needs a coach to be their best. Don't pin this load on your spouse, family member or friend … it can be too heavy a load for them.
- Alternatively, buddy up with another business owner and be each other's accountability. Make weekly commitments and check in with each other to make sure you have both followed through. Link some rewards and punishments to the tasks to increase the engagement and fun. And consider paying each other for the privilege. Now this may sound unnecessary, but my experience has been that we are neurologically wired to better value something when we've paid for it. Free is often not fully appreciated or permitted to galvanise/critique/call us out like a paid-for service can. And payment doesn't have to be with money – it can be in kind, or a trade exchange or reciprocal services.
- Accept that if you haven't got around to it within three months, it isn't going to happen without help. Pick up the phone and make the change.

#17 | Recognise and Use Difference

One of the funny things about talent and ability is that the person who has them usually doesn't know it. Because they are good at something, they just assume that everyone is good at that thing too. But we are all different, which means that some tasks and activities come easier to some people than to others.

Take some time to consider what you're good at. It will usually be the things you also enjoy. Once identified, you can then swop/trade exchange tasks with others in your spheres of influence, for example, other business owners who are at a similar stage to you and in need of your services. Of course, as the business owner you can't swap everything.

According to author Michael Gerber[26], every business owner needs a mix of skills at the start before they've got the cash to invest in a team (Figure 7.2).

Figure 7.2 *E-Myth™ Model of Entrepreneurial Development*

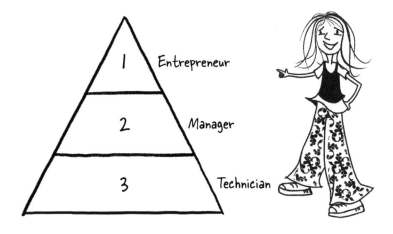

The technical skills of the offering are usually at the heart of your business – engineers start engineering businesses and chefs start restaurants. Then, there are managerial/organisational skills, which include knowing the numbers and the systems, structure and processes that keep the business running and are evident in those who've started their own business after having spent time in the corporate world. And then, finally, there are the entrepreneurial skills (selling what you actually make or do) without which no business can survive – those are the rules.

- Are there any tasks that fall outside these core categories that you could profitably and practically get someone else to help you with and who may enjoy them more than you do? If so, offload them. No need to be a martyr.
- For the 'must do' or at least 'must understand' skills, aim to improve.
- Delegate, don't abdicate. By all means engage an outsourced accountant, but don't then have nothing to do with the figures each month; reading and understanding them is still your responsibility.

#18 | View Failure as a Teacher

Failure is only failure when you quit. Everything else is feedback. Failure is your friend and, if used properly, can get you to where you want to be faster. It's certainly not something to be ashamed of or to be avoided at all costs.

When a reporter asked Thomas Edison how it felt to fail 1,000 times, he replied, "I didn't fail 1,000 times. The light bulb was an invention with 1,000 steps." And that's the truth; each 'failure' took him closer to success. Great success is built on failure, frustration, even catastrophe. Figure 7.3 is not just a feel-good meme; it illustrates common sense.

Figure 7.3 *It is Only Failure if You Don't Try*

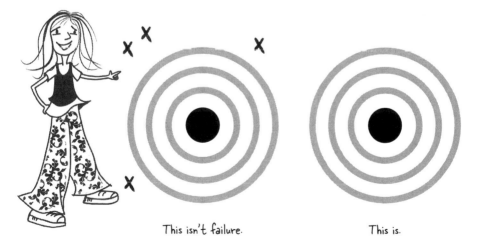

This isn't failure.   This is.

115

Failure can inform the best or next way to proceed, which can speed up success. According to Winston Churchill, success is nothing more than "the ability to go from failure to failure without losing enthusiasm." Or author Paul Coelho, who suggests that success "is about getting knocked down seven times and getting up eight."

- Think of your last 'failure' – what did it teach you? Take a moment to really lean into the situation and find that learning. The old adage of "fail fast, fail often, document what you can from it and learn relentlessly" applies.
- Read the stories of people you admire and note their setbacks and challenges and how they dealt with them. Tiger Woods has lost far more rounds of golf than the average duffer has even played. Winners don't fail less; rather, they fail more but learn and adapt their approach until they get a breakthrough.
- Keep a journal so that you can look back and see for yourself all those times when things didn't work out and what came next – it makes for positive and heartening reading.
- Intentionally search for the good that came out of your last three BIG failures.

#19 | If it's Not Scheduled it Won't Get Done

If you don't add tasks and activities from your To Do and Projects lists to your calendar and make time for them, they won't get done. If you don't make time, then it isn't important to you regardless of how much you bang on about it being a priority.

You can talk until you are blue in the face about your plans. You can make heartfelt New Year's resolutions and even set Big Hairy Audacious Goals that impress your friends, but if you stop there and don't schedule the time for action and *take* that action, then it's all for show. Good form, but no substance. Action: doing what needs to be done daily, weekly, monthly, quarterly, annually, is the only thing that will make the future you want a reality. Your chosen actions need to show up in your calendar, because action always speaks louder than words. If you value your health, your calendar will show time scheduled for the gym, or for a run, time off to relax or time blocked off to buy good food. If you value your family, your calendar will show 'date night' with your partner, concerts and family holidays scheduled in. If your actions don't demonstrate your priorities, then those priorities are just empty words.

- Have a look at your calendar; what does it tell you about your priorities?
- If you don't like what it tells you, make some changes.
- Get someone you love and respect to audit your calendar and give you feedback.

#20 | What Next?

Sometimes, you will reach a point in a Project or To Do list where no action is possible or necessary. When that happens, you have three options:

- Remove it from your current lists
- Move it to your Maybe/Someday list
- Archive it for reference.

Move on. Don't dwell on what you can't do or even what you could have done differently or better. It's done; extract any useful learning and get busy with the next tasks. Everyone has finite resources, so don't waste them going over old ground. Focus on what's next and keep moving forward.

Remember, what you focus on grows and what you tell yourself reinforces that focus. So, focus on what's next and what's possible.

- Make sure you purge your lists frequently to stay focused on what's next and not what's already done or can't be done.
- If you find yourself mentally or emotionally dwelling – get help.
- Distract yourself with something selected from your kit bag of tools that we spoke about earlier – little wins that can spark even momentary happiness.

#21 | Don't Let your Email Inbox Hijack Your Day

It is always fatal to open your email first thing in the morning; it will derail you and, even if you plan to just quickly check something, you can easily lose a couple of hours before you've even begun the tasks that are on your calendar for that day.

One thing I learned doing business in Africa is that many things really can wait until tomorrow. Don't be distracted. Plan to look at your Inbox a couple of times a day – perhaps mid-morning or lunchtime and again, late afternoon. Schedule in a set amount of time and then get back to your calendar and diary. Most of us just open our email and let the notifications draw our attention away from what's important – business by inbox!

Remember, if you answer emails after hours, before work starts and right the way through holidays, you are training everyone to misuse your time whenever they feel like it. That's your fault, not theirs. Put in some boundaries and you'll find that if you stick to them, others can become surprisingly well behaved!

- Schedule your time to review email. Stick to the timeframes you allocate and then get on with the really important stuff. Constantly checking email is a bad habit and a massive time drain. It's also a very useful tool for procrastination. Don't do it.
- Have start and finish times to your workday and stick to them – if work won't fit into them, you need to hire extra help or outsource the work.
- Delegate responsibility for tasks not done or that will be needed prior to holiday time and before you close on Fridays. Workaholism isn't attractive – it breaks up families.

#22 | Say No

We create unnecessary pressure for ourselves by putting unrealistic deadlines on tasks or letting demanding clients dictate our day by placing their urgencies on us or because of their refusal or inability to plan. We say yes to late requests and impossible timelines to please others when we should just say no.

This is your life, your time, your dream! Don't let other people rob you of your most precious resource – time.

- Make sure you really consider requests for help properly. If it is going to make your life harder, with minimal benefit to you – say no.
- A clear no is better for you and the client than a maybe that's never delivered on. Say what you mean and mean what you say.
- Make sure you have a full prospecting funnel so that badly behaving clients can be given the heave-ho. I'll discuss how in Chapter 10.

#23 | Aim to Touch any Piece of Paper Only Once

The idea here is to deal with things as you meet them. So, if you pick up a piece of work, finish it and file it. If it's a bill, schedule the payment and file it. Don't shuffle paper around your desk. Pick it up, deal with it and get rid of it.

It may be that finishing it is a three-day job and each day has a milestone you set for yourself, but don't get halfway through and then leave it. Set interim goals and finish. The world is littered with half-finished goals and tasks. Be a finisher.

Besides, your brain can easily become overloaded with partially completed or almost finished tasks. Each one is still taking up bandwidth because it can't be crossed off the list until it's done. This is often a key ingredient when we feel tired, weary and overburdened. Too much half-finished stuff, half-read books, half-done actions that sit like open tabs slowing things down and causing mental congestion. Get as much out the way as you can by aiming to touch any piece of paper only once. This is a great tool for dealing with the day-to-day stuff, on top of the other tasks that need to be done when working towards your aspirations.

- Make a tally of what is currently 90% done and diarise when you'll finish or by when it can be binned.
- Become aware of when, where and over what you dither and remember something cricketer Andrew Strauss once told me, which is, "If it takes too long to solve a problem then you're tackling the wrong problem."

• Identify a specific reward for each of the completed tasks that are currently half-done.

#24 | Plan Tomorrow's Activities Today

Another great productivity hack is to plan tomorrow's activities at the end of each day so you know in advance what you will be working on.

It ensures that you ready and aim the night before so that you can fire at the right target in the morning of the new day. Plus, it's very easy to implement. Whatever time you routinely finish your day, wind up 10 minutes earlier and spend those 10 minutes going through the next day's diary to see if you've got everything you need to get started on those tasks and/or whether you need to amend, add or delete anything.

It's akin to Abraham Lincoln's advice, where he said that if he had to spend all day chopping down trees, he'd invest time every hour sharpening his axe, or Martin Luther King's axiom that the busier his day, the longer his before-the-day started prayer time.

You will always get better results if you know in advance what you are going to focus on in the morning. Try it.

• Diarise those extra 10 minutes at the end of each day to plan for tomorrow so you can hit the road running.
• Get your team and family to adopt a similar habit of forethought and watch your collective productivity improve.
• Until it becomes a habit, set an alarm to initiate 'planning time'.

#25 | Use Watermarks and a Clear Filing System

Science has recently discovered that there is no such thing as multitasking, regardless of gender. We are all only capable of thinking about and actioning one thing at a time. What can appear like multitasking is actually just efficient switching between tasks and some people are better at this than others.

Anything that helps us maintain focus and switch quickly is therefore always going to help with productivity. One way is to ensure that you allocate time for specific activities by divvying up your day into different watermarks – one for each task group. These watermarks then sit on the calendar and to-dos are put into them. They are called watermarks because each one is always in the same place. If the slot allocated to each watermark runs out and you don't get all the tasks done, then the task moves to the appropriate watermarked slot the next day. Don't allow the task to bleed into the next slot, which is a different category or watermark.

Figure 7.4 shows my watermarks for a normal week in a four-week month. In a five-week month, I use the fifth week to prioritise marketing and selling because this is the fuel or lifeline of any business.

Figure 7.4 *My Watermarks for a Week*

	Appt Time	Mon	Tues	Wed	Thurs	Fri
1						
2	07.00 – 09.00					
3	09.00 – 10.00	1/2	3/4	5/6	7	8
4	10.00 – 10.30					
5	10.30 – 11.00					
6	11.00 – 12.00					
7	12.00 – 12.30	9	9	9		
8	12.30 – 13.30					
10	13.30 – 14.00					
11	14.00 – 15.00				My coach	
13	15.15 – 16.15					
14	16.30 – 17.00					

Group coaching	**Nine Hats of a Business Owner**	
One-on-one coaching	1/2 – Debt/Finances	
Lunch	3/4 – Sales/Marketing	
Personal/Exercise	5/6 – IT/Reading	
Daily team meeting	7 – Resource development	
Weekly/Monthly team meeting	8 – Planning	
Correspondence/Emails/Filing	9 – Own admin	
Prospecting/Client workshops		

- Take some time to work out what your watermarks might be. These are broad topics or functional buckets that you need to achieve or touch consistently and into which specific tasks and activities can be slotted to make the business successful. Use mine as a starter.
- Block out the time for the areas or watermarks and then allocate tasks to those areas strictly.
- Don't run over into the next watermark but do run over into the same watermark the next day or week.

121

Everyone has to find their own ways to get stuff done, but I have found these productivity and life hacks to be particularly effective.

Executing the 2-BEs Successfully: Their Story

Alcid John Martin, known as AJ to his clients, qualified as a chartered accountant in 2001. He worked in commerce for about 12 years as a financial manager at three larger companies in various industries before being retrenched. At 48, AJ had to decide whether to find another job, with the same job insecurity, or use his professional qualification to start his own accounting and tax practice. He opted for the latter and started AJM Financial Services Inc. in 2013, as a way to provide for his family.

It was a big decision. And the all-important starting point was to make the mental transition from an employee to a business owner. This is something that many new business owners underestimate and it's why sometimes being forced to make the jump can be a real blessing in disguise. AJ's decision was certainly made easier because of his retrenchment. He wasn't even that old and the realisation was that if it could happen to him at 48, it could happen again, and he would have no control over his future. Setting up his own business put him in charge of that future. He was also excited to see the back of corporate red tape and politics, as it would allow him to make more time for his family before they got too old. Work-life balance was therefore an important factor.

Although the risks and stresses of the two options were different, he was convinced that going his own way would be the easier option, and oh how wrong he was!

It took AJ two painful months to appreciate that his capability as an accountant was one thing and turning that into a successful business was something else altogether. AJ is a great accountant, but that skill set just got him to the start line. Essentially his skill set was AJM Financial Service's 'product'. Building a business off the back of it required a completely different skill set. It involved learning how to scale his craft, how to market his craft consistently, how to sell to customers and ensure that they could 'see' and 'feel' the value he delivered. It was about successfully transitioning from the base layer of Michael Gerber's triangle, the technician, to be able to demonstrate skill in all three layers. It was about mastering the business competencies and skills that all his years at university qualifying as a CA did NOT teach AJ.

But AJ has that unmatched quality of a great entrepreneur – he knew when he was beaten, and he wasn't afraid to put up his hand and get help – he remained teachable. After months of turning over what amounted to a fraction of his previous corporate salary, he reached out to get help and got himself a business coach – me. When I interviewed him many years later about what he'd learned, he said, "I had to learn to change my sense of who I was and then learn the skills I needed to run a business, especially when it came to sales and who my ideal target market was." These had been foreign concepts to him back then and he'd had to assume an identity that had been foreign to him too. They'd required a language that he hadn't known how to speak and he'd had to step off the professional pedestal of accountant and into the vastly more complex role of business owner. He'd also had to embrace many of the Life Hacks we've spoken about in this chapter in order to make the transition.

With my help, AJ wrestled with the mental transition – and made it. He developed a new vision for his failing practice and re-enrolled his family in a new True North. Off the back of how much he needed to make each month, we worked on him defining his target market quite specifically. He wanted to focus on small to medium businesses in his local area that needed assistance in compliance, specifically with SARS (South African Revenue Services) and the full range of financial help that sets an owner up to make great financial decisions each day, week and month.

I had to learn to change my sense of who I was and then learn the skills I needed to run a business ...

Together, we worked on creating the basic, almost-free marketing collateral, habits of action, lists of what needed to get done and a calendar, as explained earlier. Collectively, these steps created a secure foundation on which to base his steady and manageable flow of new leads when the business needed them – not just when they came in.

Off the back of his new identity as a business owner, he reprioritised and better managed his time to support his new identity as rainmaker. He became fluent in sales-speak and handling objections, as well as fluent in presenting professionally to cement his status as a reputable expert.

AJM Financial Services grew from a one-man band to a team of five employees, servicing approximately 90 clients, in various industries, with all the expected services (basic bookkeeping, payroll, tax submissions for companies and individuals, preparation and sign-off of financial statements, company secretarial services and general management consulting on the financial side of the business). AJ got to enjoy a consistent and growing turnover each month that is now up to six figures. He got himself a great red Audi, and his children were educated at their first and best choice of school, enabling them to go to university if they so chose. And, best of all, his wife was able to give up work she really didn't enjoy.

And because AJM had done the hard yards, he came through Covid and the various lockdowns relatively unharmed, stronger than before and ahead of his company's planned profit. He invested in himself and took to heart my mantra: "If you want to build a bigger, better business, you have to build a bigger, better you." He and his team have stayed updated on everything relating to finance, compliance and accounting best practice by prioritising self-education, training, online presentations and reading. And AJ has led from the front.

His advice to other business owners is simple: "The secret to success is surrounding yourself with the right support that can ensure you remain positive; forces you to make the mental shifts necessary for success; helps you learn to re-invest your time on the right things and master the essential skill of selling, which needs a constant push and strong accountability."

During the life of any business, including yours, we as owners will be required to adapt, flex and keep going with all sorts of new challenges, on top of the challenges we are already dealing with. We don't have to wait until we're sick to get better. Our economies need us, our team, suppliers and clients need us. We don't know what's around the next corner but if we get our head straight on the 2-BEs and implement the Life Hacks, we can weather many an economic storm.

CHAPTER 8

3-Ts

Now, you've got the first three of the 15 puzzle pieces that make up the foundational fulcrum of being a business owner sorted (1-ME, 2-BEs). It's time now to look at 3-Ts or three tools that will serve you well – irrespective of the business or sector you are in. Think of them as core muscles:

1. Your True North
2. Key Measurements
3. A Healthy Fuel Line.

T1: True North

Every person derives meaning from having a purposeful sense of where they are going and why. It's part of what it means to be human and why we do the Dream Chart. It's also the personal aspirational work we spoke about in Part One that is so essential for success following seismic change or disruption. When we have a strong why, purpose or guiding True North, it helps us to get up, get on and keep putting one foot in front of the other until life is the way we want it to be. Understanding our 'why' makes it easier to successfully navigate 'how' as we do life.

> Understanding our WHY makes it easier to successfully navigate HOW as we do life.

But this personal element of your True North – which is only part of your whole and complete True North as we shall see shortly – is also critical for building a business and here's why: building a business is simple, but it's anything but easy. It's a full-contact sport. It's much harder to be successful if you are broken in some way. That's why Part One is so important. You can't get to the start line damaged and limping; you need to do some pre-work to arrive ready. You may not be fighting fit, but if you have dealt with most of your immediate challenges, have squared some of the disruption in your head and know where you are heading, then you are ready for the hard work to begin.

Defining your True North gifts you with a compass that can provide moral and active direction to keep you on course to what matters and help you course-correct when needed. It's made up of two distinct but equally important elements. The first is your private and personal motivations: the WHY, which are inner reflections, deeply held beliefs and dreams that make life worth living, represented by your Dream Chart and I AMs. The visuals activate your subconscious mind and galvanise your efforts, adding inspiration to your environment to work with you not against you. Your I AMs bolster your sense of identity and self-belief when stated out loud, which can be done as often as needed.

The second element is that there is a practical, tangible point and purpose of the business that will pay for it all – the mercenary direction!

So to be complete and properly useful, your Truth North also needs a professional or public element to it. Think of this part as the all-important 'end in mind' for the business you build.

It's deciding what your business vehicle will look like when it's finished, when it's successfully funded the dreams and turned your I AMs into reality.

This element of your True North will mandate why you've got certain To Do and Project lists for action that you face bravely and get done using the 25 Life Hacks, your calendar and diary. It's about deciding or re-affirming what sort of business you actually WANT to grow, sustain, fix or use to fund your ideal life.

It's hard to build something you don't fundamentally resonate with or that clashes with your values and deep-seated beliefs. Or worse, doesn't matter to you anymore. Human beings change, life experiences change us and sometimes, even when we've created a business, we might wake up one day and realise it's just not what we want anymore. That's OK. It just means that we need to re-group and figure out what's really important now and work towards that.

And this business-minded or professional element of your True North is what you encapsulate into your Vision, Mission and Values (VMAV). Your VMAV describes, outlines and speaks to what has to be true about the type, size, turnover, profit, services, team, feel, culture, clients and efforts of the vehicle that will make you the money you need for life. It's the visual picture of what this thing you are building will look like when it's successful (as defined by you). It also includes the big-picture commitments or guiding principles, values and beliefs that you will hold 'forever true' in every aspect of the business as you build it.

Your VMAV functions as your business identity, your drawcard in the marketplace, a fixed endpoint for you and the team to aim for and a line in the sand against which you can vet those who want to join you to ensure they too are aligned to what matters.

It is foundational to your business and sits in the first stage of business building.

How did I do this?

At the end of Part One, I recommended that you revise and polish your purpose to gain greater clarity around what you wanted to create, looking specifically at the intersection between:

- What you love
- What the world needs
- What you can be paid for, and
- What you are good at.

Having decided that I didn't want to be the cat-food lady without enough to retire well and I didn't want my daughter to suffer because of her parents' mistakes, I now needed a vehicle that employed me in non-mum hours I needed to be clear about what this would look and be like when it was finished.

In my PEACE work (Part One), I had realised more clearly that I have a passion for encouraging others and a long-held belief that the world needs entrepreneurs to succeed where politicians fail. I'd tried and hated corporate life, so I definitely wanted to create a business where I was calling the shots. I was qualified in humanities and had wide-ranging, practical business experience.

I took each of these ingredients in turn. I loved working with people and helping them; that had become clear during my work as an Industrial Psychologist. I also had solid business expertise and others often told me I was good at it. I seemed to have a knack for cutting through the noise and honing in on the things that would make the difference or deliver the desired result. People often referred to me as a truth-teller or someone who didn't shy away from hard facts. I was sure that could be useful – especially in business when time really is money. I knew the world needed better business help because the statistics on business failure are still incredibly high. In my research, I'd found other people who were already successful business coaches, so the world did pay for this kind of service. And perhaps I could learn from and with them.

I had a settled sense of internal peace that I'd found something purposeful – something that I could be good at, make money from, and that the world needed. I was going to become this thing called a business coach and build a coaching business run from home, which would enable me to combine my skill sets, while honouring my time constraints as a single mum. I had done my homework on how much life would cost and therefore how big I needed to grow. And I could 'see' the final results. I had my professional or public True North.

Does what you want out of life and the life that you want bring out your inner cheetah?

If you already have a business, ask yourself, "Is my end in mind, my True North clear, public and written down? Does it reflect and encapsulate what I've discovered about what I love, what the world needs and will pay for and what I'm good at? Does it allow me to live my values and be at peace with my beliefs? Does it inspire me to get up and out of bed most days and talk with passion about what I do for others? Does it allow me to lead with confidence and strong self-belief? Is it taking me in the right direction – towards what I want out of life and creating the life that I want? Does it bring out my inner cheetah?"

If the answer to any of these is no, then the first step is to get clarity around any disconnect or misalignment and work to re-find, re-articulate, re-cost, re-shape and re-cast your VMAV. It's incredibly hard to be successful in business if none of what you have to do each day moves you towards your personal True North (your dreams and personal aspirations). It's also incredibly hard to be successful if your day-to-day effort isn't towards what's encapsulated in your professional and public True North (the vision, mission and values), which spells out to you and the rest of the world exactly what the business vehicle you are building will look like when it's all done. These are just truthful facts.

Questions to Consider Around the Legal Entity

Having decided that you're going into business and clarified what type, how big, what it will do and why this matters to you, one of the first practicalities needed to get to your professional True North and a vision for the business is to settle on how you will legally trade. Take some time to really think about the following questions:

1. Do I want to do this alone or with a business partner, and if so, what are the implications regarding legal agreements that protect each of us?
2. How will I or we work and separate ownership from employment? They are not the same.
3. What structure of business will I create? Anyone can become a sole trader, and a partnership, while straightforward, won't work well unless there is clear written agreement. Limited liability options – called different things in different jurisdictions – may be a better option. A company costs more to set up, but it offers greater protection for your personal assets should anything go wrong and can also have significant tax advantages. My suggestion – seek good legal advice early – the cost of not doing so can be huge.
4. What's the end game? Do I want to eventually sell the business, or build it to be a 'cash cow' and have someone else take over managing it for me while I step back?
5. How big, and over what geography, will it extend at scale? Will there be one or more entities?

Each of these questions will have a bearing on how you start and build the business and they need to be resolved and documented up front to prevent heartache, expense, tax complications and legal wrangles further down the line. Make sure you decide on these issues before you build something of value, especially if you are going into business with others. That way, everyone is very clear on the structure and rules of the business and what will happen in various scenarios. If these issues are agreed up front, then you reduce the chance of a fight later on. It's a bit like finalising the will or drawing up the prenuptial agreement before getting married – it's always easier to do and to agree on at the beginning of the relationship when things are new, sparkly, going well and before there's anything material of note to fight over.

What's the Number?

To have a professional and public True North and a vision for the business, you need to be clear about a number. And this number is made up of two elements: firstly, the cost of your dreams and then, secondly, the costs associated with creating, running and scaling the business vehicle that will deliver these dreams.

What will your ideal life cost? You need to allocate a completely mercenary, unapologetic, no-holds-barred price tag to your Dream Chart so that you can know what the business needs to deliver on this front. What you would like to provide for your kids and have at your disposal to spend on travel, property you want to own or enjoy, toys, vehicles, entertainment and luxuries? Come up with a number.

If you're currently in financial straits, this may be overwhelmingly out of reach. So, by all means, calculate a second number, your 'Right Now' number. What do you need to survive month-on-month right now? This may include a mortgage, other regular payments, living costs and a little extra. You can think of your Dream Chart number as the sun and the Right Now number as the stars. Articulate and outline both, but start with aiming for the Right Now number and keep your Dream Chart number there in front of you as a measure of your ultimate success.

So then, how much is enough, personally speaking? When I was calculating my number, I had no clue where to start so I found a financial planner who shared my values and beliefs. He was a qualified and certified wealth manager who worked with me to formulate an actuarial guesstimate of what the life I wanted would cost and therefore what my business had to deliver.

Having said this, there are, of course, all the other costs that need to be factored into your number, like those associated with resourcing, running and scaling your business. They include stock, salaries, overheads, cost of sales, suppliers, tax, systems, equipment, advisors, raw materials, machinery, marketing, prospecting, distribution, production, rainy day reserves, legal protection, compliance, accreditation, expansion and investments.

If you are already established, a review of your financials will provide you with this information. If you are starting out, you may not always know the answer but, with some online research guided by some good questions, you will be able to create a reasonable guess. And if all else fails, seek advice.

Some Good Questions to Help you with Your Number

1. What essential costs do I have to consider that will keep me and my dependents financially safe? For example, do I need key man insurance, income protection, life insurance, medical insurance?
2. What are my retirement costs? What savings do I need and what investments do I need to make?
3. What products and services will the business sell? How much will it cost to create or deliver these products and services?
4. What sort of help will I need when the business is up and running or what extra help will I need to scale? Do I need to hire employees?
5. What sort of equipment or capital investment, raw materials, stock and supplies will I need to run the business?
6. How much physical space will I need to operate from? Will I need to rent an office, or can I work from home initially? If you already have a business – can I downsize premises and use the saving elsewhere or do I need to upsize for growth?
7. What systems, technology, licences and software will I need to onboard and become proficient in?

8. What will the running costs of an ordinary month for this business be and how much do I need for a three-month, rainy-day reserve?
9. What are the tax implications each month?
10. Will I need to be VAT registered?
11. What marketing collateral do I need for a basic start? How much will this cost?
12. What bank accounts will I need? Pay attention to the fees and what the account allows you to do.
13. What additional paid-for help, such as legal or financial, will I need?
14. What competences/skills/learning do I need to invest in?

If you feel lost or unmotivated, a business coach and/or an accountant can help you get a handle on the business costs – the actual running, operational, scaling up and growth costs associated with the vehicle you want to build or re-build. You don't have to flail or fail in getting to the number.

As an aside, while your business vehicle is there to fund your life, please remember it cannot be your personal piggybank. The business costs have priority too. Overlooking or being ignorant of these, including tax, has caught many a business owner short. The amount you take as a salary, or salary plus dividend, is only ever a proportion of total revenue – don't forget that.

> ... while your business vehicle is there to fund your life ... it cannot be your personal piggybank.

And if you have a business already and it isn't making what you've identified you want or need, or its sucking all of your time, it's a good idea to go back and consider some of these questions and thinking to see whether the business you have needs to grow and, if so, by how much.

Vision, Mission and Values (VMAV)

Once you know your Right Now or Dream Chart number and have added in the costs of doing business via your business vehicle, you know what the business needs to deliver. But remember, nobody is going to happily work hard for you if they know that all their effort is simply going to fund your next overseas trip. That is a private motivation, not a public one, and remains in the background while your vision, mission and values (VMAV) is what is flown publicly.

Like your Dream Chart, your VMAV needs to be defined and written down. These insights can't just live in your head. They are critical, non-negotiable building blocks in securing your professional True North, which is fundamental to Stage One: your purpose-driven foundation. Each of these three elements – vision, mission and values – needs to go down on paper and then be used to enrol and inspire you and then the people you hire to help you.

Vision

Your vision is, essentially, a public, adjective-packed half-page statement that describes the business once it is successful. Think of it as reporting on what we would see if we opened the doors to your business when you've hit your most aspirational goals and targets and reached the end you've had in mind. It considers your ideal client, your offerings, your size, feel, location, team, financial success, raison d'etre and reach. It answers WHY and WHAT you are building.

Ideally your Vision should be:

- Stretchy, focused on the long-term preferred future you want to reach for – your idea of success.
- Meaningful, compelling and formatted in a way that when you read it, it brings out your inner cheetah and when others read it, it fires them up and makes them want to be a part of your business.
- Cover a span of 8 to 10 years from now; however, you need to write or verbalise it in the present tense even though it may not yet be real. Paint the picture of what your business will look like when someone visits in 8 to 10 years' time and tours it virtually.
- Strong, purposeful and definitive, so never use words like 'try', 'aim to' or 'small'. Instead, use 'are' and 'definitely'.
- Visible and descriptive to enrol and inspire you and others. Consider mentioning location, size, offerings, place, types of clients and types of teams. Don't do what many big brands do and condense their vision

down to a one-liner. Your business is probably not the sort of rocking, internationally known brand that can do that – yet! And don't be so vanilla that your vision could apply to a million different businesses.

Mission

Your mission talks more to the WHEN and HOW aspects of your business. Think of your key stakeholder groups – your clients, your suppliers and your team – and also consider what you're offering. What will be the commitments your business holds on to in relation to those stakeholder groups and what you will you deliver when it comes to the *how*? What will be the core 'doing' truth with respect to each of these?

Ideally your mission should:

• Document what you are committed to.
• Detail what products/services you will offer to what type of customers and what sort of team members you will engage with.
• Outline what your broad, non-negotiable principles are around how you will achieve your vision.
• Become a foundational part of the roadmap you and your team will follow.

Values

Business is tough for a whole host of reasons and, in the heat of battle, it can be very easy to forget who you are and what you stand for in the quest for the next sale or the next new client. Values are your WAY; they represent your 'forever trues', the principles and ideals that will always guide you in business anytime, anywhere. State your values as verbs and be creative. Use a thesaurus to find alternative words for quality, service or excellence, which are grand words, but over-used. Sketch out what you will actually see in any area of the business when these values are in operation. What will show up when you're handling a customer complaint or

> Values are your 'WAY'; they represent your 'forever trues', the principles and ideals that will always guide you in business anytime, anywhere.

firing a team member? When packing an order or asking for payment, what business values will be evident? Don't choose too many, as you will have to live them and be seen by others to be living them; otherwise, they will be pointless. Three to five values are enough.

Ideally your Values should encompass:

- What matters at the heart of your business and always will.
- What you do and how you all walk the talk.
- What your customers see and what matters to them.
- Confirmation that what counts get recognised and rewarded.
- What makes your business and its modus operandi special, different and better.

Use the Internet to research examples of what you want to build or have in mind. Search out businesses like the one you outlined in your vision. I personally looked in Australia, Canada and the UK. Check out their websites and see the sorts of vision and mission statements they use. Let this inspire your own creative thoughts. You don't need to reinvent the wheel. Borrow, echo and adapt an existing vision, mission and values that resonates with you and tweak it to make it your own. This can be just as powerful. Remember that others reading this need to be able to see what's in your mind's eye. The more descriptive your language is, the clearer your vision, mission and values will shine through.

Get this information down on no more than ONE PAGE. Less than a page and it's too short. More than a page and it's too long.

Over the years my vision, mission and values for my business, Building Best Business, have evolved and today they are:

Our Vision:

We are 'entrepreneurial evangelists' to every business we connect with. We inspire and help their owners to be the very best they can be when it comes to entrepreneurial muscle; fiscal fitness; building great teams; able and consistent prospecting; effective and resilient long-term capacity to deliver; profitability and leverage.

Our goal is 'real results for real people'. We ensure this by offering a variety of coaching processes, tested and measured intellectual property and world-class hands-on experience in businesses for owners who are keen to build to last; want to get better and bigger; clearly see their value to the economy; appreciate that overnight success isn't attainable; are investment-minded; not afraid of hard, smart work, and are willing to embrace change.

Our purpose is to Build Best Business that delivers long-term success and realised dreams for owners and their teams.

Our Mission:

- Building Best Business is a team of committed, positive, professional, business-savvy and successful individuals who work to ensure that anyone who comes in contact with the business, benefits.
- We work in co-operation with all those who operate in the SME sphere and are committed to ongoing education and an unflinching willingness to change when necessary. And we are always willing to change ourselves, our processes and our clients in ways that are practical, substantial, fun and valuable.
- Our products and services are world-class and deliver value for money and real results that give owners greater control and freedom, ignite their enthusiasm and liberate them through business development.
- Our clients understand that we are an awesome investment into their now and their future – a relationship and not a transaction. We treat each other and the coaching process, even when it gets challenging, with respect.

Our Values:

- Substance: All that we do is characterised by professional delivery, courageous ownership and fierce commitment to the highest standards of quality. We seek to exceed expectations for individual and business success.
- Resilience: Short-cut, short-term or short-changed are not in our vocabulary. We are committed to finishing strong and will not compromise on our or your long-term success for anything.
- Fun: Life is a journey to be enjoyed, appreciated and lived well and so we create an environment that is upbeat, can-do and always values a sense of humour.

- Integrity: Being a person of their word and who walks their talk, matters and so we strive to live what we teach and be the sort of example that others want to emulate and follow.
- Gratitude: We never forget to be truly grateful or lose sight of the fact that whatever we create needs to be stewarded well and shared generously.

What to Do with Your VMAV

This document is your public WHY and the professional part of your True North. It is the document you post on your website, put up on the walls in your office, hold up to the team when annual goals are set and monthly targets formulated and reviewed. It's the end point you use to galvanise action and direct decision-making to ensure that efforts are focused, accurate and working.

This VMAV is what sets you apart from your competition – it's the quest you are inviting customers, suppliers and team members to join in building and operating. It's what you use to convince talent to join you instead of your competition. It's what you use to separate prospects from suspects, so that you can convert the ones that 'get you' into customers who become part of 'your tribe'. The suspects don't 'do business like you', and that's fine. Your VMAV will attract like-minded people to your business and repel the rest, saving you both time.

Your VMAV means you stand for something, are building something specific and working towards something that others can appreciate and visualise. In standing for something publicly, you have a plumb line for everything else that doesn't resonate with you or align to your VMAV, and you can say no to the wrong customers and yes to the right ones. And you can engage like-hearted and like-minded staff and suppliers.

> Values are your 'WAY'; they represent your 'forever trues', the principles and ideals that will always guide you in business anytime, anywhere.

This plumb line also provides context to prioritise, focus and review activity daily, weekly, monthly, quarterly and annually to see if you are 'on track'. Send it out with quotations and proposals to showcase Who We Are. It helps establish trust and is a great marketing and communication tool when looking for supplier or strategic connection. It is also part of what you use to measure performance, who stays, who goes, who succeeds and how.

It matters. Get it done and put it up on the wall. Post it to your website.

T2: Key Measurements

According to business guru Peter Drucker, "You can't fix what you don't measure". This is true in sport, relationships, health, life and certainly business.

If you're going to have a functioning business vehicle to get you to where and what you need in life, you have to measure some stuff.

There are two broad measures that are relevant for every business:

1. **Strategic measures**: If this is where we are currently (our net present position) and this is where we need to be (our True North – Dream Chart for personal and VMAV for the business), what's the plan or roadmap we need to be following to get us from here to there? And are we on or off track each day, week, month, quarter and year?
2. **Sales measures**: Do we have enough money each day, week, month, quarter and year to reach our destination? Your business 'fuel' is money in the bank off the back of sales.

Strategic Measures: The One-Page Strategic Plan (1-PSP)

Before you start panicking over bad past experiences with planning, or getting overwhelmed by the idea of a strategic plan, thanks to Verne Harnish[27], we've got a workable one-page strategic plan (1-PSP) that is invaluable, easy to use and irreplaceable. Simply click the QR code on the left to visit our website www.buildingbestbusiness.com and download an example.

The 1-PSP is a business plan format, but all contained on one A3 page and not a weighty 150-page document that no one ever reads, never mind reviews. Instead, it is an action-oriented roadmap to ensure that individual and departmental efforts are channelled towards making your long- and short-term goals a reality. The problem with most strategic plans is that they are created for the long-term, but they don't optimally dig into the detail of what needs to happen over shorter time horizons to make that outcome a reality. With this version, you set out what you want to achieve 8 to 10 years from now, and then work backwards to articulate the milestones on the way against which actual progress will be measured, and revisions to the plan made accordingly.

It is therefore created once, but reviewed or updated quarterly. Although the final goal stays unchanged, what needs to happen in the next quarter or 90 days will change as you make progress towards that outcome. What needs to happen in 1 year or in 3 years' time will also change as you march relentlessly towards your chosen outcome. But don't panic. It doesn't take a college degree to be able to fill it in and it won't need an MBA to implement it. This is the ideal partnership between maintaining the significant merits of strategic planning, while also making it accessible and doable for most entrepreneurs, especially those who don't like planning because it feels too intangible. And it has worked for every business of any size, selling products or services, that we've worked with. That's how I know.

Elements of a Good Strategic Plan

Using the 1-PSP visual example downloaded from our website, you'll see that I've numbered the blocks to guide you through how to complete it, starting at 1 and working your way through to 18, in order. By the time you complete 18, you will have your 1-PSP done – and it's a great feeling. So, let's get started:

1. Business details and the date.
2. Values: Lift your three to five values from your VMAV and drop them in here.
3. The Vision for the business – your half-page crafted and compelling statement of the end you have in mind.
4. Your Big Hairy Audacious Goal – in your wildest dreams what's the one aspirational, positive mark you want your business to leave or achieve? Add that here.
5. The ONE big measure that will illustrate or be a measure of your success – is it money in the bank, a profit goal, an award won or a lifestyle achievement?

6. What's the brand promise or value proposition that customers can expect from you every time?

7. If you had 60 seconds to introduce yourself memorably to a stranger so that they'd be interested enough to give you their contact details, what would you say? Then practise this so it becomes fluent and confident.

8. Long-term goals 8 to 10 years from now, written in the present tense.

    a. Who will need to be on your team in 8 to 10 years' time to get the tasks done? (The people)

    b. What will your processes and systems need to be like to support the turnover? (Your processes)

    c. What sort of financial performance and market share will the business be enjoying each month or year by this time? (Your performance)

    d. What will be in place and functional in terms of a sales and marketing machine? (Your prospecting)

    e. What will your product or service mix be? (Your product offering)

9. In order to deliver on the 8- to 10-year goals, what will you have achieved in three years' time in each of the five categories?

    a. Who will be on your team by then?

    b. What systems and processes progress will have been made towards the 10-year goal?

    c. What level of financial performance, profit and turnover will the business be delivering?

    d. Where will the business be in terms of its ultimate prospecting ability?

    e. What will the product or service offerings look like at this point on the journey to success?

    f. Are there any critical numbers that will indicate the progress over the 3 years that make sense to watch? Turnover or market share? Perhaps it's numbers of clients or a specific production output? Maybe its monthly profit or numbers of branches opened?

10. In order to deliver on these 3-year goals, what progress will have been made in one year in each of the five categories?

    a. Who will need to be on the team by the end of year one?

    b. What systems and process progress will have been made?

c. What level of performance will we have reached financially?

d. What will have been put in place on the prospecting front – what will we be able to see in play for marketing and sales?

e. What offerings will we be selling?

f. Are there any critical numbers that will indicate the progress over one year that we'll likely find useful? If so, add them in. Things like conversion rates off the back of specific marketing strategies, goals around profitability or how much you pay management in relation to the going market rates? Perhaps it's percentage progress on finishing standard operating procedures or creating a useable library of your technical information.

11. In order to deliver on the 1-year goals, what progress will have been made in the next 90 days in each of the five categories?

a. What has to happen team-wise by the end of the next 90 days?

b. What aspect of systems and processes will it be our priority to tackle in the next quarter?

c. What level of financial performance will we set ourselves as a target for this quarter?

d. What progress on the prospecting front and building our sales muscle will we make in the next 90 days?

e. What do we need to resolve regarding our offerings to meet our financial targets?

f. Are there any critical numbers that will indicate the progress over the next 90 days that would be useful? Perhaps big to-dos that need finishing off like market research, installing CRM (client relationship management) software, finalising workable job descriptions or getting a meetings' roster up and running.

g. At this stage, also add in who will do what over the next quarter – the champions for each of the deliverables.

12. What are the top three target markets that you will aim your marketing at?

13. What marketing strategies will you put in place? You may not know until you do some reading/learning or get some help, but essentially this needs to record what you plan to do to get leads, bring in business, stay visible and have a stream of prospects to pitch to.

14. What are your marketing costs and numbers?
    a. How many leads do you need each month?
    b. How many new customers (net) do you need each month?
    c. How much are you willing to pay for each lead?
    d. How much are you wanting to pay for each customer?
    e. What is your conversion rate of leads to customers for the business, per salesperson, per type of product or from each marketing strategy?
    f. What is the average spend per customer each month? Calculate this by dividing the total sales revenue for the month by the number of invoices issued in that same month.
    g. How many repeat or returning customers do you have per month?
15. What are the numbers for the last four quarters – get them from your financial statements or your accountant.
16. What were your business goals for the previous quarter and did you achieve them – yes or no?
17. What personal development, reading, learning, training do you need to engage in to BE the best business owner you can be?
18. Now consider the strengths, weaknesses, opportunities and threats for your business and the goals you've detailed. Strengths are existing capabilities in the business that you need to optimise. Weaknesses are the gaps you may need to fill to at least neutralise any negative impact any weaknesses may have. Opportunities are the most profitable and practical things you can pursue over the coming twelve months that will allow you to exceed your targets. And threats are brutal facts or market realities that, if faced, you may be able to counter, to some degree, over the coming year.

If you get stuck on what to enter in the different blocks, get help or read *Mastering the Rockefeller Habits* by Verne Harnish.[28] It's a great book.

Once you have your plan, you can set proper quarterly, monthly, weekly and daily business goals for all aspects of the business. As you grow and develop different departments, you can have a 1-PSP for each department or branch and then one for the whole business. To have everything on one A3 piece of paper is super helpful.

And while the vision is yours by dint of the fact that it's your investment capital, your risk and your idea, the plan is something that needs team involvement to create. It is the collective roadmap for getting stuff done. Planning, once a year, to create this document is a smart move. Consider doing it over a weekend away offsite, before the new financial year starts, so that you have taken AIM before you FIRE.

Jim Rohn, and many other business philosophers of his stature, concur that money flows to the best plan and, in my experience with business owners, he's right. Those who have a clear plan on what they need to do to get from where they are to where they need to be and involving the team in creating this, do better – even if they have to change or modify the plan as they go.

The plan gives fact and traction to your vision. It provides focus, outlines priorities, keeps goals and targets top of mind for everyone, and allows you to measure your actual activity and results against the plan. The plan therefore becomes the activity-based plumb line to see if the combined efforts of the different branches, departments or team members is moving the business towards its end goal, in line with the VMAV, or not.

It also provides certainty, clarity and confidence for bank managers, investors, board members, strategic alliances, key suppliers and talent, giving the clear impression that this business knows what it's doing, where it's going and how it's going to get there. It provides an objective tool to assess performance and give feedback in a language the people understand and value.

There are many ways to do a strategic plan, but I really like this one. I find it easy to use and so do the business owners I coach. But so long as you have a plan that includes these elements, it will serve its purpose.

I can recall when a beloved deli chain hit the wall in South Africa a few years ago. People were shocked because it had been such a visible success for many years and, at the time of its demise, had 19 franchise outlets. I read an article where the business owner was being interviewed shortly after the news hit the media. She was asked what went wrong and she admitted that they'd grown organically in response to customer needs and wants but had not created or followed a proper plan. The excitement of organic growth, in place of a plan, was a mistake that cost the business. It's extremely hard, perhaps impossible, to keep control of the bigger picture and know whether you're on the right track or off track if there's no plan, particularly when you scale and grow. Without the plan, this business couldn't see the problems before it was too late. No wonder they lost their way.

Don't make the same mistake. Get your 1-PSP completed and make it visible in the business. The first one is always the hardest, but they get easier. Using this tool is one of the key measurement puzzle pieces that could just save the business. If you plan, you'll have significantly more chance of meeting your goals and hitting your targets than if you don't. Benjamin Franklin famously said, "If you fail to plan, you're planning to fail." Don't start or try and build a business without one. You may get some of the way, you may even become successful like the deli, but without a plan you are vulnerable to losing your way.

What Key Financials Matter?

Figures don't lie. As a business owner, you need key metrics to understand what is really happening in the business, beyond the stories you are told in meetings. They are also essential for good decision-making, to evaluate what's working, take right action and ensure that your business doesn't run out of money. Gut feeling or business instinct have their place, but reviewing the numbers that don't lie is irreplaceable.

And you have to listen to what they are telling you, whether you like the message or not. Assigning responsibility for the figures to an accountant is fine, but if you have no idea how to read the resulting reports, it's business suicide. A certain basic level of financial fluency and fiscal understanding is mandatory if you want to run your own business. If you don't want to become at least competent in understanding the financial basics, you can't be a business owner. If that sounds harsh it's because I've seen the chaos and trauma that can come when the effort to understand is made too late or not at all because it was 'someone else's job'.

In addition, you can't fix what you don't know or don't measure. Every weight loss journey begins with stepping on the scale. Similarly with a business, we need to know what's going on, what's working, what's not working strategy-wise, and whether we are getting a sufficient return on our money and our efforts. The only way to safely do that is to have the figures and know what they mean. Late or inaccurate financial information is like pulling a dragon's tail. It makes it far too easy to solve the symptom of a problem or, even worse, the wrong problem. For example, why chase more sales if your pricing is wrong? Why invest more money in marketing if you can't close the leads you already have? Why increase sales if the business is not efficiently collecting the money you've already invoiced?

There are three critical financial pieces of information every business owner needs each month:

Profit and Loss Statement – Actual versus Budget

This is your monthly report card that tells you what happened in the business over the previous month and how well you performed in relation to what you set out to do. It records your turnover, the routine expenses to run the business, the cost of your sales, what profit you've made or not made and how much is left over. It looks at these against your budget, what you had planned to spend and make, and is the clearest indication that your efforts are either working or not working.

Most business owners have a Profit and Loss (P&L) each month; they do read it properly and allow it to direct decisions, so it is an important document. But it is made much more useful when you record the actual numbers against a budget figure. The P&L is a backward look at the health of your business, whereas the budget is forward looking. It is also the means by which you can set your subconscious mind and employ the Law of Attraction. It has goal-like elements to it in that it draws the whole team towards the preferred financial standard or fiscal benchmark. It inspires your thinking and helps to conscientise everyone on what happens day to day with the money in the business.

With a budget, you can record the turnover you're going to chase and the expenses that will need to be paid. You can highlight what you want your cost of sales to be and how much everyone can spend on each line item, and again, many people do this. What many people don't do is budget for the profit they'd like to make in the following month, too. Adding this line item into your budgeting process promotes awareness and intentionality of your real monthly end goal – money left over. It creates something focused, positive and clear to aim for and we've already touched on why that galvanises us to behave better.

Think of your budget, inclusive of how much profit you hope to make, as your financial target each month. Set it and then check your actuals – expenses, costs, revenue and profit – against it each month. You can also measure your actual revenue and profit against your performance same time last year and against last month. Both of these measures yield different but interesting and useful information that can help you make better and more incisive decisions as you grow your business.

Balance Sheet

The balance sheet is a snapshot of the worth of the business at a given point in time. It looks at where the money has come in from (is it a loan or revenue or owner's capital investment, for example) and where it has gone out to (into stock or to pay suppliers or to run the business or to the taxman). Importantly, it also records how much is owed to you by your customers (your total debtors), how much is tied up in stock and running the business, and, finally, how much you owe to others (your total creditors).

Knowing the worth of the business and what and where the money is located, is something many business owners don't get from their accountant regularly or, if they do, they don't know how to read it. It is worth your while to go through these financials and become fluent in understanding your balance sheet.

Cash Flow

This is your crystal ball – a simple look at who is paying you what and by when and whom you need to pay, by when? It looks at what is in the bank, what you can lay your hands on if you need more cash, and allows you to plan when you'll settle your bills, which customers you need to chase, and how well the money is both coming in and going out. It is possible to be selling profitably but run out of cash. As an aside, it is also possible to have money in the bank but be worth nothing on paper. And it's also possible to be trading successfully each month and have money in the bank but be better off closing down and investing the money in stocks and shares! The latter refers to your ROI or return on investment – a number that can and should be calculated by your accountant for you regularly.

A great book to help you improve your financial competence is Steve Wilkinghoff's *Found Money*.[29] In it, he explains each of these financial instruments in greater detail, how to value your different clients financially, and how to manage the business finances more competently so that you aren't blindsided by problems you should have seen coming.

Should I Hire an Accountant?

The short answer is YES. While it may feel expensive to use a professional, the cost of not using one can be crippling. If you don't have enough money to pay for an accountant, focus on selling more so you can afford to hire one – someone who can make sure you have great financial information at your fingertips when you need it. It may be dull, but it's critical.

Don't go cheap and think you're saving money by not engaging an accountant or getting one that costs peanuts. They can do what's needed in a fraction of the time it would take you. Plus, you will know it's correct. They are not as emotionally attached to the business as you are, and they usually have staff to help them. They are also trained in finance and have to stay current in their knowledge. They know more about tax, capturing financial data and producing useful reports that you can use to manage the business better than you do. And good accountants tend to love their craft and can be a valued and trusted business advisor worth their weight in gold.

Aim to meet your accountant once a month to get a clear understanding of what the different reports mean and how the business is doing. If you can't talk to them or use what they produce, or they can't produce these reports on time, then get a new accountant.

Many business owners say they hate the planning and financial side of the business, but you can't be in business if you don't know key numbers. Even if you employ an accountant, you need to know what the reports they produce for you mean and how to take action based on the insights they offer. Feelings, opinions or gut instinct won't cut it. The numbers don't lie

Sales Measures

Just because you're a great photographer it doesn't mean that you are the owner of a great photography business. You can be a great lawyer and have a rubbish legal business. Your craft or profession is not the same as the business. Turning what you make or do into a business requires selling it to someone and getting them to gladly and consistently pay you for it.

Without sales there's no money. Without money you don't have a business – you have a charity or a hobby!

> Without sales there's no money. Without money you don't have a business – you have a charity or a hobby!

Thankfully, there are tools that can help you in this and none more so than a client relationship management system which can provide automated sales data and metrics that help make the process of selling less hard. Not easy, but less hard.

A Client Relationship Management (CRM) Software Programme

CRMs are basically database software systems that operate like a spreadsheet on steroids. They enable you to plan, action, prioritise, remember, record and engage with people whose details you collect, upload, filter and massage. Most CRMs are either free or charge a small licence fee each month. You may have heard of Hubspot, Infusionsoft, Salesforce, Zoho, Freshworks and Onepage. They're all good CRMs to try.

I use Onepage because it has all the hallmarks of a piece of software that I need for the business:

- They operate in the same time zone as I do, so there is usually a support person to speak to if I need help.
- They charge me $30 per month, which is huge value for money as it feels like having an extra person on board.
- It can link to my accounting package Xero and to Mailchimp for email blasts, so I don't have to duplicate the databases.
- It will harvest contact details for anyone who interacts with our website.
- It can be used to filter contacts by all manner of criteria – age, geography, how they heard about us, what courses they've attended and when.

- It can store notes, Office folders and documents, next actions, as well as full contact details.
- It has a facility to email via Outlook both into and out of each person's information folder, so I can have a record of email correspondence.
- I can upload prospects, clients, suppliers, personal contacts, alliances and venues – in other words, all the useful information I need at my fingertips.
- They offer really useful tutorials, a helpline in my language and are open during my working hours if all else fails.
- They typically respond to issues/queries within 48 hours.
- Their system is simple and user friendly – which is no small thing in the CRM world. Some of them are so complex it's hard to know where to start.
- It is Office compatible, so bulk uploads and exports of data are possible.
- It's cloud-based, so I and my team can access it on any number of devices, and on more than one device at a time, no matter where we are.

Before you get too far into your business building efforts, it's worth getting a CRM. If you already have a business but don't have a CRM, then consider one sooner rather than later. Have a team member or even a student help you upload and transfer your information into it and grow from there. Used with integrity and reciprocity, it is a currency that can be traded with others and has been a lifesaver for many businesses during crises like Covid. And that is true, even with today's data protection legislation.

For example, I can try out your pool cleaning products and, if they are good, I can recommend your products to my database of known, liked and trusted connections. In exchange, you come along to one of my seminars on how to improve and grow a business, and if you like the seminar, you can invite your database to the next event. I don't get your database and you don't get mine, but we swap promotions where we think there is mutual benefit for us and our customer base. One word of caution: make sure that what you are recommending to your contacts is a product/service you've tried yourself and can honestly say is worth it.

Your CRM forms a place for very focused and targeted marketing and allows you to create a community. People give their permission to be added to it and can be taken off on request. It allows you to handle multiple activities to multiple people each day by creating and posting to your desktop a to-do list or action stream. This daily updatable reminder ensures you don't forget anything or drop the ball on tasks as you grow your business. You can have different folders for different team members and the data is kept in the cloud. This means that you and they can access it from different locations and on different devices. It also means that you have access to useful, personal, detailed information that can set you apart when you are speaking to a contact, prospects, clients, or a supplier.

I'd be lost without my CRM. Whatever system you use, it will take some getting used to, but most of the good ones have easy to follow tutorials to help familiarise you with their system quickly. There is usually a helpline or online chat feature that allows for additional support. As for Onepage, while I promise I don't get any commission from them, I recommend them all the time. I also have clients who prefer Hubspot or Zoho, or who use a CRM specific to their professional sector. Just make sure you set one up and use it, preferably before you grow!

T3: Fuel Lines

The fuel line to any business is sales – essentially making sure that enough people buy the product or service you are selling. You may be the best fudge maker, accountant, photographer or quantity surveyor in town, but unless people are putting money in your bank account for what you do, the rest is irrelevant.

And there are only really two ways to grow your business:
• Increase your revenue (sell more)
• Reduce your costs (improve your margin).

Think of your fuel line as a funnel. What gets potential customers into the funnel is marketing. The business world calls this lead generation. And, for the purposes of building resilience, that includes inbound and outbound lead generation. Inbound is when others come to you by word of mouth or not as a result of your own efforts, and outbound is when you encourage or intentionally bring people into your business as a qualified lead.

But leads, even qualified leads, are not enough – you need to convert or convince these interested people to actually buy from you and become a customer. And once you've made the sale, you need to keep your customers engaged and actively purchasing what you have to offer via upselling, cross-selling and rebuying. And you need to have a strategy for lapsed customers to bring them back into the buying fold. Think, for example, seasonal ranges that invite both lapsed and existing customers back at least four times a year, or rebooking your next dental appointment before you leave this one, or the cross-sell of a maintenance contract with a swimming pool installation. Upsells are the equivalent of chocolate at the checkout in the supermarket – hard to resist and relatively inexpensive. All of this activity falls under 'Sell More'.

And then there is the reality of your margins. There is zero point in becoming great at sales and investing in marketing strategies that yield sufficient good leads to talk to, having great spend and customers returning for all the right reasons if your margins are tiny. Margins can be improved by increasing the price of the goods and services you offer and by reducing your costs.

The trick is to start with simple but effective strategies that will make you visible and compelling to those who could buy from you without breaking the bank. The simplest and most effective starting point that I introduce all my clients to is creating their digital business bio.

Your Digital Business Bio

Before you go to the expense of printing business cards and other marketing material, consider a digital business bio instead. It provides a great starting point that allows you to test and measure why people 'buy' you, and you have something material and substantial to assist you in achieving greater visibility, and sales. I get clients to put together an electronic one-page business bio that is part business card, part brochure. In a concise but compelling format, the business bio summarises:

- who you are and what you offer
- what makes your offering special, different from and better than your competition

151

- what others are saying about your product, service or business
- why the reader should contact you, how and why now
- a logo and a great photograph that communicates authenticity and warmth.

A business bio, which is more engaging than a business card and punchier than a brochure, has the added advantage of the potential to 'go viral' as people forward it, store it and pass it on. It can be designed using simple software like PowerPoint or Canva, and it's not printed, so it doesn't cost the earth. It can function as a precursor to your website and is something short and sweet that other people can pass along to those who may be interested in you. More importantly, it is quick and easy to read in situations where you may have more than one decision-maker coming to a roundtable meeting. It can contain hyperlinks and photographs that tend not to print well if you're on a budget. Essentially, your business bio is an effective and easy lead generator and conversion tool in one. In my experience, every business needs one.

And the good news is that there is a recipe for how best to put this digital business bio together. You can see some effective examples at www.buildingbestbusiness.com.

As entrepreneurs, we need to keep the fuel of the business – sales from buying customers – flowing into the business. We may also have a limited marketing and advertising budget, so we need to get maximum bang for our buck in everything we do. We need to know that everything we spend is yielding a return or delivering an outcome. And that means we can't just 'raise awareness' or merely inform our audience of our existence; we always need to be promoting to sell.

And part of what makes products and services sell is the human element behind the product or services and the value of what we sell to our target humans. People do business with people. And that is true whether your sales are business-to-consumer (B2C) or business-to-business (B2B). Your humanness and ability to connect to your target market authentically matters in selling. In fact, about as much as 80% of buying decisions have little to do with the facts and information about the product or service and everything to do with the emotional reaction of the person who is buying them.

As the world gets smaller, it also gets bigger too. We have to wade through the crowds to find our tribe – those who look, sound, dress, behave, enjoy, relate, prioritise, believe and engage like we do. Everyone is looking for their tribe and it is our humanness that indicates whether we have found our tribe or not. The one-page digital business bio is a visual representation of your business and it helps people assess your tribe quickly and if they want to be a part of it. It is a simple and effective tool to enable people to resonate with and value the WHO, not just the WHAT, and it can be easily updated without any cost.

So, with your permission, I'm going to outline the elements that you'll need to consider. Ready?

Component Parts of Your Digital Business Bio

In making yourself and your business better known, liked and trusted, a digital business bio can be very helpful, but only if it contains the right ingredients:

1. A compelling headline
2. "So, what's in it for me!" subheadings
3. Social proof
4. A strong call to action
5. A great photograph
6. A logo – placed last ... in the bottom right-hand corner.

A compelling headline

This has to be the entry point for any piece of marketing. Like a newspaper, the headline is designed to draw the reader in. You will need to test your headlines to see what works best. Research tells us that longer copy sells more than shorter copy and questions engage readers better than statements. Consider the pain points that your business offerings solve, as they are twice as likely to connect with readers than benefits or rewards. Could these pain points be turned into questions that the reader is searching for answers to – which is first prize?

What about the benefits that your offering delivers – could those be turned into questions that would resonate with your audience? For example, as a business coach I could ask, "Are you sick of working like a dog with very little to show for it? Are you fed up with corporate politics and long to strike out on your own but don't know where to start?

In my digital business bio I say: *"If Industrial Psychologist and trusted business growth expert Kathi Hyde has helped 100s of business owners build resilient, profitable businesses and entrepreneurial muscle in the last 48 months, despite tough trading in economic winter, surely she can help you?"*

Whatever headline you choose, make sure the font size is big enough so that it is the first thing the reader notices. Work hard at your opening question, statement or paragraph. Your initial job is to solve a problem or warn of an issue in such a way that your brand starts to become related to being useful and serving others.

'So, what's in it for me!' subheadings

From there, add in two to four paragraphs that cover what makes you special, different and better, but in a way that directly speaks to the reader's, "So What's in it For Me!" thoughts. One of the biggest mistakes businesses make is that they focus on themselves and not what the customers are going to get out of the exchange. If you want to talk about what great service you offer, then you also need to let the reader see what's in it for them. If you want to mention that you have a great network, tell the reader why that will benefit them. If you've got years of experience, what does this mean for them? Don't assume they will work it out or make the mental leap – spell it out.

Make your subheadings zesty and compelling so they stand out. Ensure that they are in a slightly smaller font than your heading, but bigger than what's in the paragraphs of text. With only roughly 16% of people reading everything on a page, these subheadings matter, so make sure they're there and they cover what's in it for the reader. For example, my subheadings are:

- *Award-winning reputation – gets you results.*
- *Proudly local and grown from grassroots – understands unique challenges of SMEs.*
- *International experience – ensures cutting-edge solutions.*
- *Also, a successful businessowner – walks her talk.*

The paragraphs need to have subheadings that stand out and that can also stand alone if readers skim-read them. Again, think like a newspaper editor of old. Many of us read the headlines and move on. If the headline looks interesting, we may read the intro paragraph, and if that summarises the gist of the story, that's often enough. You need to make sure that people get the gist quickly, but have the option for more depth if they want it.

Social proof

Marketing and psychology professor Robert Cialdini is best known for alerting the world to six basic, but very powerful principles of psychology that influence human behaviour.[30]

They are:

- **Reciprocity**: If we give something to someone, they will feel obligated to return the favour even if what you gave them was not something they wanted.
- **Commitment**: This is the desire to remain consistent with our earlier behaviour or commitments.
- **Social Proof**: People generally look to other people similar to themselves when making decisions.
- **Liking**: People are more likely to agree and do business with people they like. This is why it's so important to let people see you as a real human being. Let people like you and for those who don't – that's fine too.
- **Authority**: People are influenced by those in authority or perceived authority.
- **Scarcity**: People tend to want things more as they become less available.

All of these six principles are useful to consider and employ in your digital bio content, but social proof is especially powerful. When people are unsure of what to do or whether to purchase something, they will read reviews. If they find that people like them have bought something, then this social proof makes it easier for them to also buy. Authority works here too, which is why celebrity endorsements work so well. They facilitate pseudo-authority. If you are selling health products, for example, social proof from a doctor is a double whammy!

Make sure you have at least two testimonials from clients on your digital bio. Include a section called "*What clients are saying ...*" and add in two of your best comments. Ideally use ones that speak directly to your Unique Selling Point (USP) or the "what's in it for me" you're presenting. And make sure you get the clients' permission to use what they said on your marketing material. Using a picture of the client alongside what they said is also powerful because it helps to prove that it's a real, contactable person. If you don't use a picture, stating their name, company and job title can do a similar job of proving authenticity. "*Martin Jackson, CEO, Brightlights Ltd*" will always look more authentic than "*M Jackson, London*".

Examples of my current social proof are:

"*Kathi's wide range of professional skills and ability to communicate effectively at all levels deserve special mention ... I have no hesitation in recommending her.*" – Richard Hamer, Chief Geologist, Anglogold East Africa.

"*Kathi is able to give us a great healthy rhythm of reviewing and discussing the most critical aspects of our business. She's a fantastic sounding board to validate important decisions.*" – Werner Janse van Rensburg, Owner, Isoflow.

It carries much more weight to have others endorse what you are claiming about yourself.

A strong call to action

Every email, advertisement, flyer, social media post, newsletter, marketing piece, blog post, video or business bio you ever produce or send out should always tell the reader what you'd like them to do next and why they should. If you don't, they probably won't.

Cialdini's insights into scarcity and reciprocity also work well when thinking about your call to action. Making your call to action limited will put pressure on the reader to engage and call you. You could also combine scarcity with reciprocity, where you offer something free but valuable for a limited time. Perhaps a free opening session or a month's free access to software for the first 10 people who contact you. Having a deadline or a limit adds urgency to the call to action.

My call to action is:

If you're looking to:

- *Build your leadership muscle*
- *Develop winning strategies to sell in this climate*
- *Stay ahead of your competition*
- *Grow top-performing teams and exit*
- *Create operational maturity*
- *Realise real results*

Call today – your business will thank you! +27 63 624 4492

Never list just your contact details and assume people will make contact – they won't. Give them a reason and instil a sense of urgency. Never assume that because you've included a website link people will go there and buy – they probably won't. But tell people to go to the website and why, and then also make it worth their while, and they often will. I've tested it – it works.

A great photograph

In my 14 years as a divorcee, I dabbled a bit in online dating. And one lesson I learned very quickly was no photograph, no further. This may sound shallow or even callous, but this wasn't about looks – it was more about what else the picture told me. Did they hide their eyes? Did they make an effort with the picture? Was the location a place I resonated with or not? Did I like their style of dress and what could I 'feel' from the fact that they were upfront with a photo? No photo felt hidden, disquietingly so. Why wouldn't you want people to see who you are? It may have been that they were uber famous, but probably not. It just didn't feel right, honest or authentic to me.

> At a fundamental level, we all like to see who we'll be doing business with before we do business with them.

And whilst it's not exactly the same in business, there are striking parallels. At a fundamental level, we all like to see who we'll be doing business with before we do business with them. Somehow it changes things if the person is willing to be on show and to communicate, "Hey, look, I'm ordinary, safe to let into your life or house and can look you openly in the eye". So, if you run a company, put a great picture of you on your business bio. Put yourself and all your team members on the website. Let people see you. But make sure it's a professional photo, not a selfie!

What NOT to do in your business bio

Don't use CAPITAL LETTERS – they are harder to read than ordinary text and come across as shouting on the page.

Don't discount your offer – it cheapens you. Plus, it teaches your audience to wait until they get a better price instead of shop with you when you want and need them to. Research shows that, deep down, people also tend to feel ripped off by your usual and normal pricing if you can afford to slash prices by 20 or 50%. Instead, seek creative ways to add value or have your customers enjoy a benefit if they refer a friend, buy before a certain date or buy a certain volume. Obviously, this will have an impact on your bottom line in terms of an actual cost, but it has a different psychological impact on your customers, a different 'feel', and it will cost you less in the long run. Try it.

Don't put your logo upfront. Focus, instead, on the audience and what they need with a great headline question. Put your logo at the end of your marketing. We usually remember best what we read last.

Remember, everything is marketing

Behind all your marketing efforts, you need to move from being merely informative, useful and full of facts to being compelling and persuasive so that you galvanise your prospects into action. Everything is marketing. How we handle team members, what we put on our personal social media, how we drive our vehicle, the things we complain about and how we dress. It shouldn't be that way, but it is. And while visibility and brand recognition are good, marketing that actually sells is better.

Think of your digital business bio as your go-to, every-day promotion and conversion tool in one and follow the best-practice rules when putting it together.

And to save you time, in addition to creating a digital bio that you can use at various junctures in your sales and marketing process, I've listed another 15 other strategies that we've routinely used with business owners that have worked every time. Like the digital bio, they seem so simple that owners often dismiss them in the search for some form of complex magic bullet. Eventually, they relent and apply these techniques and are then happy that they did. I've lost count of the number of times these simple strategies have saved the day by keeping the fuel lines running.

While you can research more detail on implementing each and any of these, I'm going to make some brief comments and include a few pointers on each to get you going. OK?

Strategies for Increasing Revenue Through More Sales

1. Signage to Build your Brand	
2. Ask for Referrals – Don't Wait for Them	
3. Strategic Alliances with Non-Competing Businesses	Lead
4. Targeted Mailer with a Limited Time Offer	Generation
5. Collect Contact Details (Offer an Incentive)	
6. They Ask You Answer (TAYA) Blogs/Vlogs	
7. Scripts to Handle Objections	
8. Emotional Questions	Conversion
9. Before and after Evidence	
10. Order Bumping and Bundling	Increase
11. Large Size First	average spend
12. A Great Shop Window	
13. Loyalty/Membership Offer	Increase
14. Advertising your Full Range	number of
15. Reactivation	transactions

Signage to build your brand

Whether on your vehicle, outside your office, on a chalkboard, in neon lights, on your online shop or branded stationary, on the footer of all your correspondence or your email signature, your signage builds brand awareness, interpersonal trust and speaks to your audience 24/7.

Take an email signature as an example of an everyday communication that could provide greater impact at no extra cost. Many businesses and their owners just have a sign off, a designation, a logo, contact details, and possibly a disclaimer. Why not make your email signature more compelling? Using a professional head shot in your signature is a proven way to increase connection and build trust. You could include some of your values, which help attract or repel your target tribe. Or what about a link to your digital business bio? Consider creating a number of different signatures and mix them up throughout the year to keep it interesting. These can be designed for a year and rotated at very little cost.

Your messaging needs to be short, sharp, compelling, clear and noteworthy. Consider using humour to cut through and don't forget to add a strong call to action to what goes onto your vehicle, up where everyone can see it and in your email signature. Everything.

Ask for referrals – don't wait for them

When you have delivered your product or service to your customer and they are happy with what they have received and the value for money you've delivered, that's when you need to ask them if they know anyone else who would benefit from the same product or service? Why wouldn't you?

Don't wait passively for word of mouth or referrals to come in – the timing may not suit you. Rather, get into the habit of asking for referrals regularly. Pick up the phone and ask your customer for the name and contact details of someone they believe would benefit from what you offer. You could ask, "Can you think of anyone in your sphere of influence who could benefit from the same wins we've had together?" Alternatively, you could start with your own clients' top three clients and suppliers and propose to your clients that, since it's going so well between you and them, it may make good business sense for their clients and suppliers to enjoy similar benefits too. Everyone can list those off the top of their heads.

Make the referral beneficial to both the person who provides the contact and the contact themselves. Give them an exclusive referral benefit, which doesn't have to be money.

Strategic alliances with non-competing businesses

Locking shields with other non-competing, complementary entrepreneurs just makes good sense, in good times and in bad. There are businesses that are targeting the same customers as you are, but who are not in direct competition with you. Say you are a landscaper; you could create a strategic alliance with a realtor where you promote their business to clients who are looking to sell their home and they promote your business to clients who have either bought a new home, are looking to increase a sale or have moved into a new rental property.

Think about who, in your local area, is already serving customers who may be in need of your product or service but are not in direct competition. Approach that business with the offer of a strategic alliance. It's a smart move that can save you chunks of prospecting and marketing time (and money). The goal is to ensure that, on a regular basis, you put their offers to your client base, and they put yours to theirs. It's free and focused.

This strategy can even work when you are in competition. For example, I had a client who ran a couple of successful pre-schools. She has a competitor who did the same thing. They created a synergy where, if my client was full, she would recommend her competitor and if her competitor was full, she would recommend my client. They both signed an agreed code of conduct that no one stole clients or deliberately headhunted them, but that they'd both work hard to ensure that local children went to one of *their* two schools and not any of the others. I also had two accounting businesses that made a similar agreement. Ordinarily they competed, but when one was off sick, had to be away for a protracted period or they were swamped with work, the other was their agreed go-to recommendation.

Targeted mailer with a limited time offer

The reason I was so adamant about getting a CRM is because once you have a database and build it up over time, you have an extremely valuable asset that you can use to greatly assist with cost-effective marketing. Those who had databases that they could use to stay in touch with customers or clients survived Covid far better than those who did not. You could, for example, send out a targeted mailer or newsletter once a quarter to introduce a limited time special offer (not discounts), new seasonal ranges or special offers to coincide with occurrences like tax time, changes to the team or positive developments that customers would like to hear about, like new billing methods or a new outlet that's opened near them.

A local café near where I live was really struggling during Covid and I suggested that they send out a targeted mailer to everyone on their mailing list to say so. They just needed to be honest, offer home delivery or suggest to those people that they come along to the 'hatch' once a week to ensure that their favourite café was still there for them and would continue to be once the pandemic was over. People came and the business didn't just survive – it thrived.

Your database also builds the asset value of your business.

Collect contact details (offer an incentive)

If you have an office or shop that people visit, place a fishbowl on the counter and encourage people to drop their details in it, or input their details on a tablet. They may not do this for nothing though, so consider offering an incentive, like entering a prize draw where the winner each month will get something from your business free or, even better, offer a voucher that they will then need to spend in the shop. If they don't spend it you've lost nothing, but often they will spend it and buy even more. Both result in winning outcomes.

You will also need to make it clear that, if they enter the draw, they will be added to your database and will be contacted with additional future offers. And remember to always check the data privacy rules in your area before doing something like this.

They Ask You Answer (TAYA) blogs and vlogs

Increasingly, we need to attract prospects and customers online. And we need to be thinking about online lead generation. And it can be daunting. One of the best strategies I've seen is outlined in a fabulous book by Marcus

Sheridan called *They Ask You Answer*.[31] As a pool installations business owner staring bankruptcy in the face, Marcus fell upon and has since perfected the digital art of identifying what people are asking online. In his case, he figured out what people were asking Google and other search engines about swimming pool installations in his area and then answered those questions via blogs or vlogs. Because these were real search questions and queries from real people interested in installing a swimming pool (real prospects), the resultant blog or vlog ranked organically with Google and was searched for and found, often by those who'd asked those questions. Many times, the question would be the exact title of the blog.

Space that is usually occupied by researchers or trend commentary is a wasted opportunity for business owners who don't make the most of this in-between space. It's not, for example, enough to know what dishwashers are available; I'd also like to know which is the quietest one on the market currently or the smallest yet most efficient. I may also like to know who the top five suppliers are in my area, or which brand breaks down least often. And while my white-goods business owner may not sell that model or be in the top five, the fact that they have written the article or recorded the vlog means that I'll land on their site first to collect the intel I need to make an informed purchasing decision.

This immediacy and novel way to exponentially increase visibility, has been crucial in Marcus' own business and in that of so many of his clients, as his book outlines. It is well worth getting a copy, absorbing the contents and then creating and posting ten of these blogs/vlogs to sit as positive and effective Google entrapment for Joe public.

Scripts to Handle Objections

Like everything else in life, sales become easier the more you practise. Everyone who is great at sales has worked hard to perfect what they say, how they say it, when they say it and to whom they say it. They've worked hard to become confident and fluent, so much so that it sounds natural. Great sales people rarely 'wing it', even though it sounds like they do. The very best way to get great at something like sales is to practise what works, script that out and rehearse it so it becomes second nature. That way, when the business scales or you have to delegate sales to someone else, you have a winning script to follow that works too.

Having a script, especially when handling objections, can mean the difference between a yes and a no thanks. An objection, funnily enough, is a sign of interest rather than disinterest, and really is just a request for more information.

Objections are usually over:

- the price (too expensive), or
- the timing (not now), or
- the competition (we're considering two other suppliers), or
- who makes the decision (I need to ask my spouse), or
- a dispositional need to pause/check (let me sleep on it).

Having scripts or proven answers to the most common objections just gives you more confidence about giving your would-be customer the information they need to make a positive decision. It stops you fluffing things at 11.59 in the process. Why not brainstorm your top six objections and script out answers to these objections? Learn them, test them and tweak them until you have a winning script for each one and then commit them to memory – everyone in the business.

If you need more ideas and suggestions on creating great scripts, read anything by Dan Lok, Daniel Pink, Jeffrey Gitomer, Grant Cardone, Zig Ziglar, Tom Hopkins, Blair Singer, Chet Holmes, Neil Rackham, Dale Carnegie, Og Mandino, Mike Bosworth, Geoffrey James, David Schwartz and Oren Klaff. Some of the books by these authors are quite old, but their advice is timeless and still works today.

Ask Emotional Questions

Because roughly 80% of our decision to buy is based on emotion, including what we imagine that product or service will allow us to feel, it's always smart to ask the prospect two or three emotional questions that deliberately seek to tap into these aspirations. These questions can help to illicit a negative emotion they want to avoid or a positive emotion of what they will feel, either of which can encourage them to buy far more effectively than just the facts and informative copy. Consider asking questions that help the prospect to emotionally connect to what their life could be like once they are living with the benefits of your offering.

For example:

- *"What will it mean to you when we enclose the verandah and extend your living space?"*
- *"What do you hope to achieve by changing your accountant?"*
- *"What will it be worth to you once you've added the pool and landscaped the garden."*
- *"How will you feel when you know that a trustworthy security system is installed?"*
- *"What will you no longer have to worry about if you have a retirement plan in place?"*
- *"How will you feel when the freedom and profitability other business owners are enjoying has become something you can experience?"*
- *"Can you imagine how you will feel when the dust settles and this is your new entertainment area?"*

Depending on the product or service you are selling, these emotional questions are often best delivered face-to-face so that you can see the reaction, but they also work in marketing material as questions. Add in social proof and current client testimonial too, for added juice.

Create your own list.

Before and after evidence

Before and after photos and scenarios also work well to showcase what impact your product or services have had. And because the reader can now see the evidence for themselves, this transition is often even more compelling than just an image of what you do. There's something really more-ish about seeing a room before and after a makeover, or a bride and

The contrast makes the change more engaging and also makes it feel more real to your potential customer.

groom before and after they got into shape for their wedding, or the garden before and after the landscapers worked their magic.

165

The contrast makes the change more engaging and also makes it feel more real to your potential customer. They are also able to envisage the same change for themselves, with the help of your product or service, and will often mentally put themselves into the scenario.

How could you incorporate this before and after contrast into your marketing?

Order bumping and bundling

It is always easier to sell something else to a customer once they have already decided to buy and are already in the shop, online or at the checkout. Let's look at bumping first.

In supermarkets, these additional offers are often known as impulse buys, and they are stacked near the tills – for good reason! Online the same applies, where we are asked if we want to buy something else once the initial order has been placed. This order bump increases the value and is an especially effective way to get customers to spend more. It can be exercised very simply by offering, for example, the larger item or portion first or, more complicatedly, as in a DIY shop, listing other useful products a customer may want in addition to the paintbrushes. The secret is to make it easy to justify these additions in the mind of the customer. For example, if the customer has already bought vitamin supplements online, a good order bump could be simply three months' supply instead of one, which will save them time and money. Or it could be a range of complementary supplements that customers usually order with the multivitamins, like Zinc or Vitamin D. Both work.

Think about what would help your customer to get the most value from or make sense to get in addition to their original purchase? It's the equivalent of McDonalds asking, "Do you want fries with that?" Once a customer is at the counter and is ordering, they have overcome their inertia and are already committed to buying something. Making the leap to buying more or adding additional items, especially if those additions reduce the cost per unit, is a great way to grow your bottom line.

Some examples are: insurance with an air ticket, or a voucher for someone special with a purchase – offers like these that are put to everyone before they conclude buying with you. The list can be long and creative.

Just try it. You'll be amazed at how much it will increase the average spend of your customers and what impact on your profitability this will have – even if it's only a few cents every time.

The other option is order bundling, which also increases the spend before checkout by making a collection of products more appealing as a group. It's a strategy where we tie a bow around multiple items and offer a small price advantage. Instead of selling vitamin supplements individually by the type of vitamin, for example, you could create the 'Hangover Pack' or the 'Energy Pack' that contain four or five of your products for a special price that is more cost-effective than having to purchase the items singly. Or advertise the unit price for the shampoo and conditioner for just slightly less than the cost of either of the two alone.

Order bumping and bundling can happen as the customer is deliberating and before they get to the checkout. Try it.

Offer large size first

If you have a range of sizes, models or price points, always offer the biggest, best and most costly first. This is pure psychology. One of the many quirks of human nature is that we tend to anchor the first price. And anchoring can serve in two ways. If the most expensive wine is listed at the top of the wine list, everything else can look like more value for money in comparison, which is a good thing and causes many people to choose the second most expensive bottle so as not to look cheap.

Or when realtors list a substantial opening price for a property, anything offered after that by you, or me, is pressurised by this listed price. And again, you or I fear missing out by going too cheap, so we use the listed price to inform what we offer.

The same is true of your offering. I had a business coaching colleague who used to use this strategy really successfully by saying, "I usually only work with Gold Level clients where the prices are XX and upwards, but the good news is that they don't usually start there."

If you want to know more about the weird ways in which humans make sense of the world and the quirks that can help you sell more, then read *Yes! Fifty Secrets from the Science of Persuasion* by Noah Goldstein, Steve Martin and Robert Cialdini.[32]

A great shop window

Great shop window displays, online design that showcases your products and offerings, or beautiful wrapping of your service/delivery vehicles, encourage more spend by pairing, arranging or displaying things in enticing ways that advertise slices of life. Instead of just buying the jeans, you find yourself adding the belt. Or you came in for some cushions but the rug and everlasting plant work so well with them, you can't help yourself! Often customers are short of time, so if you can bundle products together and create a visual impression that suggests things they didn't necessarily have in mind when they left home, it's a win/win.

Spending time and effort on great layout, great windows and a great online window that all show slices of life montages, rather than just lines of products, can help compel, persuade and even upsell people. Ideas on what others like you also bought as part of a sales assistant script or online drop down, can help too … as can great photography. As an aside, if you are going to use visuals and photos, why not make sure these are of *your* customers, not someone else's? I once had a couple who sold boats and were adamant that their clients wouldn't want to be photographed on them. I disagreed and convinced them to ask a few. Turns out they were wrong – their clients were only too thrilled to be photographed on their new boat. After all, isn't that why people buy boats – to enjoy them and be seen enjoying them?

And for many of you service-oriented business owners who may be thinking to yourselves: "Well, that's all well and good, but I don't have any 'shop windows'," think of how a professional company uniform or a compellingly wrapped vehicle driving around could advertise what you do and provide workable and effective marketing.

In the UK, I used to frequent a local bakery that was really struggling. Their produce was genuinely amazing, but their shop window was not – a few cakes and, I kid you not, a dead spider in the corner and everything needing a lick of paint! And this lack of appeal was made even worse during Covid when people had to queue to collect their items, which gave them plenty of time to look at that dead spider! I often watched as people would express disbelief, just leave the queue and go elsewhere. As tactfully as possible, I encouraged the bakery owner to jazz up her window (and get rid of the spider). Trade turned around almost overnight. It's not rocket science!

> ... if you can bundle products together and create a visual impression that suggests things they didn't necessarily have in mind when they left home, it's a win/win.

Loyalty/Membership offer

In the 1960s, Alvin Tofler's bestselling book *Future Shock*[33] predicted that the over-choice brought on by globalisation and progress would encourage people to look for ways to belong and delimit their options. It would be about finding their tribe so that they could manage the volume of choice they would be privy to. If someone joined the cycle club, for example, then they could dress like a cyclist, buy cycling gear, talk cycling, go cycling, recreate with other cyclists and identify as a cyclist. They could also reject the myriad of other choices around sport, health, wellness and recreation. In doing so, they could limit what they focused on and make life and decision-making doable and manageable. Living in the times that Tofler was writing about back then, we see that he was right. We do work hard to find who/what we're comfortable identifying with and delimiting what we need to identify with to have both a sense of belonging and control.

Is there a way for you to create a community around your product or service? Could those that join get access to special deals, offers or events? Perhaps via a loyalty card for members or branded apparel? How can you reward your raving fans? For example, my friend at the bakery could have had a loyalty programme where customers could have chosen from a small range of offers, along with their tenth coffee or fifth weekly order – a little surprise such as a donut or custard slice. Not only does the business get recurring revenue that they can rely on, but they also get to give their special customers extra treats that showcase their range of products and create warmth and emotional connection.

Advertising your full range

I've lost count of the number of times I've heard clients of clients say to the business owner, "Oh, I didn't know you did that too." Most customers will come on board with you because they've bought a particular product or service, and it's simply not sensible to assume they know about your other offerings – play it safe and tell them!

Don't let prospects and clients guess. In newsletters, mailers, in-store and online, make sure that you present your full range of services/seasonal changes/new products. And why not tell your new team members regularly too? Out of sight IS out of mind.

Re-activate those who used to do business with you

Ex-clients can be a rich source of new business once time has lapsed. I have a client in the fruit export business who has had some of their overseas markets decimated by the war in Ukraine. Fortunately, they have a good history of investing in relationships in Vietnam, the Philippines and Malaysia, which they can now reactivate to create replacement business.

It is always wise to stay in touch with ex-clients or lapsed customers periodically as part of your strategic communication. Have them on your database and, with their permission, send them useful snippets every now and then. Don't bombard them or include them in all communication. Be selective and offer real value to encourage them to purchase again.

Okay – that's about it on some great selling strategies

So, while this isn't an exhaustive list, it is a good audit or start point. Any of these that you aren't currently doing will help. And do them first. When things get tough, our temptation is to cost-cut our way out of trouble, but this is second prize. First prize is always how can we sell our way out of trouble. More business, more orders, more customers – they are what protect and create resilient business.

That said, all sales are not created equal and watching the costs, ensuring that money isn't being wasted down the plughole, and preserving your margins, is key owner work. Again, I'm not saying this in an exhaustive list; however, it is a useful list of strategies that work for most, usually. Use it to shortcut what to do if you're under pressure, or audit what you're currently doing and then as a resource to fill in the gaps. Also, read more about these strategies to get sufficient and good operational intel to ensure a great return on your effort.

Strategies to Improve Margins

1. Stick to your payment terms.
2. Negotiate favourable supply chain terms.
3. Train your team.
4. Secure a good deposit.
5. Seek out efficiencies.

> **If they aren't paying, they aren't a customer or client.**

Stick to your Payment Terms

A customer who doesn't pay, who pays really late or not without haggling and nagging, isn't really a customer. They're a pain in the backside that is costing you money in the long run. Not paying you on time, or with much moaning when you have delivered, is disrespectful.

As a general principle, if clients don't pay, stop supply as soon as you can, have a debt process to follow, terminate the relationship if they still don't pay routinely and then hand them over to a collections agency. You don't want to be chasing up debtors when there are businesses out there who are better equipped to get the job done for you for a percentage of what they can recover. Nor do you want to be holding your breath each month, hoping and praying that difficult clients will cough up.

I had a client who designs websites. If you didn't settle his bill, you weren't able to go online. I had another client in software development and your programme would swirl down an alarming pink plug hole to a black screen if you went past your payment due date. It certainly had people ringing him to sort things out.

Exceptions to this rule are those who seek you out, 'fess up to a short-term hiccup and work with you to settle their outstanding debt on a repayment plan. For these sorts of clients, have compassion and be flexible with how you can help. That they have faced you and negotiated a workable way forward is customer gold! After all, we all can get into a pickle with our suppliers at some point in our entrepreneurial journey. It's life.

Negotiate Favourable Supply Chain Terms

A cash gap is often created between when you pay your suppliers and when your clients pay you, which can cause cashflow problems if it's not managed properly. If your terms are 30 days, then ensure that this matches what you have negotiated with your suppliers. If you can't, arrange shorter payment terms with your clients or introduce part-payments, monthly retainer fees and/or deposits to ensure that when you need to pay money out to suppliers, some has come in. While it is okay, when your business is still small, to 'carry' customers without a deposit or cost of sales invoices from suppliers fall due before your customers have paid you, this won't cut it when you scale. Bigger customers and bigger orders mean bigger supply chain bills, more tax and greater pressure on your cash flow. Start with the end in mind and structure this flow well so that you aren't the piggy in the middle carrying the can.

As a rule, pay yourself first, then put what will be due in tax out of reach (it's not your money) and pay everyone else after that. Why? It is harder to have to tell staff, the taxman or your suppliers why you aren't paying them when you've short-changed or wrong-footed prospecting and now don't have enough. It acts as a powerful motivator to fix the sales instead of doing what so many business owners do when sales are insufficient, and that is to go without, themselves.

Learn to date or woo your supply chain, rather than just engage or do business with them. They are part of your business success, so having them know, like and rely on you can be a real competitive advantage. They also need to be privy to your plans for the future and the vision for your business. Forewarn them too of the upcoming flow/level of your business so that they come prepared and able. It's a compliment to them and helps to secure you in their eyes as a business priority. With supply chains under pressure, who will they service first? You who they know, like and are clear about the future with ... or someone else? And if, for any reason, you run into difficulties or need to call in a favour, you will always have more leeway if you have nurtured a strong, interpersonal relationship with them.

Train your Team

Someone once asked Richard Branson, "What do I do if I train my team and they leave?" to which he famously replied, "And if you don't and they stay, then what?" Good answer. Trying to run a business with a team that is not optimally skilled and competent will soon become a heavy weight that bears down on you, rather than gifting you with wings that provide personal leverage.

> Teams should gift you with wings not weights.

Adults learn by doing and through experience. Samples of work and work shadowing, where a new team member can watch and learn from those who are good at what they do, are examples of smart techniques to build capability in your team. So, too, are show-and-tell videos, role plays and opportunities for the team to try and practise. The more skilled the team, the fewer the mistakes and the better the margin. Where possible, let them have access to scripts that work and your standard operating procedures that detail, step by step, how things are done so that they can get it right first time. These should always be written down or recorded – visually or audibly – somewhere for easy access by everyone who works for you.

Don't forget, too, to secure the information so that when team members do leave, this intel doesn't leave with them!

Secure a Good Deposit

If you have cost of sales, always get a healthy deposit from your clients – ideally, more than 60% as a sign of mutual commitment. For example, I have clients who sell to the installation market and have to buy materials on behalf of their clients, so they ask for a 70 or 75% deposit. Anyone who raises an eyebrow at this request needs to be given two good reasons why it's important and necessary:

1. Firstly, remind your clients of the volatility in the international supply chain and that it is your job to ensure that you secure reliable goods for them at decent prices. If you are able to negotiate, buy in bulk and do so early in the life of the project by shopping with the money from the

deposit, it increases the prospects of getting the best deal for them. By entrusting their deposit to you, you are enabled to shop around, link up with other current orders and exercise more buying muscle, which is ultimately good for the client.

2. Secondly, in this day and age of easy yeses and escalating money constraints, a deposit is a show of commitment from both parties. Clients have peace of mind knowing that your business has prioritised them and you have peace of mind that the client is serious about the collaboration and isn't going to change their mind. In short, it provides certainty for both parties – rather like an engagement ring!

Seek out Efficiencies

Business owners who don't budget and engage in critical test and measure each month, miss out on engaging their subconscious, setting up the Law of Attraction and securing better financial results. If they don't have an idea of what they need or expect to achieve each month, it's very hard to measure progress or look for inefficiencies in the supply chain as well as in the team and systems in the office.

Whilst we touched on this earlier, it is a margin strategy to look regularly at your outgoing payments and cost of sales and ask where you can trim costs or improve processes without impacting quality and perceived value. Where can you do better, make fewer mistakes, and accrue some savings? If you can improve your margins without constraining or negatively impacting the business vehicle, do.

Summary

Business logic, supported by good test and measure rules, is a good strategy to employ. There is no point putting in place more effort with your sales by improving your conversion rate if the numbers are showing that you aren't getting the money in on time and in sufficient amounts. There is zero point in wasting time on beefing up your website and electronic flyers to improve your marketing efforts and bring in more leads if you haven't learned how to turn an interested person into a sale because you 'don't like selling'.

Get the money in!

174

Additionally, there is the hard business truth that not all strategies work for every business. It's about finding the handful of ones that do, and working those into a business rhythm of consistent action. Many a business has failed because the owner has used the wrong strategy or because they didn't employ enough strategies. Failures can also be because it was the right strategy, but wrongly or badly executed or, quite simply, because the business just didn't keep the strategies they chose going long enough to be able to reap the rewards. Growing or fixing a business is a marathon or a steady plod, not a sprint. Consistency is often the key, rather than creative brilliance. Most strategies have to be in place and monitored for at least three months, but usually six, before the results can give you a steer on whether to continue or not.

So, get the right financials on time and understand them. Have strategies that have been tested and measured to generate leads for you. Fine-tune your conversion to ensure that you are securing enough sales and getting in the necessary monies.

Executing the 3-Ts Successfully: Their Story

Christy-Lyn Dosé started learning the harp when she was 25 years old. In three short years, her talent and hard work paid off and she mastered the instrument, passed her Grade 8, and was officially a performing, teaching and composing Harpist, with a palpable and infectious love for what she did.

However, as with so many musicians, turning this passion into something she could make a living from eluded her. She was resigned to doing weddings and events, working when everyone else was off, teaching one-on-one or composing with the million-to-one odds of ever becoming the next Michael Bublé or Ed Sheeran of the harp world!

In 2017, she vowed: "I have to get myself a business coach because my number one problem is I have no idea how to turn what I do into a profitable livelihood that can support me."

Flash forward three years and she and her two sisters, Megan and Cara, now run a business called Learning The Harp that turns over six figures a month, employs 10 staff and has over 1 000 clients, many on retainer – most of whom do not live on the same continent as Christy-Lyn.

Christy-Lyn and Cara are based in Cape Town, with premises that now boast a swish, new recording studio; Megan 'runs the show' from Croatia, where she and her husband Slaven live; and the other seven staff work in Cape Town, producing what's needed to keep the largely American harp players and learners enthralled, paying each month with joy, and coming back for more.

So, how did they do it?

First up, Christy-Lyn needed my help to appreciate that, like AJ, she was a technician. Her skill set was harp playing. She also needed to learn to package and sell what she does and formulate the sort of business plan that could get her from where she found herself to where she needed to be. She needed to dare to envision and then build the kind of future she wanted for herself and, lastly, to identify and then master the basic business competencies and tools that she needed to become profitable. She, by her own admission, had no clue about any of this. Our paths crossed at one of my workshops and we began the exhilarating journey of her transitioning from a solo performer working every weekend for a pittance, to where she and her sisters find themselves today, running a thriving, profitable business.

And during this business journey and extraordinary growth period, two of the three sisters got married and the third sister had her first baby. And no, they didn't have any loans or family money; in fact, Christy-Lyn was barely making a living when we first met and they started the business. They knew there were no silver bullets or fast tracks to success and knuckled down to do the hard work. And the help I gave them was paid for by the growth of the business. If the owners and the coach know what they are doing – and we did – this can work well for cash-strapped businesses.

Learning the Harp has steadily and systematically kept on growing each month by implementing the best practices each year as they follow their plan, roll out operations according to their vision, keep their pipelines full and use their business collateral and competencies. In short, they have all worked hard with me to grow a business from scratch in an impossible industry, in impossible times, against the odds, using best practice (which exists) and everyday tools and strategies that anyone can use. And, in spite of everything, they are a success.

Every business needs to be able to work profitably without the owner having to be there 24/7, and this is not a defunct rule, because Christy-Lyn is a musician. As I stressed in the 3-Ts, as a business owner you still need a life, and your business is a vehicle to fund that life. It must be built to deliver that. If it is failing to deliver, then something has to change.

Christy-Lyn, Megan and Cara also had to appreciate that they needed to sell something different from the usual performances at events, live gigs, CDs and one-on-one lessons that most musicians sell. With only one of the three of them being a musician, Learning the Harp had to move from an 'I' self-employment to a 'we' business.

From there, the Learning the Harp owners realised that they needed a vision that would give wings to Christy-Lyn's dream to build something more than simply 'being a musician'. This would include stretch goals for all of them, uncomfortable though they were at times, so they could move into new territory for the business. All three of them felt that they needed a strong, able, trustworthy hand to hold on to. As Christians, they had always held on to God's hand and prayed before making decisions and taking action – part of that peace we spoke about in the first section of this book. And the next hand they took hold of was mine, for that so essential and missing business help that they also needed.

Christy-Lyn started as a sole practitioner and, through a truly compelling Vision, Mission and Values, was able to 'sell' the idea to her sisters – first Megan and then Cara – to come on board as joint owners of her newly minted, fledgling enterprise. Expansion then extended to Cara's husband, Kevin Smuts, who is an experienced, internationally recognised composer, responsible for works like the music score for the Oscar-winning *My Octopus Teacher*. It also involved Christy-Lyn's husband Jonny Dosé, a highly respected guitar teacher and recording studio owner, in creating their own recording capability and international online presence. Truly, a family business.

Together, they created their one-page strategic plan (1-PSP) which has been a map to deciding priorities, growing the team, packaging new offerings, responding to the marketplace, increasing their paying client base and expanding their teaching capacity. By developing their kit bag of marketing tools and a compelling list of offerings, the three sisters not only birthed and grew Learning The Harp to employ all of them profitably, but they were all able to withstand the catastrophic impact of Covid and actually grow. Their results continue to inspire them to have the courage to dare to dream BIG and maintain a positive attitude throughout the ups and downs; to promote and sell what they do profitably and sustainably; to create a revamped 'grocery shelf' of offerings that includes a novel lesson format and other product lines that complement playing the harp that now form their growing merchandise section; and they have learnt how to tackle strategic alliances that increase their global visibility, impact their pipeline and enable them to continue to grow month on month.

They have been disciplined in their accountability to me, always following through on what they've committed to do. They have been courageous in identifying a daring but sensible business structure, as well as putting strategies in place each month to acquire more members, get in more business, grow their social media audiences and improve their capacity to deliver. They have applied their combined talents on systems, technology, video production, music-making, harp expertise, mastering YouTube and novel marketing to keep the pipeline full of clients and attract the talent that now makes up their team, all of which helps them to continue to deliver to the highest standards and on a global stage.

They have used a CRM and tech to create business collateral and lead generation. They have packaged their offerings and sold them well. They have learned the sort of business competencies that we've outlined in this chapter and applied many of the strategies listed here. They have an accountant and receive proper financial reports every month. They watch their marketing numbers and know what's working and what's not because of rigorous and consistent test and measure. They distribute their Business Bio regularly and their YouTube presence is strong.

"We no longer listen to those musicians who tell us they live from hand to mouth and give up weekends to eke out a living," says Christy-Lyn. Instead, they've become an inspiration to other musicians about what's possible and a real encouragement to both the harp and business world.

If they can, you can.

CHAPTER 9

4-Cs

━━━━

Now that you have 6 of the 15 puzzle pieces of a successful business (1-ME, 2-BEs, 3-Ts) under your belt, it's time for the 4-Cs. Without exception, when I start working with a business leader, especially if that leader is having problems, the root cause is very often people and invariably relates back to one of these 4-Cs:

- **Clarity**: Is everyone in the business really clear about the purpose and objective of the business and what their individual and collective tasks, responsibilities, standards of execution and deliverables are?
- **Competence**: Does everyone in the business have the required expertise and competence to do the job they are required to do and deliver on what they need to? Do they know how and is there a performance management system to identify and plug performance weaknesses or gaps with appropriate training? Could business coaching help you, your business and your senior people?
- **Consequences**: Do your people know the outcomes or consequences if they deliver or fail to deliver on their responsibilities? Do you celebrate the wins and reward those involved? And what happens to those who underperform? Critically, are these consistently operationalised?
- **Character**: Are your people in the right place and come from the right tribe? Does their character fit with what you are asking of them, and do they fit with your VMAV, ambitions and goals?

The 4-Cs are all about people. People ARE our business.

Whether we sell to them, buy from them, dream and build for them, work with them, prospect to them, employ them or live with them – the bottom line is that whatever business we build, we are in the people business.

Getting good at relating to, working with and managing people is key to any business resilience. And whilst this is straightforward, it is anything but easy. People are unpredictable, squishy, emotionally complex, non-task, non-binary human beings. They make mistakes, they can be infuriating, they can agree to all sorts of things they have no intention of doing and sometimes they are just not the right fit for your business. Sometimes it's your fault, sometimes it's their fault, and sometimes it's no one's fault.

Get the people side of your business right and everything becomes easier, even though people are people. Get the people side of your business wrong and you can get mired in industrial relations disputes and misery in the blink of an eye. You can follow a wonderful recruitment system and still make a mistake. And, yes, I've actually seen the opposite truth where the boss from hell has fabulous support and world-class delivery from teams who stay and can't explain why!

Whatever business we build, we are in the people business.

Most business leaders have experienced the classic recruitment story where they take someone on board who seems perfect, only for that person to end up being a disaster. And if you haven't experienced that yet, then buckle up; it's coming. It's inevitable. The good news is that there are predictable patterns that always help to get the people side of business right, first time, most times. So, before we unpack the 4-Cs, it's worth taking some time to explore what you can do straight off the bat to reduce people mistakes.

Start with You

There is a great quote from Andrew Stanley, Senior Pastor at North Point Ministries and author of more than 20 books, that's relevant to business owners seeking to recruit the right people: "Be the kind of person that the kind of person you are looking for, is looking for." Stanley said this in relation to dating and finding a life partner, but it is equally true in the world of attracting and retaining worthwhile talent. If you want a ripped and energetic girlfriend, then be the sort of partner who will attract that sort of a woman. Being an overweight couch potato or a barfly is extremely unlikely to attract, let alone hold on to, someone who's idea of fun is to get up at sunrise and jump on her gravel bike!

Similarly, at work and in the world of business, if you want to attract a world-class salesperson you need to be the sort of person a world-class salesperson would choose to work for. Someone with a clear vision, resources for the right sales tools, someone who has invested in a great product and service that people want, who offers significant commissions, public acknowledgement, a ladder of success to climb, and non-moving goal posts. That's who awesome salespeople will gravitate towards and stay with!

If you want the best PA, then you need to be the sort of boss who would attract that kind of PA. Someone who gives clear instructions in a dignified and respectful way, who appreciates competence and the willingness to go the extra mile, and someone who is easy to like and connect with, and who is reasonable in their demands. Someone who gives regular feedback, invests in their employees, lays out a clear career path, acknowledges their 'right-hand' publicly and values them. Someone who has their back and won't throw them under the bus at the first sign of trouble, who pays well, remembers their special occasions and never forgets Secretary's Day. That's who an awesome PA will choose to work for.

In essence, it's back to the Law of Attraction. If you suck as a business owner and don't do your job well, if you don't lead by example, then you may be able to initially attract talent, but they won't stay. Unless you are the kind of person that the kind of person you are looking for is looking for, you won't retain that talent and your front door will become a revolving door of attrition. Or they may stay, but their performance will be underwhelming or grudging because they will tend to mirror your own underperformance. Neither is good for staff morale. Neither is good for your bank balance or your confidence. And neither is good for your business reputation.

What are Your Key Tasks?

There is always an element of fit between you as the business leader and the people you hire but, beyond that, if you want to be the leader who attracts the best people, you need to know what your key tasks or main responsibilities are – and deliver on them. As the business owner who holds a senior, or even the top position in the business, it means that you need to demonstrate competency. In what? Well, in each of the following for starters:

Planning: Are you able to explain your business purpose, objectives and targets to your team and why they are important? Do you know where you are going, why and how you are all going to get there? This plan comes off the back of your personal Dream Chart and business VMAV – your True North – but it is also your job to position that vision in a way that is inviting and inspires others to want to join you for their own reasons. And once you are aligned towards the same outcome, possibly for different reasons, and travelling in the same direction together, the plan is what holds you on course. And while the eventual plan is almost always created cooperatively with everyone's input for maximum buy-in, you lead in terms of getting the plan implemented.

Rainmaking: As the business owner/leader, you will always be a – if not *the* – key rainmaker, ensuring that there are enough sales. This means focusing on sales yourself and then delegating what you have perfected to others as you scale, empowering and championing them to succeed in this too. As the owner, you may never truly step away from prospecting and should always keep your muscles well-exercised. Look at every situation as a possible marketing situation to increase visibility, reputation or leads, even if you then pass on those leads to a salesperson to action. Your team will always respect you more if you maintain your connection to, and competence in, sales and lead from the front.

The other rainmaking role of the business leader is around talent. It will always be your job to pay attention to people and note great talent when you see it. Invite them to consider joining the business, even if there is no obvious or immediate need now. Good people are harder to find than you think, so it's your job to be gathering contact details and adding them to the talent funnel before you need them.

You may have a sales and marketing department to assist you with execution, or outsourced human resources help, but getting enough sales and the right people is fundamentally your responsibility. It's on you if either the sales or talent funnels dry up. It's on you to fix it.

ROI: Being the kind of person people want to work for includes being comfortable with the financials and knowing whether the business investment is or is not delivering a return. Knowing what expenses, effort and relationships deliver the most or best return is part of your job. When people know that you know, they also know there is nowhere to hide. As the owner and leader, it's your job to be watching these things on a monthly basis and to get rid of the things that don't deliver a positive ROI. You are not a charity.

Chief Attitude Officer: No one likes a negative nelly or constant complainer, least of all in the top dog position. Your job is to be the most positive, passionate person in the room – every time. Your attitude is infectious and, because you are the leader, it carries more weight with the team than anyone else's. It's also a critical building block to good self-belief and helping others to believe in the business too. If you aren't seen as believing in yourself and what you are trying to achieve with your business, how can you expect others to?

Problem Solver: Your job is to see the big picture and the detail, seek out problems, ask for input and resolve what gets in the way each day, week, month, quarter and year. Empower others to do the same and be a sounding board so that you create an open, problem-solving and innovative culture. People will mess up and not all solutions will work, but if everyone in the business knows that you support ongoing problem-solving and ingenuity then they won't be afraid to try. If this is hard for you, find a coach or someone who can help you become unstuck on this.

If you have a habit of procrastinating, then know that this won't result in you being respected by the team. The whole point of any manager is to resolve and solve what the team can't. And the buck stops with you, at the top of the pile. If anyone can, you can, must and should.

Being the Leader: The buck stops with you. This means leading by example, which includes doing everything that you want others to do – if you won't, neither will they. If your people see you avoiding sales, they will too! If they see you short-changing or shirking in your role, they will do likewise. Being the leader is about being the general who actually goes to war, rather than sits behind a desk issuing instructions. If you want people to do their best and go the extra mile in their jobs, you need to do the same in your job. In your own business, you'll quickly find that others won't do what you say, they'll do what you do. So, if you slack off and do the minimum, over time so will they. If you make excuses for targets not reached or work not completed, in time you will start to hear similar excuses coming from your team. Your people will end up mirroring you, so make sure they are mirroring the best in you.

Leading in Learning: Each new stage of the business will mean learning and doing stuff you may not have done before. Demonstrate your own ability and willingness to keep learning new competencies, finding new solutions and coming up with new ideas and new ways of doing stuff. Be a reader, encourage and reward others to do the same and share their new learning with the business. Have a business book library. Foster a learning culture and make sure that your people know that you don't expect perfection straight off the bat, as there will always be a learning curve when any of you are developing new skills. That's OK. You can't build a bigger, better business unless you build a bigger, better you and encourage others to do the same. All the talent in the world won't cut it unless you are also teachable. Stay teachable – it's an essential asset, especially in uncertain times when the environment can change so quickly and without warning. Think Covid!

> It's your business so do your right job, right – even as a shareholder, you are always a role model.

When you get bigger and can afford a management team, some of these responsibilities can be delegated, or at the least, their execution can be shared. But, as the owner, you must demonstrate the traits you want to foster in others. Even as a shareholder who is no longer working in the business, you will always be a role model.

Have a Proper Recruitment Process

Finding, attracting and holding on to good talent is not luck. The right time to look for talent is *always*. Job applicants may not be in short supply, but talent is. The last thing you want to be doing is looking for talent when there is an urgency to fill a gap.

When people resign, they may have to give a month's notice, but one month is rarely enough time to properly search for, find and onboard someone good – unless you're incredibly lucky! So, if you haven't already been looking at people who impress you, people who've come into your sphere of influence, or have served you well in a different business, you'll find yourself under pressure to settle on someone who may not be right. And if your process has been non-existent or shambolic, you're setting yourself up to repel the very people you want to recruit.

> Talent will always have a choice and it is up to you to sell your business to them and explain why they need to work for you and not your competitionl.

If you have a proper recruitment process in place, you can be running it even if there isn't currently a job to be filled. Recruitment advertising is fundamentally marketing!

Talent will always have a choice and it is up to you to sell your business to them and explain why they need to work for you and not your competition. Below are 12 tips it may behoove you to consider to ensure that your recruitment marketing attracts the right people.

#1 | Use Your Vision, Mission and Values (VMAV)

Your VMAV helps to position your business and sells the big picture dream and ultimate destination. It outlines the purpose that directs the individual positions in the business and will give the role meaning to the right person who shares your vision, mission and values. You want people who are aligned to your VMAV for their own reasons, so that coming to work and doing their best work is aspirational and meaningful to them as well as to you.

#2 | Get the Recruitment Advert Right

Don't just focus on what you want in terms of skills and experience and list it under a boring job title like Bookkeeper or Project Manager; instead, focus on what's in it for the applicant and who they need to be to join you in your quest. Inspire them to join you.

Think of your job title as a newspaper headline designed to attract your perfect candidate. I worked with an accounting practice that was looking for an administrator to also handle the company secretarial stuff for clients. The perfect candidate needed to be someone who had some legal training but was probably not a fully fledged attorney, because it wouldn't be a challenging enough role for them. The person needed to be organised and detail-focused, but it was more than an administrative role because of the specialised knowledge that was needed. If we advertised for a lawyer or an administrator, both were likely to miss the mark, so our chosen headline was:

"Legally experienced and fed up with being undervalued where you are currently? If so, why not consider this newly created opportunity to handle the A-Z of company secretarial needs for our clients in our vibrant, trusted accountancy practice?"

Our hope was to attract the paralegal/secretarial/junior person working under an attorney who is often overworked and underappreciated. And it worked.

In another business, my client was looking for someone to work in the front office of a gas shop. The person would be doing some customer service, some selling, but also some admin like answering the phone and cashing up. It was hard to give a definite name to the role, so we opted for a headline that used some descriptive words to keep the net wide open.

"Do these seven characteristics describe you:

- *Sunny-natured*
- *Persuasive*
- *Pays attention to detail*
- *Goes the extra mile*

- *Has great verbal communication skills*
- *Is fluent in Microsoft*
- *Is willing to work a 5½ day week?*

If so, then this well-paid, responsible position as our first and most important point of contact in our busy, bijou retail outlet selling gas to loyal customers and newcomers, Monday to Saturday, with two others to help, could be a great long-term opportunity for you."

The business had struggled to keep this role filled. People came and went and there was no continuity. They wanted to find someone long-term. Given the location of the shop, we decided our best bet was to attract a single mum who lived in the area, had kids in the local high school and wanted secure, steady employment. This wasn't prejudiced; it was just practical. We didn't preclude men from applying, and our deliberate use of the words 'sunny-natured' and 'bijou' meant that we would only attract the right type of applicant – male or female – one who would hopefully stick around. Again, it worked, and it was an eye-opener how many applicants spoke about the attractiveness of the advertisement. Marketing job well done!

As well as a great headline that speaks exactly to your target audience, your advertisement also needs to include responsibilities and key attributes to prospective applicants, outlining what they will need to be able to do and what type of person you need them to be. Both matter. The advert must also detail what the applicant needs to deliver and what they will receive in return. And, like all good marketing, the advert should end with a strong call to action, together with a deadline, in order to create urgency.

We have some examples of Dos and Don't Dos on the website – have a look – www.buildingbestbusiness.com

Top 10 Free or Almost Free Options on Where to Advertise:

1. Send the advert to your entire database – customers, suppliers, alliances, prospects, service providers, ex-clients, team members – they know your business and have experience on the sort of people you currently have.
2. Ask your clients or suppliers if they would email your advert to everyone on their database, as this will extend the pool you're dipping into.

3. Ask your community. Put the advert up on noticeboards, websites or in newsletters for the library, the gym, your local sports club, your church, your vet/doctor/hairdresser, your children's school – especially if geography matters.

4. Send an email directly to people whose performance impressed you with a simple request: "I loved the work you did, and we are looking to hire. Do you know of anyone like you who may be interested in the role?" People usually hang out with people like them, so they may refer you some top talent. The added bonus of this technique is that if the person is looking for employment themselves, then they will obviously refer themselves but, if not, it will make their day that someone else has noticed their skill set. Note: It's never good form to poach staff from another business, so always ask permission from the employer first to contact their team member.

5. List the advert on your social media platforms and narrow the area of visibility – Facebook and LinkedIn are our favourites.

6. Word of mouth – tell EVERYONE you're looking to hire.

7. Approach the relevant departments at your local secondary and tertiary educational institutions. You could exchange some free lectures, career advice sessions or job shadowing, internship opportunities for the right to advertise the role to the students or, more importantly, the alumni.

8. Add the advert to your website. Ask your strategic alliances and any professional associations linked to what you do, if you can add the advert to their website homepage for a couple of weeks. Try to make it beneficial for them too. Offer something of value in return.

9. Advertise with voluntary organisations who specialise in specific niche groups, as they could have just the kind of person you're looking for. Migrants, artisans or single parents, reformed prisoners or disabled individuals are examples we've used before. I had a client who sold and serviced white goods and when they were looking for a great receptionist, we chatted about this specific strategy. They ended up hiring a blind chap who could identify me from the sound of my walk, even though I was one of literally hundreds of annual visitors to the business. It was remarkable and quite a talking point. He did an amazing job for the

business, was always warm and welcoming and was thrilled to have been given such an opportunity. A real win-win.

10. Advertise, on a paid basis, on professional online platforms such as LinkedIn or Indeed. They're not free but are a good alternative option if options 1–9 don't yield any candidates.

#3 | Use an Application Form

Direct all applicants to your website to download an application form. Instruct them to fill it in and submit the form, by a particular date, and disregard anyone who just sends a CV. Chances are the form will duplicate parts of their CV, but it serves as a good 'prospective employee test'. It's a little more work, but if they are not prepared to make that little extra effort to follow your explicit instructions, then the chances are that they probably wouldn't be the right candidate for you. The real test is whether they are able to follow your instructions. They don't have to like it; they don't have to agree with it, but they do have to be willing to do it.

The Application Form format that I recommend requires some biographical details that help you circumvent industrial action later on (like health status, criminal background, availability and the like) and provides for full contact details that aren't always on CVs. But, most importantly, the form reduces the huge variability of CV information, and the myriad of ways it can be presented, into one directly comparable format by asking all candidates three good questions:

1. Why you?
2. Why us?
3. Why now?

And, finally, it seeks permission for the last places of employment to be contacted and supplies details of who to speak to there. These are the references you want to contact, not the references on the CV (more on this in #7).

It's also wise to manage expectations upfront to make less admin work for yourself in the form of fielding unnecessary calls from candidates who are unsure whether their application has been successful or not.

On the Application Form, add a message:

"Please note, if your application is successful, you will be notified by [Date] and you will be invited to attend an interview and receive an introduction to our business and coffee on [Date and Time]. Make sure you are available." And also add, *"If you haven't heard back from us by [Date], please know that your application has not been successful, and we wish you well in your job-hunting endeavours."*

There is nothing worse than applying for a job and then hearing nothing. It's unfair, but it takes time that you may not have, so stating what will happen in the Application Form lets everyone know the score.

If you'd like an example of a great form, scan the QR code on the right to go to our website www.buildingbestbusiness.com and download ours for free. Add your logo and the correct deadline and off you go.

#4 | Interview on a Saturday

There are two major benefits to this strategy. First, your ordinary working day isn't interrupted (and neither is theirs!) and the interview process doesn't interrupt or distract other employees.

Second, it tests commitment and flexibility. If the candidate comes up with all sorts of reasons why they can't make it, they will probably come up with all sorts of reasons why they can't do all sorts of tasks that you may ask of them in the course of their employment. You want open, adaptable people who agree to requests rather than find problems. The only exception to this may be if they are already working over a weekend.

#5 | Use Great Interview Questions

You only need to ask five to eight good questions in an average interview and make sure you ask all applicants the same questions, in the same order, to allow for useful comparisons. 'Good questions' in this context are questions that will require the candidate to provide an example of behaviours – what they have actually done in their previous roles, rather than their opinion.

190

For example, if you are wanting to hire a production planner, it stands to reason that they must be the sort of person who is organised, detail-focused and systematic. So, rather than ask whether they have these traits, which is just their opinion, ask them a question that requires them to demonstrate these traits: something like, *"Tell me, what did you do to prepare for today?"*

Genuine planners, from experience, admit to stalking you online, visiting your website and social media platforms to learn more about the company and what people are saying about it. They tell you how they drove to your office several days before the interview or worked out what train or bus they needed to get and rode the route to make sure they gave themselves enough time on the day. They talk of shopping for an appropriate outfit, visiting the hairdresser and organising childcare, making sure to allow for more than enough time in case the interview went on longer than expected. And they've usually made a list of questions that they want to ask you. Candidates who say they are planners, but where planning is not necessarily part of their innate nature, tend to be far less detailed in their description of their preparations.

- If you want someone to evidence innovation, ask them, *"What did you do to improve your last job?"*
- If you want someone to evidence responsibility, ask them, *"Describe a time in your last role when something didn't go well or as expected. What did you do and how did you handle it?"*
- If you want someone to evidence leadership, ask them, *"Describe a time in your last role where you needed to take charge – how did it work out?"*
- If you want someone to evidence people skills, ask them, *"Describe a time when you conflicted with a colleague, what happened, did you resolve it and how? And then what about a time with a subordinate?"*

We've put a Great Interview Guide on the website www.buildingbestbusiness.com and, of course, you can download it for free. We've clustered questions under different attributes so you can pick and mix ... and add your own!

#6 | Try Before You Buy

Interviewing on a Saturday, with good questions, will help to narrow down your candidate field considerably, leaving you with only the strong contenders. Next, you want to see those contenders in action via a try-before-you-buy or role-play exercise.

Let's assume you have a vacancy for a workshop manager and you're interviewing five people. These five will have been invited to attend an interview, get an introduction to the business and be given coffee, as specified on the Application Form.

This is primarily a marketing exercise, so you will need to pay a few of your existing staff to attend on the Saturday morning if they are not already working that day. You may like to kick off with a brief overview of the VMAV of your business and their role as you envision it. Then, you could have five stations, like a gym circuit, that each applicant circles through:

1. Coffee and something yummy to eat, with the supervisor – never underestimate the role of good food in marketing!
2. A computer task (completing a job card or putting a quotation together) with your administrator.
3. A tour with any member of staff. I like to use someone junior because it gives them a boost and you can also tell a lot about a person based on the way they treat someone they perceive as junior, subordinate or less qualified than them.
4. A first interview with you, the business owner/boss.
5. A practical task with a member of the team, who will be reporting to this newbie manager.

Finish off with everyone back together again to receive a thank you and a Next Steps Brief.

Not only does it leverage your time, but this sort of process allows for the Holy Grail of any recruitment process – direct comparison. It also helps to get buy-in from the team who will be working with the successful candidate; they feel included and listened to and it can help to onboard the winning candidate well. Plus, it alerts applicants to the fact that they are not the only contender for the job. A bit of competition can usually spark better or best behaviour. We all step up when there are others watching or the stakes are higher.

Once the sessions and interviews are over and the candidates have left, ask the team members who supervised or were involved in each session to rank all five of them in order of how excellently they handled each task from 1–5 (5 being best).

For example, the five candidates are listed along the top and you total the rankings on each element of the recruitment process for each one:

Exercise	Jim	Bob	Mary	Fred	Belinda
Coffee and general discussion – are they our 'tribe'?	5	2	4	3	1
Computer task and digital fluency	4	3	2	5	1
A tour of the place with a junior staff member	3	2	1	5	4
First interview with you as the owner	4	3	5	2	1
A practical task to evidence technical skills	4	3	2	5	1

You can add to this rating form by scoring the five candidates on other aspects that are key to the role, like the ones below, and again rank them in order of 5 being excellent and 1 not so:

Exercise	Jim	Bob	Mary	Fred	Belinda
Coffee and general chitchat – are they our 'tribe'?	5	2	4	3	1
Computer task and digital fluency	4	3	2	5	1
A tour of the place with a junior staff member	3	2	1	5	4
First interview with you as the owner	4	3	5	2	1
A practical task to evidence technical skills	4	3	2	5	1
Geography – who lives closest to the business?	1	2	4	5	3
Previous salary in relation to what you're offering	1	3	4	5	2
Relevance/usefulness of past skills training	2	4	3	5	1

Exercise (continued)	Jim	Bob	Mary	Fred	Belinda
Age in relation to your ideal candidate	1	2	3	4	5
Previous job experience that relates to this role	4	5	3	2	1
First impression	3	2	4	5	1
Their references	5	4	3	2	1
Their DISC profile in relation to the role	4	2	5	3	1
Their appearance in relation to your expectations	3	1	2	4	5
Second interview with you and perhaps a team member	3	4	2	1	5
TOTAL	47	42	47	56	33

And then total up the scores. It's fascinating who comes out on top and it's a great way to stay objective, enroll the team in the eventual choice and have ammunition should any candidate query your final decision.

#7 Check References

As I alluded to earlier, I'm always a little dubious about references listed on a CV. No one is going to include a negative reference, are they? What you really need is objective input from the people who worked with, or even better, managed that candidate in their previous roles.

When you have shortlisted your candidates to the top two or three, make contact with all their previous direct bosses – not the HR department. Some people can be a bit cagey when asked about past staff members and there is liability to consider.

Start by saying that a past employee, Jim, has applied for a job, and you would like to simply verify some CV information with a couple of simple Yes/No questions – would that be okay? Then ask two or three questions such as:

- *"Jim tells me he worked for you as a bookkeeper in charge of debtors – is that correct?"*
- *"Jim says he was earning roughly $34,000 when he left you – is that accurate?"*
- *"Jim advises he was in this job for 10 years – does that sound about right?"*

Then hit them with the only question you really want an answer to:

- *"If you could, would you rehire Jim?"*

If they hesitate, then you know something's up and you need to ask Jim about it at the next interview. Most people will not go into the detail, but it doesn't matter; the content of the story or situation is not the 'give-away', the hesitation is. You need to find out more. Don't just assume the worst of the candidate, however, as sometimes it's the other party or business that behaved badly. But if there was hesitation, when you speak to the candidate again you need to find out more. You may say, for example: *"Jim, as promised, I rang all the places you worked at before and Bob from your previous employ expressed reluctance to rehire you, what was that about?"* And then go from there.

I once interviewed a bloke who seemed perfect, but his referee had hesitated when I'd asked the big question. When I queried it with him, it turned out he'd been in jail for two years for GBH. Totally not what I'd been expecting, but how he handled it was a real learning curve for me. He looked me straight in the eyes, his own welling up with tears, and told me that he knew what he'd done was wrong, but he had served his time and had a family who needed him to step up. He told me he'd kept his nose clean (other references backed that up, as did his parole officer) and if I would give him a second chance, I wouldn't be sorry. I did. And I wasn't!

In my experience, you only ever get two responses to the big re-hire question. They say yes immediately and often wax lyrical about how sorry they were when the person left, or they hesitate. Both are great outcomes, because they allow you to get closer to finding out key information that will help you get to the perfect candidate, and it is often the truth. It's also better for the candidate. In the instance above, my GBH ex-jailbird was relieved that I knew the truth and hired him anyway and was even more diligent and committed as a result of needing to prove himself.

There is, of course, a problem if they've only had one job and the current employer doesn't know they're looking for another. Then, this modus operandi for reference checking obviously won't work and you'll have to resort to obtaining feedback from people like their teachers, youth pastors, sports coaches or neighbours.

#8 | Personality Profiling

I've lost count of the times I've heard business owners tell me that investing in a profile is expensive. What's actually expensive is hiring the wrong person. Investing in a profile for key personnel is just smart business, saving you time, money and preventing the plummeting morale that so often happens after a bad-fit hire.

Research has shown that:

- The average cost of a bad hire is 30% of that hire's annual salary.
- A single bad hire costs companies an average of $14,900.
- The average cost to hire an employee is $4,425.
- It generally takes at least six months for companies to break even on new hires.[34]

My preferred profiling tool is DISC (more on that later in the chapter), but there are many others. They offer a unique insight into what's under the hood of your potential recruit, because they illuminate traits and characteristics that may be hidden from view in the interview process.

#9 | Make an Offer

Once you've made your decision on the final candidate you'd really like to have on the team, make the official offer.

Rush it and you run the risk of cutting key corners, coming across as desperate and settling for someone who is not ideal but will do. Take too long and talent will assume that they aren't a priority and chances are that someone else will nab them first. There is nothing more frustrating than going through the process, taking too long and then, when you finally make your offer, your chosen candidate says, "*Sorry, I hadn't heard back from you, so I accepted another offer.*" And then you have to start all over again or take your second choice.

#10 | Maintain a Recruitment Mindset

Finding the right people at the right time is not always easy. One way to reduce the risk is to stay open to recruitment all the time. You may not need anyone specific right now, but if you come across people who impress you, tell them about your business, your vision for the future, what sort of people you are likely to need as you expand, and ask for their details so that you can get in touch when opportunities arise. Most people will be flattered and will acquiesce with enthusiasm.

This also works if you want to hire a number of people from your recruitment drive, but not all right away. As long as you are upfront about your needs and the timeframe, it may work for some people. For example, you may say, *"You're great and we'd love to have you; can we cement the transition for the start of the new year/the start of the new financial year/the start of the new quarter?"* As a strong negotiating position and a practical way to manage the flow of talent – providing you've done a good sell on the vision of the business – it is responsible and proactive, two things that talent will definitely be able to appreciate.

I had a client who runs a couple of nursery schools, and she had a team of 60 that included teaching assistants who, for various reasons, were often not able to come to work at short notice. They had to deal with public transport, their own family commitments, and many were at the entry level of employment where life stresses can loom large. Because no sane parents would drop off their kids without staff on site, she had to be ready at a moment's notice to fill any gaps on the team. In dealing with this problem, during our coaching sessions we resolved that she would recruit every single Wednesday afternoon. This gave her the opportunity always to be looking at entry-level talent, putting them through her process at her leisure, informing them about how and why her schools worked the way they did regarding teaching assistants, and then creating a list of people she could phone and onboard at short notice.

She kept a permanent list of five names, adding to it as people dropped off it or were hired by her, either as a temporary fill-in or permanently. And really, without exception, those who ended up on that list were grateful for the opportunity to try out with a view to a more permanent role. She had more choices, so we did not have to manage the PR nightmare of staff gaps and the process could be run by different people as it became part of the system. It also meant that forward-planning school leavers could apply early. It was a win for everyone involved – including the kids and parents.

#11 | Day 1 Matters

Someone once said: "You only get one chance to make a good first impression," and they were correct. The first day is everything. Going back to the nursery schools owner, we worked very, very hard at making sure new staff were wowed on their first day, even if they were temporary. They were respected, valued and made to feel special.

The owner was always there to greet them on their first day and, before they arrived, their snapshot had been put up on the wall in Reception under the title of 'Our Family', and a coffee mug and bunch of flowers had been ordered for them. The Standard Operating Procedures Manual had been printed out, together with all the take-on forms.

Each new start was appointed a buddy to show them around, accompany them to tea and lunch and introduce them by name to everyone they would need to interact with on their first day. Log-on details and access to software were handled with the administrator after tea. And after lunch, the owner would reappear and say that as the first day is usually stressful, she was treating the new employee to an Uber ride home so that they could put up their feet for the afternoon, read the information at leisure and absorb everything that had happened. She'd see them the next day, bright and breezy!

It was a hit. The new recruit felt valued and appreciated and was ready to start Day Two with passion and enthusiasm.

Consider what you can do to make your new recruits feel welcome, valued and respected in ways that would be special and different to anything that they may have experienced before.

#12 | Use a Structured Induction

Day One is all about making the new start feel welcomed and valued, and induction is about helping them to become settled and productive as quickly as possible.

There is always an onboarding uptake curve for even the most able new employee. Any change is stressful, and a new job is right up there. We owe it to our business to make the transition from new start to settled team player as smooth and as fast as possible. And it all comes down to having a proper, structured induction process, as opposed to throwing them in the deep end and hoping for the best or letting them just find their own way as they go.

I often play a card game with clients and their teams to illustrate the value of induction. In groups of four, they have to play against one another in a simple game of securing the most tricks with one of the four suits as trumps and highest card wins. There is a set of detailed rules that they are all encouraged to read and then, when the game starts, they are forced to stop talking. All other forms of communication are allowed, but it is interesting how many people do not take advantage of writing notes! At the end of the game, the top two winners move to the next table. The same set of rules applies there too, but few bother to read them because they look so similar – why bother? The game starts again and deteriorates into immediate chaos. What no one knows at the time is that, hidden in the bulk of what looks like identical rules, is one line right near the bottom of the page that specifies which suit is trumps. It's different at each table.

What happens, usually every time, is chaos, which is exacerbated by not being able to talk. When we debrief afterwards, we explore how even though everyone knew how to play the game, at the coalface there were issues that needed induction. We identify the truth that, in the absence of these shared and known rules, people default to what they know and used in their past (which is often different to now) and three things always suffer: enjoyment, pace and results.

The only way to be clear about "how things are done around here" is to ensure that expectations are properly communicated to everyone from the start, via a thorough induction process. Make it awesome. Make it immediate. Make it useful. It's an investment in ensuring that you enrol all newcomers into your wider business tribe as soon as possible, make the transition as painless as possible for them and as profitable as possible for the business.

These 12 tips help to ensure that you get the right people on the bus.

The 4-Cs – our next set of puzzle pieces – make sure that they are equipped with what they need to deliver and that they become an investment with a great return.

The 4-Cs are:

- Clarity
- Competence
- Consequences
- Character.

C1: Clarity

In my experience, so much of what goes wrong in life – and certainly in business – can be avoided with clarity: clarity of communication and expectations so that everyone involved in the business knows exactly what's expected of them. The biggest problem is that too many businesses already believe that clarity is in place. However, scrape the surface and it's not.

This first C – Clarity – is therefore the puzzle piece that ensures that everyone knows exactly what has to get done, by whom, how, by when, how often and with what tangible outcome. This clarity starts with a detailed job description for each and every role in the business and every employee.

Job Descriptions

I have seen hundreds, possibly thousands, of job descriptions in my time, but I can count on two hands how many good job descriptions I've seen. I think this is because business owners are generally very busy and/or they don't see the import of being absolutely non-negotiable about creating these documents optimally, and the idea of adding what can seem like unnecessary admin to their day is unappealing. As a result, there is either no job description or it's been cobbled together from a bog-standard online version, or an employee is asked to write something, or it's just a one-page, high-level aspirational document, none of which deliver clarity. Having no clear, detailed job descriptions is a fast track to confusion and chaos.

The acid test of whether a job description is a good job description is whether it is used to actually impact, improve, measure and change an employee's performance on the job. If the answer is yes, it's a great job description. If not, then more work is needed. That said, it shouldn't run to 20 pages; however, it should cover all the bases and be as clear and succinct as possible.

The other reason that job descriptions don't get done in business is because owners just don't know how to write them. The key is to work out what is really important to you in the execution of the role and to make sure the detail of that execution is contained clearly in the job description. And this is much more easily said than done – trust me.

For example, I worked with a client who was complaining that the receptionist they had hired was not answering the phone to their satisfaction, which struck me as too vague. So, I suggested we look at her job description. True, the document did specify *"answer the phone by the third ring with good morning, XXX here, how may I help you?"* But when I questioned the owner, 'answer' was the wrong verb. What the owner actually wanted the receptionist to do was *"answer all incoming calls and resolve or escalate them the same day."* The boss took the receptionist aside, apologised for not having made the job description clear enough and restated what he actually required and, as a result, he got the behaviour he wanted.

With this renewed clarity, the issue was solved almost immediately. The new receptionist was clear about what was required and able to deliver to the boss's satisfaction.

When two human beings interact with each other, the one thing that can pretty much be guaranteed is that there will be occasions when what one person believes they have said, is not what the other person believes they have heard. We think we are being clear, and the other person may even nod and look like they agree, but unless you are clear about exactly what you expect, and clear that the other person is able to relay those expectations back to you as you intended them, then nothing is clear. Into the gap goes wasted time, missed opportunity, frustration, wrong outcomes and hurt.

> When two human beings interact with each other, the one thing that can pretty much be guaranteed is that there will be occasions when what one person believes they have said is not what the other person believes they heard.

So, before you jump to conclusions about an employee's ability or suitability for their role, do they have a job description that outlines exactly what you expect of them? If not, then you can't really be annoyed at what is, effectively, your own shortcoming! Check in with them: "What did you and I understand had to get done, how, and by when?" You will probably find out that the reason things are not getting done the way you expected or hoped is because those expectations were not spelt out clearly enough in the job description for the employee to understand them the way that you intended they should. Once people have that clarity, their performance almost always improves and, if it doesn't, you have the written documentation to initiate procedures to manage them to change or leave.

Job descriptions done well are used to assess, manage and improve performance, so it follows that they should seek to be crystal clear about:

- what has to be done (the right verb),
- by when (any deadlines),
- with what frequency or other conditions,
- with what tangible outcome (that we can all see),
- to what standard/template/example,
- and following what checklist/process/standard operating procedure/ statutory requirement.

Think it through, write it down, break the list down into a group of these new, clear tasks for each person and see how people clashes, team frustrations, poor performance and relational disappointments can be massively reduced.

You can find 'before and after job descriptions' for various roles on our website www.buildingbestbusiness.com. You can see how little clarity is contained in the first, original job descriptions and how much more clarity is locked into the second, revised version for each role.

The second in each case is an example of a properly written job description to base yours on, so feel free to download them and get cracking on yours.

Job Description Writing Best Practice

Below are the 18 best-practice rules for writing great and workable job descriptions that ensure that you and your employee are on the same page regarding tasks, responsibilities and skill set. That way, you both know what is expected and the employee knows what they will be assessed and measured against.

1. The verb is everything. After all, it is a job description so the actions/ behaviours rule. Make sure it accurately describes what you want to see happening if you were to watch the employee doing that job brilliantly. Really think about it. Use a thesaurus if necessary to find the best, most accurate words to express what actions you want to see being executed.

2. Steer clear of vague verbs such as 'assist', 'handle', 'ensure', 'manage', 'motivate' and the worst of all, 'try'. Also, avoid what I call on-the-way verbs. For example, if you 'order' and 'settle' payment for consumables, use something like 'procure' which involves both. If I have to 'review' something, I don't also need to 'check' it because that's implied in the review.

3. Have a concrete, visible, tangible outcome for each job task. There has to be a point where any objective third party can see "Yes, that's now finished". Spell this out and don't be afraid of descriptive adjectives to give additional colour, detail and clarity to this outcome.

4. Include a timeline that explains by when various tasks and activities need to be completed. This is one of the most frequently forgotten elements in verbal and written instructions. I can't tell you how many times I've heard bosses complain about something not getting done on time only to go silent when I've queried, "Did you spell out the deadline expectation?" No, they did not.

5. If it's not clear, it won't be followed. People may learn over time what isn't being said, but it's no way to manage, relate, scale or invest in your team as a common business-building practice. The clearer you are about your time expectations – in fact all your expectations – from the start, the more likely your team will meet them.

6. Include adjectives that amplify the outcome (don't be afraid of a long list of these, as they are 'seeing' words and help others visualise what you mean), the deadline and the standard that the task or activities need to meet. They can all be made clearer with the right adjective. Include some adverbs that colour up the verb for the same reason.

7. Capitalise important documents or meeting schedules so that the employee knows:

   a. They are a 'thing' at your business, with a source that outlines what is acceptable.

   b. How to meet those requirements and that previous examples can be found on a shared platform or resource to view.

   c. They have to become familiar with all the terminology that is being used, as it forms part of the business 'lingo'.

8. Use active not passive language.

9. Job descriptions are the sum total of the tasks that need to get done by someone, or a group of people, to enable the projected turnover to be reached each month and year. A great way to create strong, cohesive job descriptions is to start with a Master Task List for the business. Brain dump all the tasks and activities that need to happen to deliver what the business does each month at scale across each of the functional buckets of the business – General Management, Finance, Human Resources, Marketing, Sales, Operations, Admin and Research and Development. Start with the thought:

   • "If I had one customer, one sale, and was producing one widget, what would the tasks be?"

   • Then add to this thinking: "What have I left out of this task list when this business is up at scale and turning over $XK per month and per year?

   • Then consider: "What has to happen daily, weekly, monthly, quarterly, annually in each of these buckets to get stuff done?" Think tasks, not what the person in the role currently does.

   • Once you've got the tasks, ask yourself: "What, if anything, have I left off from the past/flawed/incomplete job descriptions?"

   • Now that you have a completed Master List, go back and colour-code who of your people currently in the business is doing what. You'll very quickly see whether everything is covered and whether every task has someone who is responsible for that task or activity … or not!

If you go to our website www.buildingbestbusiness.com, there are two examples of one of these Master Task List brain dumps that you can look at to see if you're on the right track or not.

10. Avoid words like 'continuously', 'always', 'never' and search for the reasonable frequency that would be exhibited by a competent person and use that instead. Be clear, but also realistic.

11. Kill off any mention of 'either/or', 'etc', 'as required', 'when necessary', 'periodically' and, instead, spell out what this refers to. If you don't, you'll leave it to the discretion of the employee and before you know it, there will be a disagreement. If it matters, spell it out. If it doesn't matter, don't add it to the job description.

12. Don't make each individual job description longer than one page. Any longer and it's almost certainly more than one person can accomplish productively and without undue stress. Stay focused on the tasks that only the person in this role can and must do in order for the business to be successful.

13. Don't list experience, skills, attributes and training separately; instead, weave them into the outcomes-based task list. Do the same with key performance indicators (KPIs). Having these separate or in addition to a job description, creates almost too much to watch. With an outcomes-based job description, the details, standard and frequency are already identified in the task list and additional KPIs shouldn't be required. Keep things simple, concise and clear.

14. As a practical benchmark, if a seasoned manager cannot walk into your business, look at the existing job descriptions and direct the team to get stuff done, then your job descriptions need revision.

15. Ensure crystal-clear accountability. Often, there may be two or three people in a business doing the same work. It's important to apportion that work so each person is responsible for their defined bit of the total load. For example, there may be two people in accounts who invoice customers, one may invoice customers A–M and the other N–Z. If this isn't possible, then it's about who has overall responsibility for the outcome in question. This may result in breaking one task down into a couple of sub-tasks so that each person can be responsible for their bit.

16. If there is no one to do a task, then see if there is someone the task can be passed on to. Can it be done by a more junior person in the team? If not, then it has to go into the bucket of tasks for a new hire.

17. Link performance to salary and, if applicable, bonuses. Once you've got a crystal-clear job description, it is easy to have employees and teams rate themselves on a scale of 1–10 each quarter, give you a tangible why they have done this, and enable you both to reach an objective agreement on their score. Two great authors who've done some good research on this that is both practical and entrepreneur-friendly, are Michael Gerber and John Warrillow. Both have also done great work on long-term incentives and outline neat ways to link the ratings on performance appraisals and work done to money.

18. Use the job descriptions as building blocks for a meaningful organisational structure to determine which roles or groups of tasks fall under the purview of which boss. Remember, each person can work with others and even provide services to others, but must have only one boss! Also, make sure that equally valuable roles are on the same level of seniority and pay to avoid griping, and that no one in a particular role has more than six to seven other people reporting to them. Stretching key players too far with a more-than-practical number of subordinates isn't smart – for you, them or the business. We've got two examples on our website www.buildingbestbusiness.com of how the building blocks have been placed into an organisational structure, with hierarchy (who reports to who) and parity (which roles are on similar levels of seniority) evidenced.

You can also use job descriptions, slotted into a structure of seniority and who reports to whom, as the basis to work out your meetings roster (who meets whom and when), design your recruitment advertisements, handle job interviews, induct new employees, settle disciplinary disputes and structure the best type of training – all competency-based.

And because you've used a flexible format like Excel to brain dump your exhaustive Master Task List, as the business scales you can revisit, update and revise this document to ensure that it accurately reflects what needs to happen to get the required results. As staff members come and go, their tasks can be regrouped, tweaked, rearranged and redone to suit the business as a whole.

Try it.

Clarity is the first place to start when reviewing outcomes and getting the most from your people. Most people want to do a good job and feel they have made a valuable contribution that is noticed and rewarded. This is virtually impossible without clarity.

It's also deeply unfair to chastise employees on tasks not done to your standard when neither you nor they can put hands on your hearts that you have shared what that standard or expectation is, and that they have received this communication with crystal clarity.

So, do the work and get those functional job descriptions created for everyone. And if you feel like you are too busy, get help. Every day that you leave this unattended to is another day of suboptimal performance, an advantage worn away, an opportunity missed, and bad habits formed by everyone.

C2: Competence

Once all the job descriptions are done correctly, each person in the business, including you, has absolute clarity. There is now zero misunderstanding about who, what, how, by when, the frequency and to what standard each task needs to be done. That these tasks are also linked to remuneration underlines to everyone that they matter.

Next is Competence. To have a great business, the team needs to be competent in the performance of its tasks. Like everything else in business, competence has to be measured in order to make sure it's maintained, and you must be alerted to any shortfalls that need addressing. There are two great tools to help measure and monitor competence that I get my clients to master:

- Meetings:
  - A Daily Stand Up
  - A Weekly Huddle
  - The Monthly Actual vs Budget
  - Quarterly Strategic Planning (QSP)
  - An Annual Long-Term Strategic Planning Session
  - A New Business Development Think Tank
- Standard Operating Procedures (SOPs)

Meetings

Consider the job description as each team member's starting place, their marching orders of what has to be done, by when, how and to what standard. Meetings are the place where you get to find out how each team member is measuring up to their marching orders so progress can be checked, corrected and improved.

French philosopher René Descartes once said, "I think, therefore I am." In other words, we think something and then act in a way that determines who we become. If these actions are repeated often enough, they create habits.

Competence or skill in anything, be it photography, recruitment or welding, is a practised behaviour or habit. Positive actions repeated over time become habits which, if engaged in for long enough, lead to mastery.

> Without regular, good meetings, teams may practise the wrong way of doing their job which then becomes habit and hard to change – for them and you.

Because behaviour is habitual, it stands to reason that whatever we practise regularly is what we'll end up doing habitually. If someone joins your team and is left to their own devices without a clear job description or induction, they may learn the wrong way of doing their job or do it the way they did it in their last place of work. However, if they practise what is now required often enough, it becomes their habitual way of working. Nevertheless, if there are no meetings to check on progress and performance, then you may not find out which of these two realities are occurring at the coalface until it's too late.

Essentially then, we build competence and incompetence by the way we review and check in with the behaviour and actions of others. What we leave to gather momentum unchecked and unchanged will become "the way things are done around here". If that's world-class – wonderful. If it's not, it will quickly become a problem.

Meetings are therefore the perfect place to measure what is getting done against expectations and to pick up an issue as early as possible – and certainly before poor habits are formed. Meetings, when conducted correctly, can be brilliant for accountability and celebration. They can also help to collectively find different and better ways of doing things. Meetings can be safe places to sort out choke points and create positive momentum around the right behaviour.

Verne Harnish is my go-to guru when it comes to creating productive and powerhouse meetings. In his excellent book, *Mastering the Rockerfeller Habits*,[35] he speaks of making sense of these different but equally important types of meetings and how to connect them so that no one suffers from what Patrick Lencioni calls 'death by meeting'.

In my 30 years as a business growth expert working with large and small organisations, I've seen variations on Verne's model that enable the business to really breathe and develop. After all, if there is sufficient and consistent communication about behaviours, and if these behaviours are measured against expectations, the work of the business gets done and the business moves forward. So, let's elaborate on Verne Harnish:

A Daily Stand Up

As the name would suggest, this is a 5–10 minute daily debrief between you and your direct reports, ideally held at the start of each day. The only agenda items are what's happening today and what, if anything, could cause problems. It can happen over WhatsApp or Zoom if you are in different locations, but it needs to happen. People at the coalface need to know that each day they have a place that helps them anticipate and solve any problems; a place where they can ask the dumb question, deal with the niggles, sort out their indecision, handle the gap left by someone who isn't in, or manage the crisis. In fact, the only reason they have a boss is not to oversee them or ensure they get the work done but, rather, to help them solve the problems they can't – the problems that get in the way of them doing their job.

No Minutes are needed for this type of meeting. It's the locker room chat between captain and team. Nobody else. That's why doing your job descriptions first matters because it also gives clarity about what roles report into which captain and manager. The only way the team can see who is in each Daily Stand Up is by having a clear organisational structure. The boss or business owner has their Daily Stand Up with their main managers. And then each manager has their Daily Stand Up with their direct reports and so on down the business. If teams have to get out first thing, you can have tomorrow's Daily Stand Up with your direct reports 15 minutes before you close today, and your direct reports can meet their team first thing. Choose a time for your Daily Stand Up and stick to it so that it becomes habitual.

These short Daily Stand Up meetings ensure everyone in the business knows their priorities for the day and has help to resolve any potential problems before they arise. And they need to take place four days a week.

A Weekly Huddle

On the fifth day, the Daily Stand Up is replaced with a Weekly Huddle. You can decide what days of the week are for Daily Stand Ups and which day is allocated to the Weekly Huddle but, once you've decided, stick with these days.

The Weekly Huddle is a longer meeting but should still only take 20–30 minutes, certainly once you get used to the format. Its primary function is to look across the different departments to check that the business is on track to make the weekly business deliverables. This could be the number of closed sales, or installed pools, or erected stands or transported pallets of goods. It could also be the number of completed SOPs or the filing of archive accounts or reconciled supplier accounts. It could also be market share or stock turn around. Whatever you choose, it is a meaningful measure for your business on whether things are progressing as you had forecast or not. These weekly numbers or deliverable milestones are, of course, derived from what the business needs to achieve monthly which, in turn, is one third of the quarterly business goals. In this way, the deliverables make sense as milestones themselves and also incremental milestones in the larger business objectives, which helps underline the purpose of the goals to the entire team. Each person is able to see how they contribute to the larger business objectives.

The Weekly Huddle should include informed representation from each department or project that needs to be moving forward. Attendance can be rotated between team members at the same level. This means that the same people aren't always tied up in meetings and all the team members get the opportunity to grow 'good meetings' muscles. Good meetings are just another habit – we need to practise them to get good at them and make them a positive habit, instead of an irritating and unproductive time-suck.

Like the Daily Stand Up, the Weekly Huddle is operational. It is looking at the coalface and what is getting done against what needs to be getting done across the business. If anything more strategic or long-term crops up in these meetings, park it and add it to the agenda for a more appropriate forum. One of the most common reasons meetings don't work is because the content is mixed up or attendees try to cover all the outstanding issues in one meeting. Keep the meetings focused on what they are about – for the Daily Stand Up and Weekly Huddle, it's operational issues only: what is getting done and what is causing impediments and delays to task completion.

Make sure you minute the Weekly Huddle as an accountability record for the following week, with a WWW Outcome – Who's got to do What by When – to meet the deliverables.

The Monthly Actual vs Budget

Next comes the monthly meeting to look at actual action versus budgeted action. This needs to happen every fourth week of each month and in that week, it replaces the Weekly Huddle. This is a 2- to 3-hour investment run by you as the business owner, where you systematically review the budget of each department, project, branch and sector of the business. Specifically, you're looking at:

1. What was supposed to happen – i.e. with regard to the budget?
2. What actually happened. Look at the hard numbers and facts only. No blame, as it wastes time and ruffles feathers.
3. What does the Head of Department, Project Lead, Branch Manager, champion or outsourced expert recommend to resolve the problem/s?

I've counselled clients to have each of the attendees send in a Round Up Report 48 hours prior to this meeting in which they detail these three things. Each round up should be no more than one page and include an executive summary of what's happened and what can be done to get back on track if necessary. Depending on the size of your business, you may go into the monthly budget meeting with anywhere between five and twenty one-page overviews of each department or project.

You need your leaders to come to the table prepared to offer up good solutions and help make good decisions so that they leave the meeting having resolved these issues in ways that can help the whole business. This means they'll have to have received and read through these round ups prior to getting together.

Part of growing good management talent is to get the team practised in applying their minds, using common sense, general business experience and intuition, as well as making key decisions regarding all areas of the business, not just in their own area of expertise ... so don't be shy about getting everyone into the habit of doing some intentional preparation prior to meetings.

This meeting is part-operational and part-strategic. It's where the longer-term goals meet execution and the work that make these goals a reality on the ground. Minutes should be taken so that progress can be charted each month. Again, at the start when it's new, it can feel clunky and take longer than hoped; however, it should improve if you stick to the recipe. Get help if you need it and practise.

Quarterly Strategic Planning (QSP)

Once a quarter, the meeting schedule is augmented by a quarterly strategic planning (QSP) session, which can replace a monthly actual vs budget if time is short. It's for shareholding owners and executive management to decide whether the business is securing an adequate return on investment, sufficient profit and turnover are being consistently achieved, the longer-term goals are still appropriate or need to be tweaked, and to ascertain whether there is viable progress being made towards achieving these objectives. It happens every 90 days, because research shows that's the length of time most teams can progress positively before they are in need of feedback on how things are going, how they are doing, are things on track or not, and where/how do we need to improve to safeguard things that matter. Think of it like a team resting point on a hike, a half-time locker room chat or the essential finish line to all the hard work that the team has put in over the last quarter to cross it, so that they don't lose heart, can pause for breath, celebrate some progress and recalibrate if necessary.

For you, it's equally but differently important. It is your opportunity to remove yourself from the business for a day every quarter to look up, back, forward ... and it gives you the time to think! Ignore or postpone this because you're 'too busy' and you disqualify yourself from a proven business advantage. As business philosophers the world-over are fond of reminding us: "We out-think our competition long before we out-perform them." It's imperative that you make the time to do this.

And when you get back from your off-site QSP with your key team, invest an hour or so updating the entire business on the outcomes from it. Perhaps hold a morning coffee or order in pizza and some beer at the end of the week and let everyone know the outcome and ask questions. Consider sharing:

- What happened vs what should have happened and what got in the way – don't make excuses or lay blame.
- What the business did well and not so well – keep it factual and positive; take responsibility.
- What this means for everyone – good and bad news, as well as viable tools in the communal kit bag.
- What the next quarterly goals look like and why.
- What you're all playing for – WIIFM (what's in it for me – people are individually motivated).
- Who was exceptional and deserves public mention?
- What can we be grateful for?
- What are we celebrating today?

Annual Long-Term Strategic Planning Session

As your business scales, you have a team and your turnover is now well beyond that of a start up, your size will warrant taking your senior management or perhaps the whole team away for a weekend to put together a longer-term strategic plan. You could, for example, roll the fourth quarterly planning session into this weekend planning session to leverage time. This longer planning session completes the rhythm of meetings for the year.

I recommend using the One-Page Strategic Plan (1-PSP) format I outlined in Chapter 8 for this meeting. It can be filled in at a departmental or project level first and then worked into one master document as an outcome of the last meeting.

A New Business Development Think Tank

Think Tank Weekends are particularly useful in fast-paced sectors, but they can be beneficial for all business. This is a time for facilitated brainstorming, where invited representatives take time out to look at trends, research, new developments, what different markets are doing, what the competition is up to, different products and offerings that may have come on to the market, upgrades/changes that need to be considered, customer requests and suggestions, and good ideas that can make money. It is not usually in place of one of the other meetings, but in addition to them.

Business owners tackle this sort of meeting in a variety of ways. Some do it fairly frequently, like once a quarter, and keep it in-house with contained audits and personal research. Others piggyback on events in the sector that run once or twice a year and get involved in something much bigger than themselves. Still others do it by surfing online and collating findings, without having to meet up. And there are those who need to go on a walkabout/travel to get intel and make connections. Whatever makes sense for your business, this "Ant Brigade"[36] as Seth Godin calls it, is essential to prevent the business becoming blindsided by missing something seismic in the marketplace or slipping into irrelevance.

Godin tells a story about ants foraging for food in new surrounds. They set off in a circular route of the area to be explored and then, once inside it, they lay down a faint scent in a seemingly random but very efficient manner that covers this new area. As soon as they find food, they head back in a direct route, laying down a different trail that says to all the other ants, "This is the way to food and water". This movement and exploration into new areas is critical to their survival. The same is true in business. To do this well, Godin recommends mandating a small percentage of staff or staff time to play, experiment and create in the field of the unknown as your Ant Brigade!

Once you've sorted out all your meeting types, put them all onto a Master Meetings Roster. Publish this a year in advance and ensure that everyone blocks out the time to meet – no excuses. For the first few months, these meetings may be a drag and you may even complain about them being a 'time suck', but you will soon get used to the rhythm and the results – when they come – will ensure that you won't want to stop. Trust me. Try it.

Standard Operating Procedures (SOPs)

The right meetings schedule will illuminate competence and help you fill in any gaps. The other tool for ensuring competence is standard operating procedures. It's the point where most businesses find space to cement a demonstrable, definable competitive edge and the place where quality standards are forged and sustained.

As the business owner, you have the privilege of detailing how you want things done because you put in the risk capital and worked hard to create the business in the first place. Making sure that the way things are done around here is the way you want them done, starts with job descriptions and is fleshed out by standard operating procedures (SOPs). SOPs are essential, especially when there is a process that has to be followed to ensure a particular outcome: if there is specific technical content to consider; if there is a specific way/outcome that is legally correct or simply if I, as the owner, want to ensure consistent high standards. Think of it as a library of competence that the team can tap into when you are not there. This library will walk them through the specific 'how to' of all the required tasks.

Job Description Tasks First

If you focus on the tasks outlined in job descriptions first, it will soon become apparent which tasks need an SOP and which don't. It will also become clear who is best placed to detail the SOP – it's usually the person doing that task most frequently and currently doing it very well.

An SOP is a step-by-step best practised, idiot guide to completing any task in the business and, together, they form a library that is then available to newcomers who can quickly gain the required competence in any and all tasks.

These can be written, or you may also want to use video or a screen recording while using and demonstrating software, for example. These can be stored electronically in a central place with access protocols, just like a library. That way, staff can dip into the SOPs when they need a refresher on how to do something or want to double check that they are doing the task correctly.

SOPs also form a wonderful asset for a business, which will be particularly valuable should you want to sell. They're a great training resource and a brilliant way to on-board new recruits. Staff love them as they give them a road map that they can refer to whenever they want. They feel happier because they can learn what they need when they need it, and not feel as though they have to interrupt you or a senior manager to get assistance to get on with their job.

Recording the "way things are done around here" as standard operating procedures – whatever your medium of choice – isn't only hard work; it's a team road map, a safeguard on quality and a business asset.

I was coaching a restaurant owner once, who detested doing this sort of admin and his adult ADHD got in the way of any sort of bookwork. His response to my "get some SOPs done" was uncooperative, to say the least. When I asked him what his biggest time-waster was, he immediately said it was chivvying the kitchen to have it tidy at the end of each shift. But his definition of tidy was not what his kitchen staff thought. I suggested that he take detailed photographs of what the kitchen needed to look like at the end of each shift if those shift workers wanted to be paid on Friday, caption the picture in the four languages that his staff spoke, and stick it on the kitchen wall.

It solved the problem! It wasn't that the staff were being deliberately difficult or lazy; they just hadn't understood exactly what he'd meant by clean and tidy. Once they did, they could replicate it!

I had another client who kept putting off the creation of an SOP library. I suggested that when the team couldn't go out to install on rainy days, he could use his most outstanding employees to 'star' in some SOP videos to show others how it was done. It was fascinating to hear how team members enjoyed this public affirmation.

Be creative, use tech, have fun with it, but get it done.

C3: Consequences

When people know what is expected of them and understand what competence in that task looks like, then they will either deliver or not. Either way, there needs to be consequences if the behaviours are to be fixed or sustained.

Broadly speaking, consequences can be divided into two categories: 'towards' and 'away from', known more colloquially as 'carrots and sticks'. Carrots are things we want, stuff we pursue and the rewards we'd like to get. Sticks are things we want to avoid, ensure we never get, and punishments.

Carrots tend to pull us positively toward engagement with various tasks. They are welcome and tend to invite us to stretch our capabilities to become better. They are usually something that matters to us, so we engage our best self, our best efforts and our competitive spirit. Things like a trophy, money in the bank, a great figure or applause are examples of carrots. Sticks push us away from a negative, sanctioning result that we want to avoid. Things like missing out on a bonus or being last in the performance league table, are good examples.

Carrots and sticks both work but for different reasons, and they will work differently on different people. We are not all motivated by the same things.

Extrinsic and intrinsic motivation also plays a role. Extrinsic factors are things outside of us like money, applause (carrot) or demotion (stick) that we find motivational. Intrinsic rewards, however, are found within us, like knowing we did our best or feeling a sense of increased confidence (carrot) or, conversely, guilt and regret (stick).

Tversky and Kahneman[37] noted that we value avoiding losses about 2.3 times more than achieving gains of the same value, underlining that sticks are twice more likely to work in shaping our choices than carrots. And Clive Mottaz's[38] research underlines that intrinsic motivation trumps extrinsic when it comes to work satisfaction over the longer term. People usually immediately assume that the carrot of motivation is money, but it's not necessarily. Giving people the opportunity to do purposeful work that feeds their self-confidence, while allowing them to cushion themselves from a glum retirement, is likely to be far more motivational than even a stick.

Herzberg's Theory of Motivation[39] also bears mention. He found that only some elements or variables can motivate. He divided things that impact an individual's performance and happiness at work into two groups: Hygiene Factors and Motivating Factors (see Figure 9.1).

Figure 9.1 *Herzberg's Theory of Motivation*

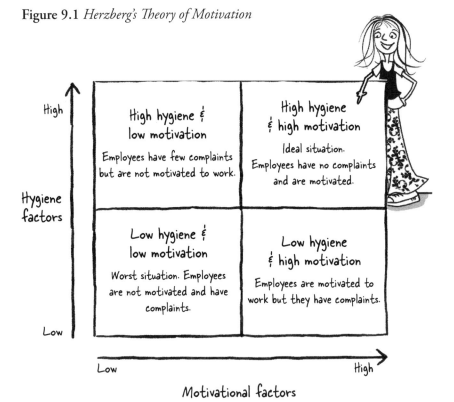

Hygiene factors create satisfaction when they are present and dissatisfaction when they are absent. Money is a good example of this. When a staff member is paid well, they are usually a happy team player and, when it's absent, they are usually dissatisfied and will complain. However, it doesn't

218

necessarily follow that with extra money they will become more motivated. This is a function of other factors. Money is therefore an extrinsic carrot that may keep people satisfied but not necessarily motivated.

Other examples of what actually motivates and what keeps dissatisfaction at bay are:

Figure 9.2 *Motivators versus Dissatisfiers*

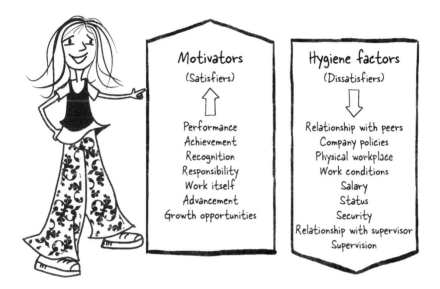

Suffice to say that carrots and sticks are both needed in the motivational mix. The key is to get to know your people and make the carrots meaningful to them so that they can tap into their own intrinsic motivation.

Link Carrots and Sticks to Specific Outcomes

If you don't link consequence to the specific behaviour you want to encourage or discourage, you are wasting your time. Salaries, training, bonuses, feedback and performance management are all examples of carrots that show up in entrepreneurial businesses, but they can be time-consuming and expensive. You also can't keep increasing a key employee's remuneration forever. At a certain point of seniority, certainly in a small business, it just isn't affordable. The only way you can stay current with the money over the long haul with valuable individuals is to link their renumeration to a performance or profit bonus where, if they and the business do well, the sky's the limit.

This has the added bonus of giving good people 'skin in the game' – which is a clever, golden handcuff for great and valuable team players. However, it needs to be linked to clear performance targets, so that everyone is on the same page about the consequences of delivery (and failure to deliver). You don't want to be stuck paying bonuses to poor performers just because of their level of seniority, or become embroiled in arguments over what and who deserves which bonus or slice of the profits.

You also need a clear policy for wrongdoing – and this needs to be enacted every time. It's called discipline and most of us hate it, but unless consequences are followed through on each and every time someone doesn't behave right, you'll have problems. The message of inconsistent delivery of consequences to the poor performers is that they have got away with it and the message to the good performers is that it doesn't matter. Neither is good for your business.

Clarity, competence and consequences work together. It is certainly much easier to sanction clearly communicated tasks in a job description with an SOP, than it is to have a discussion with an employee about what you think isn't working. The evidence will speak for itself, because you can point to objective facts around what the person agreed to deliver versus what they have delivered and let the evident gap do the talking for you. It's always easier to confront non-performance if you get the 4-Cs right. And if that gap can't be filled, then you have the ammunition to manage them out of the business without a fuss.

C4: Character

Okay, so now you've cycled through the first three Cs. You have a team member who is crystal-clear about what has to be done. He has a thorough and well-thought-out job description that is working – for you and him. His competence is beyond doubt, and he is a skilled, confident operator. He has benefitted from training and is nobody's fool. There have been consequences when he mucked up and rewards when he exceeded expectations, but it hasn't made for a motivated, happy team member. He remains a square peg in a round hole. It's like he doesn't fit and that often just comes down to Character – the fourth C.

This is a harder problem to deal with. But it is essential to contend with it as early as possible, especially in a small business where everyone is working so closely together. There simply isn't room for team members who are not aligned with what you are doing and building or who don't fit in. It isn't a discipline issue and it's often no one's fault, but it needs to be addressed – fast.

The best plan is to avoid the situation happening in the first place and this can certainly be helped by the robust recruitment process mentioned earlier. It is also wise to invest in personality profiling tools – especially for key hires.

Use Personality Profiling Tools to Assess Character

My preference is DISC, a behavioral self-assessment tool developed by psychologist William Moulton Marston.[40] The DISC theory describes personality through four central traits (see Figure 9.3).

I like DISC because of its simplicity, its reputation for reliable results, and the way that teams can relate to and use the information. That I choose to represent each of the four elements in the diagram with a different dog breed adds a dose of humor. It also provides a good recall trigger and an easy analogy to aid in the identification of different clusters of traits by management, white- and blue-collar team members alike. It allows for a less pointed means to discuss interpersonal differences that can underpin team conflict. The fact that it's been validated on normative population samples in the places I do business, and how easily business owners can become fluent in its usage also helps me commend it. That I'm a registered psychologist means that my clients can use licensed copies under my supervision, and we tick all the boxes. It's safe, reliable, useful, legal in the event of a dispute, reputable in terms of feedback to the applicant, and valuable. It basically increases the chances of a right hire from 50% to around 80% and is massively helpful when it comes to improving/fixing/changing your team culture and self-awareness or performance management in general. Now those are odds worth paying for.

Figure 9.3 *DISC Traits*

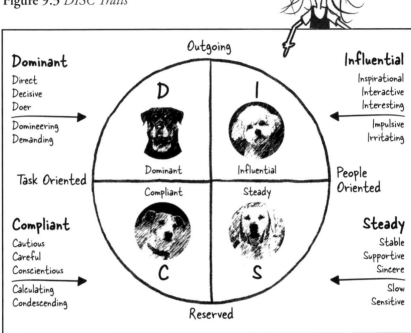

If you'd like to access DISCs for your recruitment, go to our website www.buildingbestbusiness.com. We have a preferential rate for clients and use it broadly when it comes to their teams, but non-clients can also purchase access to the tool to improve their recruitment procedures and ensure that their candidate's character is going to fit in with the business.

DISC takes about 10 minutes to fill in and about the same amount of time to score. The result is then factored into and delivered via a multiple-page report that assesses their fit for the job role, what they will bring to the position, how they are likely to handle conflict and stress, and what sort of environment plays to their strengths. It is a professional and impressive gift to your top one or two candidates, and it's always a smart recruitment investment because it looks 'under the hood' of possible recruits so that you can assess their likely fit ahead of time.

I have a friend who went for an interview as a senior marketer for one of Australia's leading banks. In the interview, she asked the interviewer, "If the bank were an animal, what animal would it be?" He immediately said, "A fat brown and white cow." At the end of the interview, my friend was thanked for her time but told by her interviewer, "I really don't think you'd like working for a fat brown and white cow!" And he was right. They both knew it, because the question had allowed them both to recognise that although she had the qualification, the skill set and the ability to do the job, there was no fit. Profiling allows you to measure that fit ahead of time, so you reduce the odds of having to manage someone out.

There are many profiling tools on the market, but you need to find one that is affordable and user-friendly. Make sure it is easily available, complies with the law, and has been validated and deemed reliable for your population groups.

Profiling is a really great way of ticking that last box – 'character' and therefore fit. Once you have narrowed the field down to a couple of recruitment possibilities, especially in senior roles, then profiling those candidates can help you separate them to identify the right person for your business. Not just the job but your vision, mission and values (VMAV), culture, ethos and philosophy.

Getting the 4-Cs right will improve your business performance and the speed your business can scale – guaranteed.

Executing the 4-Cs Successfully: Their Story

Realtors based in Durbanville, Cape Town, founded by Manja Kritzinger in 1996, started modestly and over the last quarter of a century has grown, expanded its areas of operation, gained in profitability and reputation and become a well-known name in the industry. Passionate and disciplined about building up a sought-after service in the northern suburbs of the Western Cape in South Africa, Manja recognised early on that she and her son Andre weren't just realtors, they were also business owners who would not be able to do it alone.

Exuding that old-fashioned passion for knowing their clients personally, combined with their family values of integrity, innovation, transparency and excellence, they have now become a force to be reckoned with. But they will be the first to tell you that it hasn't always been easy or fun, and there have been significant people challenges along the way.

Sustained success, with this level of operation, is all about how well the team functions. Running a personable, sought-after service, where you know the clients and they know you, is fine when it's just you. Securing sufficient stock and closing enough sales each month is also fine when it's just you. But when you have to create a team and a culture that can do this as well as you, and also have enough houses/stock incoming to warrant the team, that is very different.

Manja will be the first to tell you that people are complex. People are not always easy. Talent isn't that easy to find and doesn't always stay. It is vulnerable to being poached by the competition and it isn't cheap. Fifty-four staff is a handful by anyone's standard.

People challenges are top of mind for most businesses. How do I find, grow, keep and manage enough of the right talent so that we can make the right amount of money consistently? How do I get the team to work well together and not have to police them? How do I instill and enjoy a sense of ownership in team members, so they stay because they want to? These are questions that, at some stage or another, most business owners need to ask.

And so Manja and Andre, together with the other two owners of the business Charlene and Rumé, all had to knuckle down to getting the 4-Cs back on track.

For starters, their vision for the future had run out. They'd arrived at the place Manja had envisioned all those years ago and now needed something fresh. They were established and profitable but had started losing sight of their end-in-mind or, more truthfully, had not updated it once they'd achieved those initial goals and as the business developed. Resolving this first hurdle was crucial. All four owners therefore created a professional True North that all four were willing to fight for. And having thrashed this out, we all had the essential destination, which included a presence overseas.

It provided the missing context to work back from and to ask some critical questions about the team and the tasks they needed to embrace, master and deliver on. This, then, turned into a six-month project of brainstorming, writing, re-writing, adding to, deleting, re-writing, editing, sleeping on, changing again and plenty of robust debate among the four of them on their Master Task List. It sounds like an easy thing to do, but it's not. For starters, it is terribly tempting to think about different individuals and what they do, rather than considering the vision and what needs to be done to deliver that.

It's also easy, as the owner, to gloss over the detail of what needs doing – all the things that fall into our unconscious competencies. Things that we don't think about and so don't articulate because they happen almost automatically, without effort on our part. This, however, is not the case when someone younger, less experienced, new to our game or more junior is in the driving seat. Brainstorming for this clarity has to be sufficiently detailed and appropriate for both old-hands and newbies. It is a BIG task in an already-established business.

The second challenge to getting this Master Task List finished, was for each of the owners to be sufficiently disciplined in avoiding the passive tense, searching for just the right verb that would ensure 100% clarity, thinking through the conditions around how/when/to what standard each task needed to be performed to warrant a salary and noting them, and also settling on a tangible outcome for each task. In giving it their highest and best over most of a year, they finally – and to their relief – got the list done.

And it made such a difference. The owners had been experiencing duplication of effort and messy reporting lines, which left team members unsure of who to go to with various issues. It also saw variable results. A lack of clarity around what exactly was expected of them by management had led to frustrations on all sides and slipping standards of work. It became hard work to differentiate between someone not actually knowing and therefore needing training versus non-performance by someone simply slacking on the job. Usual carrots, like great commission splits, weren't motivating consistent results and the weight of staff, who should have given the business wings, was compounded by the devastation of lockdowns, work-from-home rules and a halt in trading during the Covid pandemic.

In short, the team wasn't a dream team.

So, after getting to their True North and enrolling the team to the new vision, sharing the values that they wanted to see expressed and being demonstrated in every area of the business, and what their commitments would be, all the realtors were excited. They were then focused and galvanised to work hard on that master list of tasks, which then formed the content of good, visible job descriptions that are the first step in gifting everyone with clarity and the business with a proper structure.

From there, they were able to group these tasks into different levels of seniority and under different roles, which gifted them an organisational structure. They were then able to slot who was currently doing what into this organisational structure to create crystal-clear clarity across the board. Duplication was spotted and stopped; some tasks were moved to new owners; tasks that were not being done were assigned an owner; they were able to create a hierarchy and clear reporting lines and then establish who needed to meet with who daily, weekly and monthly to get the job done.

For the first time, every team member had a list of what they needed to do as their bit to deliver on the vision. For the first time, they also had a clear boss and clear subordinates. There was clear parity on who was senior to whom and who was on a similar level to whom. For the first time, it was clear who needed to meet whom, over what and when. A roster could be drawn up and the first tent peg in managing day-to-day performance was nailed down.

Because performance is essentially behaviour in action, catching this when it's wrong needs to happen fast and early if you want to avoid wrong stuff becoming a habit. If you wait for a couple of months to correct an employee, it's harder for both you and them to change.

Other wins included a published standard and norm on expectations, against which actual performance day-to-day could be compared. Instead of hearing that they hadn't lived up to management's expectation or had been disappointing/underwhelming/not worth the full bonus, team members were now able to rate themselves against a tangible, observable task outline and answer for themselves, "Have I done this task completely, well enough and as I was asked to, or not?" This objective and visible line in the sand became the standard against which the actual could be fairly and consistently assessed. It became easier, then, to decide what was genuine incompetence, what was a real training need and what was disciplinable poor performance.

This, in turn, meant that consequences could be more fairly, consistently and confidently applied which, in turn, positively impacted motivation and respect for management. Talent has been able to practically aspire to more senior positions because the next-level task list is public and clear.

It has also been a game-changer with respect to advertising for new staff. What they need to do and who they need to be is now systematised in the form of great job descriptions, so the work of recruiting, inducting and onboarding has been streamlined.

Additionally, quarterly performance appraisals, without having to 'police' the essential behavioural changes that come out of them, are possible because line managers can oversee self-assessments and ask team members to explain why they rated themselves as they did, and what needs to change or happen to improve their ratings.

It has also been easier to have those hard conversations with team members who don't fit. Having assured all parties about what needs to be done and to what standard, the Realtors team now finds it easier to appreciate who can or can't do the job. Once this is no longer in dispute, consequences for not doing the job, while not enjoyed, can't be ignored or considered unfair. Likewise, who gets rewarded becomes less subjective and open to criticism. What each team member has to do or do better to enjoy similar rewards to other A-team players, also becomes clearer and less subjective.

And the 54 team members in a fast-paced, competitive industry of property are now working better. The vision is clear and all the tasks that need to get done to deliver on that vision are assigned to the right people. Lines in the sand have been drawn and those who don't fit can be managed out faster. This has positioned Realtors to enjoy good growth, targeted recruitment, being a magnet for talent, and the sort of ROI that makes the effort worthwhile.

They have an enviable commitment to in-house training and, because of their efforts, they are able to onboard and intern people with a level of involvement that is living their values and gifting them success.

And all this while so many are complaining, "You just can't find good people anymore."

CHAPTER 10

5-Ps

The last puzzle pieces for building a powerhouse business are the 5-Ps. They are all about promoting you, the business, what you do and making money, but, specifically, they are about how to turbo-boost sales. You can have the best business in the world, but if you can't make consistent sales then the business – and the life it funds, which is primarily yours – will not survive.

The 5-Ps are:

- **Proposition**: Not just what your product is or the service that you're offering, but who it will appeal to and why.
- **Prospects**: Who will buy, how often, how much and how many?
- **Process**: What are the steps to follow to successfully 'date' prospects and find and close sales?
- **Preparation**: What tools, scripts, emotional questions and prep pre-work will help secure you an edge?
- **Practice**: Role play, review call recordings, committed learning for better results and the like that turn those who can't into great rainmakers.

When implemented in your business, these last five remaining puzzle pieces and the deliverables associated with them will go a long way in helping you smooth out the scary financial or cashflow peaks and troughs of business as usual, so that you can secure and maintain a strong, predictable and consistent monthly income.

It may be tempting to look at the 5-Ps and think: "This is the crux of the issue; we need to make more money so I'm going to start with the 5-Ps." Please don't; there is a sequential reality around building and scaling a business and it really does start with YOU and, specifically, the PEACE puzzle pieces in Part One. We all need to arrive at the business start line as a largely whole, fully functioning adult. And that means finding some measure of peace with who we are and where we are right now, so that we can focus on the future, not the past, and be ready, willing and able to do whatever it takes.

Then, we need to be sure that we are mentally ready and have sufficient business collateral to keep us working at the 5-Ps when we may be tempted to give up. The 5-Ps are deliberately positioned next after the foundational stage and the necessary thinking that precedes every great sales strategy. Getting sales right, and especially resiliently so, relies on getting the other puzzle pieces in place first. It's the only way I can pretty much guarantee owners that once this has been done, sales become less hard. Never easy, but definitely less hard.

So, let's get to it …

P1: Proposition

Proposition embraces two important components. Firstly, what are the offerings on your Grocery Shelf? And secondly, who will these products or services appeal to, and why – your Value Proposition.

Your Grocery Shelf

You don't need to have premises or a storefront to have a grocery shelf; any business – or even a service – can ensure that they offer a range of products or services that their customers know about and can 'see'. Customers want visible, easy-to-buy choices and it is always easier to sell if there is a range of offerings on view that they can choose from. Additionally, customers want value. They want to know they have bought something that will make their lives better in some way. The 'so, what' of what we do, therefore, becomes critical.

So, what is on your grocery shelf? When you sell each of your products or services, is it enough to get you the monthly turnover you need to fund the life you have identified that you want? Is what's on your grocery shelf visible and clear to your customers so that they can easily browse and make a choice? Do they know about your full range? Are your offerings packaged thoughtfully? Are the offerings compelling? These questions are as relevant for services as they are for products.

For example, say you're a landscaper looking to build your landscaping business. Your grocery shelf of offerings could include some pre-landscaping services such as tree felling, site clearance, out-building demolition or helping to secure planning permission. The landscaping business would obviously include a range of more typical landscaping offerings like monthly maintenance for a small, medium or large garden, the provision of different design themes like English Country Garden or Tuscan Garden, through to family-friendly, pet-friendly, easy-to-maintain or water-wise options.

The proposition could also include post-landscaping options, like regular maintenance and pre-season upsell specials on additional services that become relevant around the changing seasons. It could include things like cleaning down pipes, leaf disposal, pruning and fertilisation. And finally, your grocery shelf could include allied services like decking, pool installation, awning installations, outdoor furniture, barbeque or braai facilities – none of which you actually offer yourself, but you may get a finder's fee or commission for bringing customers to those businesses.

Now your landscaping business has a wide and varied range of offerings that make optimal use of different pricing options and your time. Some of the services you do, some others do. Some of what you sell is service- or time-based and some is product-based. Considering this much more extensive grocery shelf also introduces options and wiggle room when it comes to negotiating with a prospect. It also helps prospects pick and mix from your offerings to suit their requirements and budget, thus reducing the chances of your getting an outright "no" from any prospect.

Make sure that your offerings are clearly illustrated on a website if you have one, and/or in-store if you have one. Revisit *T3: Fuel Lines* in Chapter 8 to increase the chance of sales. The landscaper could, for example, add before and after images to his website to showcase results, or bundle often-bought services together to make it easier for his customers to get exactly what they want at a price that works for them and still delivers value.

As the business owner of this landscaping business, you may have done your sums and worked out that you need to secure three big garden projects and six smaller ones each month to keep the business ticking along. Everything else is therefore icing on the turnover cake. Having a diverse grocery list just ensures multiple opportunities for sales and multiple streams of income, so you are seldom cornered.

So, what's on your grocery list? Be creative and put on your thinking cap. And once you have this list, package the items on it into different offerings, relegate some to spontaneous add-ons at various times of the year and have things you can upsell when you need to increase income.

The key to creating an extensive grocery shelf is to really lean into your offerings and think outside the box.

If customers want your goods and services packaged in ways that make it easy to buy, with sufficient choice and range, and a "so what" they can resonate with – give it to them.

1. Identify your top-shelf core products or services.
2. Take each one in turn and consider what else could you offer that would make that product or service more valuable or immediately useable.
3. Could you link up with other businesses that are not competing with you, but who are speaking to the same sorts of customers so that you can provide a trusted network of suppliers to your customer that will also provide you with additional income? If this is possible, make sure that you agree on terms and expectations with these other businesses. These 'strategic alliances' will often be viewed as an extension of your business, so do your due diligence and make sure you align with companies you admire.
4. Think about what customers or would-be customers may need before they are in the market for your product or service. Could you provide this?
5. Are there any products or accessories that you could offer as upsells that would add value to your offering?
6. Thinking about the outcome your customer is after, what else could you provide that would help them achieve that outcome faster?

7. Are there any after-sales opportunities for you? Will what you have sold to your customer need ongoing servicing or checking in the future? Is there a possibility for ongoing maintenance or a safety check of some sorts?

Remember, everything that is true of a product grocery shelf is also true for services. As a business coach, I offer one-on-one sessions and also various group coaching options. The group work runs over a year and is initially focused on getting those involved to the point of predictable income and hiring their first team. The second stage is focused on scaling up the business. And I am associated with a network of trusted professionals, including wealth planners, labour advisors, recruiters and accountants who refer me to clients whom they believe could benefit from my involvement, and vice versa.

I also run regular workshops for clients of my clients and suppliers. Not only does this add value and my clients are viewed in a good light by their own customers, but it also routinely brings me more leads and great business contacts. I offer annual strategic planning, sales training, team alignments and DISC profiling as product offerings to clients, and I'm also available as a guest speaker at client events. Any money I earn from these speaking engagements I gift to a non-profit organisation of the client's choice.

My hairdresser, gym, cycling club, swimming group, church, library, bond originator, business banker, mechanic and beautician know what I do and how to get hold of me for clients and friends of theirs who are my target market and need my help. And I refer my clients to them.

Your Value Proposition

Your value proposition incorporates what makes you special, different and better than the rest, and is the 'so what?' of why those who buy from you do. It answers what is the problem that will be solved, or the benefit gained by buying this or that from you?

If you are unsure of what your value proposition is, ask your raving fans why they chose you and the products and services they bought from you, and what it meant/gifted them. They'll tell you.

Good Questions to Ask to Identify your Value Proposition:

- What problems will our product or service solve for our target market?
- What negative consequences will our target avoid if they buy our product or service?
- What benefits will our target experience from buying our product or service?
- What is the cost to our target of not using our product or service? What will they miss out on?
- What value will our product or service deliver that matters to our target?
- Who is currently experiencing the benefits of our offering and what do they say is special about our product or service?
- What results have the product or service generated for users? Can we quote those results in our marketing?
- What trend, season, movement or current hot topic does our product or service tap into?
- Who can endorse or recommend our product or service to our target?

You don't want to be competing on price alone. You want to know, and want others to know, what those things are about your product or service that add real value to your customers, the things they are most grateful for and what it has meant to them. And then you want to incorporate this into your sales muscle.

Going back to our landscape business example, the following aspects of their work make them special:

1. We're in your hood, so can optimise transport costs and keep them low.
2. We're trusted family team members and will treat you and your family as we would our own.
3. We have a range of options to suit all needs, tastes and budgets and can maintain your garden after we've worked our magic.
4. We have a range of allied services that offer customers preferential terms.
5. We have products and accessories to save you time and hassle.
6. We have a range of maintenance offerings that will keep your investment in great shape.

7. We'll complete a comprehensive design document and rendered plan, along with a detailed plant list that you will get to keep once the work is done.

It's imperative to take some time and really drill into what makes your business offering special in comparison to your competition. What do you do better? What do you focus on that is often missed? Once you've identified these differentiating factors, you need to spell them out for customers. If you don't, they may not make the leap between what you offer and what that means for them.

Together, your grocery shelf and value proposition are part of your business foundation. Deciding what you sell, what else you could sell to augment your core offerings and how to package all of this into a range or choice of options for your target markets, is all part of building a strong foundation for your business.

P2: Prospects

Like all the other puzzle pieces, prospecting has its place. It's the activity you engage in when you're clear about what you sell. And let's face it, once you are clear about what you have on your grocery shelf and what it means, it's much easier to identify who will be your 'who'.

Time and time again, when I ask business owners who they are targeting or who their product or service is focused on, they will either try to convince me that 'everyone needs it' or they will waffle.

Most of the business owners I deal with have not got this element of their business sorted. Working out who your target market is and compiling a list of names of at least 10 people or businesses – which you replenish as you convert them or they drop off – that fall into your identified target markets are essential for getting sales traction, building your sales expertise and keeping the pipeline healthy.

I worked with a vet, spa and grooming business that had rented space in a shopping centre. The rent was significant, and they were struggling to grow the retail side of the business. The first step was to figure out their target markets. To do this, we revisited the story from another coach who'd worked with a dog food business owner operating in a mall. They had identified two different but essential markets. First, they considered who owned big dogs (because they ate more) and hit on security firms. The dogs are part of their service offering and therefore a business asset and they need to be in the best of health. Security firms would therefore order large quantities of food on a regular basis, but the owners would be unlikely to visit the shopping centre. To attract that market, the owner hired an assistant who had worked in a vet practice and therefore had some affinity with animals. When the security firms ordered their dog food from the store, they were offered a complimentary 10-point health check for each dog because the assistant who made the deliveries could do it. For anyone who has ever tried to check the teeth of an Alsatian or get pills down the throat of a Rottweiler, this is an attractive value-add. The security firm owner scored with having great food delivered monthly and their dogs pre-checked medically, while the dog food business got to secure a loyal clientele who got more bang for their buck than they would have from the competition.

But this target market didn't visit the shopping centre, so both the owner and the coach had to identify a market that did come in and, ideally, off-peak. The answer was old-age pensioners (OAPs). They came in around 10 am when the mall was less crowded and it was easier to find parking, plus they avoided all the kids after school. Makes sense, right?

For the OAPs, their dogs tended to be small and fluffy. They were much loved, but money was tight. At 10 am every morning, the shop owner put out a small desktop sign, with a cute photo of Fluffy, together with a compelling invitation to "Pssssssst, ask about the special refer-a-friend campaign when you get to the till."

If Fluffy's owner referred a friend who also had a small, much-loved dog at home, and if that owner bought their dog food from the store, Fluffy's owner received a giveaway sample pack, every day for a week, that had been gifted free of charge from the manufacturers. The result: a repeatable, affordable

> Who is your who – it's a critical business question that will save you time, money, effort and disappointment.

marketing campaign that was dead easy and almost free to implement and brought in results which far outweighed the costs associated with running it.

I have used a variation on this tactic with many different clients to bring more people into their store and encourage them to buy more. We have given away samples, vouchers, strategic alliance products, small and inexpensive add-ons that are seen as valuable by the customers, and limited-time special offers, all in return for referring customers. In short, we have rewarded the customer behaviour we want to encourage and done so in ways that communicate value to the target market and are infinitely repeatable because the results outweigh the cost.

The lesson in this anecdote is simply that the value proposition for OAP dog owners who came into the store was very different from that of the security firms. The former were interested in freebies that would benefit the love of their life, a great return in exchange for telling a friend, and securing a good deal for themselves. The latter was about quality, well-priced food being delivered on time and within budget every month by a reputable, reliable supplier who offered an additional service that made saying yes to them and not others a shrewd business decision.

If the owner had focused on traditional selling points like quality, excellence, reliability, price and personable service, they would have missed both the security firms and the OAPs.

Target Markets: Who are Your Whos?

Who are your Fluffy owners? Who are your security firms?

Do you have a detailed list of your ideal target markets and how your offer will appeal to each market? Various aspects of your offering are likely to appeal differently to different markets.

We can't market and sell to everyone – and nor should we either need or want to. It just stretches our budget, time and effort too thin, and we end up with diluted impact. Identifying your various target markets in detail is essential so that you can focus your marketing efforts – and not-unlimited resources – on that market, with the right message for them that actively works to improve sales. It doesn't preclude others who aren't in that group from buying from you. In fact, paying attention to the demographic or characteristics of your current customers may help you identify new markets. Each market will prioritise your offering and the various elements of your value proposition differently, and your job is to speak directly to the drivers within each of them in ways that will get you the best results most consistently.

Once you've identified your target markets, it's time to add some detail around their physical, social, psychological and geographical attributes:

1. How old are they?
2. Are they educated? If so, to what level?
3. What do they do for a living?
4. What stage of life are they in?
5. What sort of disposable income do they have?
6. What do they do for enjoyment and to relax?
7. What are their interests?
8. What matters to them?
9. Where do they hang out and what sort of media do they engage with?
10. What do they like to read, watch or listen to?
11. Who do they know?
12. Where do they live, holiday, spend recreation time and commute to?
13. What could they appreciate about your product/service especially?
14. What pain point would what you make or do solve for them?

The outcome of this thinking exercise is that you come up with a working description of your 'ideal customer'. Use your existing raving fans and people who love what you make or do, as the starting point. Engage with them and find the answers to the above questions from them. Don't assume you know the answers. Don't answer on their behalf or guess – have a discussion. Often, we are not our target and while we need to be our first fan, we may not be our ideal customer either. So, it follows that what we think, feel or believe about things may NOT be the same as our prospects and those we are targeting.

Get creative. Think about who you need to speak to and how else you might reach those people.

For example, I met the then editor of *Your Business Magazine* through The Businesswomen's Association of Cape Town (BWA) and was drawn to their excellent work. Their target market was pretty much exactly the same as my target market. Like all magazines, they were always on the lookout for quality content and good stories to share with their readers. So, I arranged to write a series of articles over 18 months that offered value to those business readers, while also keeping my name top-of-mind to that readership. That effort ended up bringing me a consistent flow of the right sort of businesses – my tribe.

The additional credibility that came from being associated with a publication of that calibre, and the ability for readers to get to know, like and trust me through those articles, was gold. I also repurposed the articles, using them as objective testimony that also allowed many of my clients to enjoy similar visibility by showcasing *their* results.

It's been a win/win/win for everyone involved. The magazine got useful content for their readership, I got free advertising, and my clients got some brand awareness and marketing juice. And it's still going. Our current series is titled 'If They Can, You Can'. I have written about who they are; what they do so well; what their challenges were before, through and after Covid; and, most importantly, what I as the business coach and they as the business owner did to ensure that they had some of their best-ever trading years.

> For many entrepreneurs, when we face seismic changes in the market, we find that it underlines and showcases what we know we should have got round to doing but didn't.

Some of those featured businesses have been included in this book to inspire you and give you hope. For each of them, what was truly interesting was that Covid wasn't a death knell; it just exposed and accelerated problems that were already there. Instead of folding under the challenging new conditions, they used the lull and my help to take bold and decisive steps to solve their challenges. This helped them survive and has contributed to making their businesses more resilient over the longer term.

For many entrepreneurs, when we face seismic changes in the market, we find that it underlines and showcases what we know we should have got around to doing, but didn't. And, if we are brutally honest with ourselves, it is this procrastination and inaction – not the actual event itself – that has been the cause of what's gone wrong.

In the abovementioned series of articles, I was able to get this critical point across and talk about best practice to ensure that each of these businesses came through stronger than ever. It has been wonderful publicity. It has also been inspiring and hope-building for a business community that needed to hear good-news business stories of success over adversity.

List of Names

Once you've got clear on who your target markets are and have devised a detailed description of your ideal customer from within these, start compiling a list of names of real people that you know who fall within these parameters that you can contact.

They can fall into one of two lists – either people you know personally or people who are in direct and regular contact with the people you already know. People with whom you have no connection, come off a list you purchased, or were the result of an online search, are harder to access. Think like dating! If sales is new to you, start with the easier lists first. And remember, you can always turn a stranger into a connection by exploring who else you know who knows them.

Who do you know that can go on your list of prospects to call and have coffee with tomorrow? It may be the names of business owners like a hairdresser or a gym, where people in your target market already visit and that you know by name and can pop in to see. It may be the editor of a publication your target market reads, like my business magazine editor friend whom I was able to meet and have coffee with, which ultimately resulted in my being able to provide value to her readership while also generating leads for my own business.

It may be someone with a voice that your target market already listens to, like a radio presenter or an influencer that you know well because of a lucky personal connection. I had a client whose son was best friends with a world-record holder for mountain bike racing. He was the perfect person to open the new BMX track at their game lodge and spa business.

It may be a vocational interest, like the SPCA or Mountain Rescue, that puts you in touch with the right people. It may also be a location, like a specific holiday resort or destination, to which your target market or ideal customer regularly travels in large numbers.

I remember hearing the story of a wealth planner who loved fly fishing. He therefore targeted a couple of resorts in the Scottish Highlands, became well-known at them and ensured that whenever certain types of people checked in, the management notified him and booked him a room for those weekends. Talk about a smart overlapping of one's social and business life!

It may be a specific sport that attracts your target market in numbers, like a dive school or a hiking club. It may simply be the school car park or your church. My minister is a fan of what I can do and for anyone in our congregation who is in need of business help, he has no hesitation in letting them know who I am and how to get hold of me, or even better, letting me know whom I should connect with.

The truly important thing is that you are now armed and able to compile a list of actual people that you can talk to, inform, compel and connect with. People who, if they aren't the right ones, can point you to those who are. And each week, month and quarter, you can add to this list so that it stays plump and current.

Every business needs a list like this. As business owners, we have to be filling up our pipeline all the time and that starts with knowing who the next person is that you are going to ring, meet up and have coffee with.

> Chasing down a sales prospect to a successful close is a dating process – if it wouldn't work with a hot date, then don't try it in selling!

And once you have your list, you need to set up that coffee date. But do some research beforehand. This means checking out the business and/or individual online or on social media. Find out what sort of person they are, their interests, and who else you know knows them. Have a look at their website and, if possible, sample their products or service.

It seems obvious, but it is important to flesh out whether this person should be on your list or not by doing some research. LinkedIn, your network, Facebook, Instagram and the Internet may offer more insights and help you to get to know your prospect and their business. Don't be lazy or half-hearted. Put in the effort.

List Resistance

When I talk to clients about the need for making this list, there is list resistance. The most common objection is that they don't need a list because their word-of-mouth referrals keep them busy. But what happens when it doesn't? Or they tell me they just don't like selling and prefer to rely on their website, google optimisation, enquiries or incoming calls. But what happens when these stop for some reason or numbers fall? I have lost count of the number of business owners who've told me that they don't need to worry about building their sales muscle to a great, robust pipeline.

These lucky business owners have had the privilege of operating in 'economic summer'. Usually as technicians who were good at making or doing something, they had the opportunity to start their own business at a time when there was a surplus of work. As a result, they developed a false sense of security that business would always be that way. But it isn't.

While word-of-mouth and referrals from happy and satisfied customers is wonderful, and incoming enquiries sparked by your online presence are to be encouraged, nurtured and relished, they alone do not futureproof any business from economic downturns and arid pipelines.

There are many good reasons why normally healthy, plump pipelines run dry – apart from things going wrong in the marketplace like new competition, recession, downturn or obsolesence – things like getting into a comfort zone, neglect, incompetence, wrong priorities, distaste, ignorance or being too busy. But it's usually the point at which business owners suddenly realise that they should have developed that sales muscle. They are now able to appreciate that they don't have that key ability to turn on a sale. They haven't tested and measured workable ways to identify, attract and compel their targets to buy ahead of actually needing them to. They haven't learned the language of sales or tested how long it takes to convert leads into paying customers. They haven't invested in customer retention strategies or consistently talked to their customers, ex-customers and prospective customers to gain greater sales insight. And now they have a problem.

No business owner should be in the position where they can't turn on their sales tap when it is needed. And word-of-mouth just won't cut it. It's helps, but you have no control over it; it's inbound. You need to be proficient in prospecting where you and the business go out, find and convert sales. But if you're resting on your laurels because you have a great website and social media following – beware.

A great website and functioning social media presence across multiple platforms gift you with visibility, engagement and community, but won't necessarily result in a productive pipeline. Investing in a great website means that you have an online home that functions like a great shop window to showcase your business, but it's only useful for sales if your target market is also online, knows about your website, and your conversion strategies are in place and working to turn visitors into buyers. My experience is that a great website can't fill up your pipeline on its own.

It's the same with social media. It has been, in my experience and that of most of my clients, almost universally fantastic for informing people and communicating compelling testimony. It is a super tool to help you build community and increase your visibility and customer engagement. It's incredibly helpful if what you make or do requires educating the public, but it's still the poor relative to other more robust strategies when it comes to converting leads. The prevailing percentage of turning online leads into online customers remains stubbornly low.

Clearly, well-designed websites get better returns than those created by novices. And you certainly need to optimise your website and understand online algorithms, keywords, SEO and what your target market is searching for. Some type of social media strategy is better than no social media strategy, but being online is not some magic silver bullet. Most businesses will still need other lead-generating and lead-converting strategies. It's a case of both-and.

P2: Process

Next comes the absolute need to have a comprehensive sales process. Your sales process will always work more efficiently after you've done your pre-sale thinking work (proposition and prospects). That way, you are clear about what you are selling and whom you are targeting.

You may believe that you have the best products and services in the world, but they won't sell themselves. Far too many business owners still hold the delusional beliefs that:

- We just need to be open and stock up and people will come. This is the 'Field of Dreams' fallacy – 'Build it and they will come'. They won't!
- Customers used to come, so if we just keep on doing what we've always done, customers will come again.
- Some outside force (Covid/the recession/political change) is to blame; it has nothing to do with what we are doing or not doing.
- It's just bad luck; if we can just hang on, the tide will turn in our favour again.
- We've never targeted or marketed before, so why do we need it now?
- 'Quality' and 'excellence' will be enough to attract sales.
- We are not salespeople and shouldn't have to sully ourselves with sales. That is someone else's job.

If you are the business owner of a small to medium enterprise, sales are always your job. Too often, business owners see themselves as technicians or experts. Their focus is on making or doing something optimally, but at the expense of prioritising sales. And the more professionally qualified the business owner, the more this anathema seems to occur. Over my last 30 years in business, I've witnessed a proportional relationship between hating sales and the level of professional expertise and seniority of the person being asked to sell. But there is no point beavering away to make a product or service better if no one is buying it. Learning how to sell it and getting good at selling it, are always more important than adding extra bells and whistles to the offering in the hopes that will sell it for you. No one is exempt from selling – not now, not in these tough times.

Bottomline: I know many coaches who are better than me. I know many competent and renowned psychologists and I know more able and experienced business advisors than me. But they can't or won't sell and that creates levels of pressure and stress in their lives that I just don't want in mine. I have watched many peers enjoy dizzying highs and truly alarming lows; the excitement of securing a big, well-known client and the massive financial hole that was left when that relationship came to an end. I decided, early on in my career, that the stress wasn't worth it. Instead, I learned sales and got really good at the 5-Ps, which has meant that my order book has been consistently full for over a decade. That has gifted me the sort of predictable, stable and reliable income that has made others in my field sit up and take notice. Being able to build a business that yields the amount we want and need every single month, year in and year out, despite the economic weather, is the Holy Grail of business.

And if I can learn how to do sales, so can you.

It is best to learn early and to keep on developing those skills. It's also advisable to ensure that everyone in the business is sales-attuned, even if it is not their primary role. However, this will never happen unless you, as the business owner, set the example.

Most entrepreneurs start the prospecting process by printing business cards and stationery but, even if they meet a prospect and exchange business cards, what happens then? More often than not, you run the risk of not hearing from each other again. Or you ring and they 'aren't available' and they ghost you until you go away. Don't waste money, initially, on creating business cards; instead, a much more effective and lucrative approach is to become a business card collector. When someone says, "*Why don't you give me your card?*", it is often just a polite way to bring the conversation to a close. Instead of handing one over, never to hear from them again, say, "*I don't have one with me, but how about I take one of yours and I'll give you a call.*" That way, you have the contact details and retain control of the process, instead of handing control over to the other person. And you save money on printing costs too.

Sales is a process, never a once-off, even for great salespeople. Be ready to follow at least six to seven steps as your investment into getting to a successful close.

The other avoidance tactic that business owners gravitate towards, instead of implementing a prospecting process and sticking with it, is to run a social media campaign or jazz up their website, assuming that this will be sufficient to open the sales flood gates. But these actions are at best brand-building activities and points of contact and enquiry that will assist and add momentum to increased leads and prospective sales.

Most of the businesses I work with are on the small side of SME and therefore don't need to turn over millions a month. If you are one of those businesses, then it's far harder to be noticed online amongst millions of websites than it is to identify a list of names of individuals or businesses in your area that would appreciate what you are selling and call them up. I call this stalking, but it's a legitimate lead-generator for many businesses. And once you have the leads, online generated or not, you have to date them to ensure that at the end of the dating process there's a business marriage.

Don't Think Selling, Think Dating

To date well, you have to follow a process. Think about actual dating in a romantic sense. You would never send out an email blast and hope to secure an awesome date. And you certainly wouldn't expect a marriage proposal from one contact! Instead, getting to know someone is a gradual process and it takes time to build mutual understanding and trust.

Almost every client I've worked with, once they appreciate that sales is the result of a process not a one-off hit, and they actually do the hard yards and build a sales process, confirm that they tune into an unspoken language. It's the sales speak of knowing when to push towards, when to back off, when something feels 'too soon' or 'just not right' in a sales situation and that this does, indeed, feel very similar to their dating experiences.

As with dating, successful selling and prospecting usually involves its own moments of anticipation, awkwardness and, potentially, rejection. And as with dating, it takes time and can't be rushed. In fact, in my experience, easy to close usually means that the customer doesn't stay.

The other critical element in your process is to know what the goal or outcome of each step in it is. Beginners to selling often have unclear or unrealistic hopes off the back of their first phone call, second email or their first meeting. They want to run before they can walk and therefore jump prematurely into providing information and offering quotation content and pricing way too early. It's the dating equivalent of, "Let me tell you about my family and what kind of marriage I want," after the first coffee. Or they are unrealistically ambitious in their hopes that one email will yield a sale and so are devastated and demotivated when it doesn't – the dating equivalent of "I thought we had something" after a one-night stand. Neither works. Setting interim goals for each stage of your process takes the pressure off and allows the joy of little, incremental wins. It also forces you to pace yourself and not run ahead prematurely or engage too infrequently to secure a solid and confident yes.

The Prospect Dating Process

Having used the information and resources you've accumulated from your proposition and prospecting work, it's now time to create your sales process.

1. Ring them up

Take each contact on your list and start by calling them. Don't email as a first point of contact. Often, we want to tread lightly, or we don't want to interrupt the person, or we are unsure what we are going to say, so email is viewed as a 'safer' option. Just call.

Try using first names in a brief, direct and confident way:

"Hi, it's Kathi here for Joe, can you put me through please?"

This has worked for me. Waffling and wordiness communicate inexperience and a lack of confidence. If they do ask what it's in connection with, I follow it up with something truthful and simple like:

"I'm trusting he'll remember" or "I met him last week and promised I'd give him a call."

I'm being deliberately opaque on whether it is personal or not. And obviously this only works if the marketing strategy involves an initial face-to-face exchange or if you have found the right name in your online research.

If you haven't actually met the prospect yet, another successful tactic is to reference a mutual third party. I therefore may say:

"Hi, it's Kathi here for Joe. I promised Yvonne Jennings I'd give him a call – can you put me through please."

Mentioning money has also worked with a good number of clients who've mastered getting past the gatekeeper.

"Hi, it's Kathi here, for Joe. Yvonne Jennings from ABC company thought he would like to hear about the margin wins we've helped her make in their business, so I said I'd give him a call. Can you put me through to him please?"

Big doors swing on little hinges so, as a business strategy, always also get the name of the person who answers the phone and use it in the conversation. If you can meet any of the gatekeepers in person, invest some time in striking up a relationship with them. I always seek to engage in a little bit of social chitchat that I know will endear me to that person and make me more memorable to them.

So, briefly comment on things like:

- their accent
- their name, if it's unusual
- what happened to 'so and so' – only if there's been a staff change
- traffic
- a current affairs topic that everyone is interested in, like a train strike or the cost of fuel
- the weather
- the busyness of their switchboard and how that must feel
- a genuine compliment on their friendliness, warmth, manner, efficiency or help.

There are lots of podcasts out there with ideas on how to make great sales calls. A YouTube search will yield a rich supply of these resources, which are quick and easy go-tos. Find the people who evidence your style (or one that resonates with you), work in your type of industry and have a track record of success. Go for those who SHOW you about sales, with great samples of actual interactions and practical, interpersonal examples.

2. Get permission to send your one-page digital bio

When I get through to my prospect, my goal is not to do anything other than get their permission to send an email with my one-page digital bio (see Chapter 8 for a refresher). If I were to send an introductory email, as so many of us do, without their permission, I'd just be hijacking their inbox and vulnerable to them deleting or sidelining the message.

Think on this for a moment: when we get an uninvited email, our natural reaction is, "*I didn't ask for this and I'm too busy, so I'm just going to File 13 it.*"

Getting permission is polite and shows respect, but it's also compelling. It also massively increases the probability of the prospect opening and reading the email.

For this reason, I usually say something along the lines of, *"Hi Joe, I'm the business coach Yvonne spoke to you about who's helped her make the margin improvements she's so pleased with. She thought there may be some synergies between what we do, so I thought I'd call you to find out a bit more about what the business does and get your permission to email you my one-page digital bio – is now a good time to chat?"*

Resist the temptation of getting into pricing, details of a current order they may be interested in, or being put off at this stage with "We're not buying now" signals. Be clear with them that it's about establishing contact and confirming potential synergies now or later … or not.

3. Email the one-pager, with an engaging subject line and a sign-off that keeps you in control!

Email your one-page digital bio so that your prospect receives a compelling, well-crafted, persuasive and professional electronic document that they can read to learn more about you *and* forward to other people in their sphere of influence. This can also be forwarded to other decision-makers, perhaps in the management team or on the Board. It means that instead of my prospect selling me, I get to sell myself directly. And this resource remains a click away for my prospect to send to others they know or may meet in the future.

To help ensure that the email is opened, make the Subject obvious and compelling.

To help ensure that the email is opened, make the Subject obvious and compelling. For example, I usually add, *"As discussed, here's my one-page digital bio for your reading pleasure!"* In the body of the email, I also state that I'll call back within the next 24 hours to make sure that the email arrived. And then I do.

4. Follow-up phone call

If you say you will call back within 24 hours, then make sure that you do. It's a small but tangible way to communicate that you have integrity and will do what you say you'll do.

This time, when you ring back, you will know the gatekeeper's name and they will probably also remember you. You might therefore say:

"Hi Kerry, it's Kathi for Joe. I promised I'd give him a quick call today to follow up on an email he had me send him yesterday. Is now a good time to speak to him?"

When you get through, restrict yourself to confirming that they got your email and finding out their thoughts on your one-pager with something like, *"What did you think of it?"* This usually prompts some discussion and a conversation. If it does, try to secure a catch-up over coffee or a virtual coffee to discuss further. For example, I say:

"It looks as if Yvonne was right and there do seem to be some possible synergies. How about we push the boat out and connect over a coffee or virtual coffee to discuss this further?"

5. Coffee meetup

This can be in person or virtually and should take no more than 20 minutes. This is the 'date' component of prospecting and involves you getting to know each other a little better.

Coffee always starts with chitchat and how they got into the business and ends with a next step. If you are naturally sociable, like people and are curious about their story, this can make life easier. But anyone can learn to be more sociable, especially when armed with the right questions. Ask about their dissatisfactions in the business and what they'd like to fix. This is especially useful if your product or service can help solve those problems. Just let the other person talk and air their frustrations. Pay attention and ask questions that open up the conversation even more. As part of this coffee discussion, look for ways to paint a vision for the prospect of how they would feel if those problems were solved and recount client stories that illustrate what could happen if they were. Alternating between the two is a powerful persuader.

Seek to then segue naturally into a next, clear action step:

- *"Well, it seems that you may benefit from ..."*
- *"Well, it sounds like it may be a good idea to ..."*
- *"How about if ..."*

Offer up your potential solution – which could be a written quotation, a proposal, a meeting with decision-makers or an on-site walk around. Ask if it's OK for you to put together a proposal and send it to them or, better yet, offer to hand it in to them. There are varying percentages on this, but usually around 70% of conversational cues and building rapport are non-verbal. Meeting in person is key to closing well. There has to be some point in the process where you and they come face-to-face.

6. Send the proposal or quotation

Keep your proposal compelling and focused on the prospect, not you. Make sure it's informative and answers the most commonly asked questions, the problems they may be experiencing, their spoken wishes from your coffee time and what would need to happen next and by when.

At this juncture, you may wish to include testimony from similar clients who have already bought from you, as well as the contact details of one or two clients whom they could ring. Testimony is social proof that what you are claiming about your products and services is actually true.

Think about calling it an Investment Plan or Proposal and be sure to itemise the returns on saying yes, as well as the cost of saying no or delaying a response.

Alternatively, you could consider using a digital proposal platform like Pandadoc, which has a proven impact on conversions and the speed with which prospects get to a yes signature over traditional proposals. Sites like these also allow you to embed media and track your prospective clients' progress through the proposal via useful analytics.

7. Confirm receipt of a proposal or quotation or hand-deliver it and handle the objections then and there.

Although this follow-up call is positioned as a call to confirm receipt, it's really an opportunity to answer more questions and handle objections.

However, use it if hand delivery is, quite simply, not possible. Certainly, in the early stages of perfecting your sales ability, face-to-face quotation delivery rules, because you get practice in responding to hesitations and queries. I've had clients prioritise flying up-country to deliver a quotation. It's expensive but, for a large quotation and the impact it can have on their sales close rate, it's invaluable.

As an aside, if you position well upfront in the coffee meetup or in the proposal stage that you deliver quotations to ensure that any concerns or queries are ironed out early on and ask when it would be a convenient time to connect, this makes it easier to get in or see the prospect online with your offer when the time comes.

Remember, too, objections are always better than a flat out "no". They are a sign of interest, despite how they may feel. When people offer up objections they are, in fact, asking for more information or permission. The secret is in being prepared for them and well-versed in how you will respond to them (we covered this in Chapter 8). It is such a good opportunity for you to be confident, clear and articulate about how your product or service can help the prospect achieve their goals. Confidence sells, and competently giving the prospect permission to move forward to a yes is a good example of this in action. Don't fluff it having got this far!

In addition, people are exceptionally uncreative in how they object, so if you script your response to all the major objections, you will soon feel comfortable handling anything that's thrown at you.

8. Close the sale

Once you have handled all the objections and answered any further requests for information, you need to ask for the sale. Actually ask, with a smile:

"So, assuming you have no further concerns, are we going to be doing business together?" or *"So, shall we get started then?"*

As you finesse your process and test it out on real prospects, you'll find yourself fine-tuning some of the steps or deciding to add additional steps. For example, several steps before the close I invite people to attend a free Business Building Workshop so they can see me in action. I always send an email three days before the event to clarify the venue and start time.

I also send a quick WhatsApp message the day before to remind them that we've booked them a seat, put on the kettle and turned away others to accommodate them, so we look forward to hosting them – come rain or shine. Holding a free workshop is a great way for people to experience what you have to offer as a service-based business, and to demonstrate the delivery of value, before they commit to working with you. What 'freebie' trial offering could you consider?

Test your process and measure the results, fine-tune it as you go and make sure it's written down and communicated through the business so that everyone is following the same prospecting process. Make sure your sales process is filed under 'S' in the Standard Operating Procedures Manual or cloud-based folder.

Share results and invite input and suggestions for improvement from your team. Share the wins and the learnings. Never delegate sales until you have demonstrated to yourself and your team that you are proficient in sales too. It helps both your credibility as a business owner and your credibility as a general manager if you've walked your sales talk with a reliable sales process. Plus, professional salespeople tend to be gifted communicators and therefore can be really good at bullsh*t. To prevent them taking you for a ride or running rings around you, it helps to know first-hand what's possible in a normal sales day, how the market tends to respond and how long a sale typically takes to make or close. That way, you can question any invalid excuses and show, by example, how to resolve problems that have stumped them. Use the learning to onboard others quickly in the sales process and always look for ways to refine and improve upon it. And remember to make sure that all your prospect interactions are updated on the CRM. Use it to capture each step of your sales process and record progress made. Your CRM can then produce a list of steps and actions that need to be completed each day and ensure that you don't forget anything or anyone. A CRM often feels like an extra pair of hands!

> Never delegate sales until you have demonstrated to yourself and your team that you are proficient in sales too. It helps both your credibility as a business owner and your credibility as a general manager if you've walked your sales talk with a reliable sales process.

P4: Preparation

Successful business owners and people who can sell well, often make it look effortless. And although it looks effortless now, that ease is actually built on thorough preparation.

So, when great salespeople are making it look like they are winging it and it comes naturally, it doesn't, and they aren't. It's a little like a great actor – their performance can look magical and completely 'in the moment', but a look at their preparation over the months prior to being on set would tell a very different story. They have prepared so much that their performance has moved from clumsy, conscious incompetence to professional unconscious competence.

Be prepared – it's not only a Scouts thing … it's essential in good sales.

The same is true of brilliant salespeople. Preparation and practise are the keys to great sales skills.

Be prepared – like a good boy scout. Record the best person doing their thing and let everyone use this as a learning tool and a plumb line. The hallmark of great selling is great scripts and brilliant, work-every-time emotional questions. (Recap on these in Chapter 8.)

18 Preparation Tips – What to Formulate, Document, Role Play and then Fine-Tune

1. Your elevator pitch: Work out the best possible answer to the question, "So, what do you do?" Make sure everyone in the business knows that elevator pitch and that it's word-perfect when delivered.

2. All known ways to get past gatekeepers, so everyone has a range of options to try that have worked in the past. These people are blocking your access to your ideal customer, so learning how to get past them is important.

3. All the objections that you and your salespeople have ever heard when selling your offerings, as well as the most effective responses to counter those objections. Keep adding to and updating this document.

4. The best ways to reactivate clients who used to do business with you but don't any more or haven't bought for a while. What is the reactivation process? Again, fine-tune and improve on this all the time.

5. How best to ask a raving client for a referral – everything that has ever worked.

6. The solutions that your product or service delivers, so that everyone is able to counter client problems and frustrations with specific offerings and demonstrate the connection.

7. All the ways your salespeople have asked successfully for a sale.

8. Why you price your goods and services the way you do, so that everyone can explain this clearly if asked.

9. In a folder, ideally online so that other team members can access it, testimonials so that you can match one from a happy, existing customer/client with your current prospect. When a business like their business has got results, this is even more persuasive than a business from a different industry.

10. How to handle a direct and definite "no thank you" with grace and without sounding desperate or 'snippy'.

11. All the FAQs that your customers have ever asked. Keep adding to the list and fine-tune and update the answers.

12. How to brief and onboard a successful, working, strategic-alliance partner.

13. Why you have the terms and conditions you do and what's in it for your customers to stick to them.

14. The rules of successful engagement, so that your customers know how to get the most out of your product or service. Make sure they know these.

15. Your customer onboarding process, so that they can get the most from your product or service as fast as possible and feel like they belong.

16. Your vision, mission and values – VMAV – so that it can be emailed to customers without hesitation. Make sure that everyone in your business, and the prospects you speak to, know your VMAV.

17. Your ideal customer and what target markets they belong to.

18. Your one-page digital bio in the cloud, so that anyone in the business can access and send it when needed. Review it at least once a year to update or amend it.

Prospects are People

It is easy to forget, in the stress and pressure of sales, especially in the learning phase, that prospects are people. People we have met, established some links with and people we are getting to know. People with whom we build relationships and who, over time, buy from us because they know, like and trust us and what we make or do.

The nirvana of any business is repeat customers – those who buy regularly. But customers who feel hassled, manipulated, neglected, tolerated or pressured are unlikely to turn into repeat buyers. Even if they love your product or service, if they don't also feel comfortable buying from you then they won't come back. Never lose sight of what you are doing; as Dan Pinker[41] puts it, you are "professionally helping people to buy."

People have choices and it is your job to ensure that, if they are to be included as part of your tribe, they get to hear about your business, your solutions, and how these can help make their lives easier, better or solve a problem that they have. If you are proud of what you create or deliver, you owe it to those who could benefit from your offering to tell them about it and make it easy for them to enjoy the benefits.

And people don't have to be threatening. Get used to delivering your elevator pitch in the car park, in the bank queue or while waiting for the library to open. Start by remarking to the person next to you, "*Well, it seems that we're stuck here for a bit. I'm Kathi … and you are?*" Then ask them what they do and, if they don't ask you back, smile and ask, "*Would you like to hear what I do?*" I've never had a "no".

The very best time to start prospecting is when you don't need to. Diarise a few coffees. Start with one a week and simply ask prospects in your target market, "*How's business going?*" Brian Grazer, the Hollywood producer, does something similar, although he calls them 'curiosity conversations'.[42] Instead of selling, he just makes dates with people who know things about topics he's interested in but doesn't know much about. Think of your coffee dates like that   your way of acquiring information and getting to know something that you don't already know about your prospect and their business.

Just about every client I've convinced to try this has found it odd and uncomfortable at first but, after a couple of months, what felt so hard at the beginning, is less hard and the buzz they get from actually interacting positively and successfully with prospects, encourages them to go out again. Even the anti-sales business owners discover that the 5-Ps work and they close sales.

I was reminded of these 5-Ps when I was watching Wim Hof, the father of cold-water swimming and the power of breath, talking to various celebrities in his TV show. He laughed out loud when Gaby Logan and Tamsin Outhwaite exclaimed, "It's freezing!" as they jumped into a cold shower. "Of course it is," said Wim, "what did you expect? It's the Italian Alps, the rivers are frozen and there's snow everywhere. It doesn't get less cold and it won't get less cold. You just get better at it. It's all in the mind; you decide!"[43]

The same is true of sales. It doesn't get less challenging, it's just that we become better at it. Get armed, get prepared, have your tools, do your homework, write your scripts, role play, make your calls, follow your process and keep at it. What's the worst that can happen? Someone can say no? Big deal!

Sales is about building relationships. Gone are the days when we could just inform our intended audience what our opening hours were and what we sold, and they arrived at the door (Figure 10.1)

Figure 10.1 *Relationship-building Over Selling*

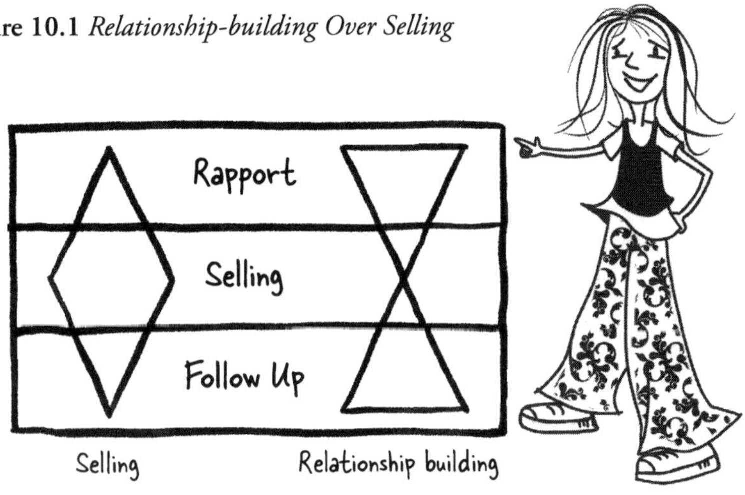

Rapport

Selling

Follow Up

Selling   Relationship building

With the choices customers have, we have to move away from flogging a product or service toward buildings relationships with our customers who will then, in turn, buy our product or service. At any time that the economy is shrinking or under pressure – when 'economic winter' sets in – knowing how to prospect or sell well is what will keep the roof over our head and the wolf from our door.

If we run out of people to buy our awesome products or services, everything else becomes academic. We have to learn and get good at sales. It's that simple.

P5: Practice

I've said it a few times already, but business – and especially sales – really is a full-contact sport. It involves the andragogic reality of learning by doing. Andragogy is the science of how adults learn and it's best done by doing or by experience. The old-fashioned apprenticeship where one learned at the knee of a master, was good stuff. Alas, it is in short supply these days, although mentoring forms similar rhythms. We cannot teach sales as well as we can show or demonstrate sales.

Remember, as a business owner, you must lead from the front when it comes to sales – at least initially. Role plays, recording calls, setting goals you can control and listening to sales mastery podcasts are great ways to help take your practising to a new level so that you can demonstrate sales mastery to your people and encourage the same behaviour in them.

Role Play

Various role-play selling scenarios can be found online on YouTube or in selling podcasts. These are learning dynamite. Watch as many of them as you can and find your heroes who look and sound the way you want to. I'm a huge fan of Dan Lok[44] because of his settled sense of mastery in the sale and his laconic, laid-back style. In training yourself and team members, the role play separates the masters from the rest and what better place to start than by copying those who can demonstrate that mastery?

Learning a successful sales process is a lot like learning a new language – we become fluent by using it. Putting ourselves into different selling scenarios and practising how best to react, allows us to develop new neural pathways that make the selling process easier over time. When we encounter that scenario in 'real life', we know what to do because we have practised and rehearsed it. And just like rock climbing or playing bridge or icing a cake – we don't get good by reading about it; we get good by doing it, paying attention to what happens and fine-tuning our approach, so the doing gets better. We master the art of selling by selling.

Role Plays to Practise

- Different ways to get past a gatekeeper.
- Handling objections.
- Different ways to close the sale.
- Dealing with particularly difficult customers.
- Building interpersonal rapport.

It's also worth checking out your competition. How are they making a sale? How are they closing the sale or handling objections? Try buying from your competition and see what they do very well and what they do badly that you can improve on. And pay attention to all the sales calls that you ever receive from now on. Pay attention to what they do well – could you incorporate that into your own sales process?

Record Your Sales Meetings and Calls

While it may make you cringe, the best way to learn is via feedback on how you sound. Push record on your phone at a sales meeting and listen to it when you get back to the office. You'll very quickly hear whether you:

- Established rapport or jumped into business mode too quickly.
- Asked enough questions or did all the talking.
- Listened to what others were actually asking and answered their questions or just pressed on with your 'pitch'.
- Timed your offer or asked for the sale well or not.

- Covered dissatisfaction and vision and got to the next step clearly and eloquently so that, even if you didn't close the sale, you knew what had to happen next.
- Missed the gap.
- Made a friend but not a sale.

What about your call to get past the gatekeeper? Record that too and listen to it once the call is finished to see how you can improve next time you want to persuade a prospect or onboard a strategic alliance.

These feedback loops are essential if you are to get better at sales. Without them we can delude ourselves that it's going well, but unless the numbers are improving, it may not be going as well as you think. And to work smarter, you first have to know where the problems lie. Assuming that your product and service are top-notch, then it's going to come down to whether you've found and are engaging with your target market in the right way or not.

It really is that simple. Not easy, but simple.

Set Goals You Can Control

Too often, when it comes to sales, business owners set sales targets – how many of what needs to be sold. And while this is important, it's not the most important thing.

Every business needs to know how much they sell each month. Restaurants need daily revenue targets and manufacturing needs daily outputs to meet sales. If you sell in different regions, or you sell a range of products and services, each needs its monthly, weekly, or daily target so that progress can be matched against them.

But the final result of any sale is also related to the person on the other end of the interaction, and no one can control that part of the equation. What's therefore more useful for you and your business is to also have goals around what you can control that, when done, will increase success. These are called behavioural drivers – the actions that will increase the probability of sales results.

For example, how many gatekeepers do you need to get past each week? How many coffee dates do you need to schedule in a week? How many follow-up phone calls do you have to make every day? These are targets you have control over and, if they are consistently met, that activity will turn into the sales you are after. You can't always control whether someone will buy, but you can always control your activity that will make those sales more likely.

Learn Through Sales Podcasts, Presentations and Books

So much of my thinking and relearning has been shaped by great books I've read, podcasts I've listened to and conference presenters doing their stuff. This stream of input has been, by far, the easiest and cheapest way to educate myself, change my mind about things, help me unlearn what is no longer helpful and master what is. I hope this book can help you unlearn and master a few things too. But there are also some really great audio resources – and yes, this book is available in audio format too! – and speaker opportunities that can be easier to fit into a busy life than reading a book. You may like to try audiobooks or the vast array of sales and business podcasts, in addition to falling in love with building your go-to library of useful reads.

> If you'll learn by doing and reading before you do, you'll find that practise really does make perfect with regard to sales… and, once practised, you'll be better at it and then it really IS less hard.

As our business goes through growth and new stages, defeats and setbacks, we will have to master new stuff. We will have to read up on various topics we may know nothing about, such as search engine optimisation and how social media works. We'll need to learn how to draft a good flyer until we can afford to hire someone to do it for us. And, even then, we will need to be able to critically assess what's being done against current best practice.

Practise helps, but we need to be practising the right things and that means constantly learning and maintaining an open mind to change and adaptation. Remember what Einstein said: "The definition of insanity is doing the same thing over and over again and expecting a different result."

Be brave and confront what you don't know, so that you can learn and improve. Build what works into your processes and make sure everyone in the business knows what you've learned. Encourage everyone to adopt a learning mindset and build a learning culture, with a good go-to library of resources, in the business.

Executing the 5-Ps Successfully: Their Story

At age 28, Godfrey qualified as a Master Mariner, capable of taking command of any ocean-going vessel, and elected to take up a career in the Port Services in Cape Town. Cumbersome bureaucracy quickly took the shine off that career option, and he decided to opt for the exciting prospect of creating his own business instead.

In April 1998, Godfrey launched his marine services company that offered a wide range of services, all related to towing and salvage, purchase and sale of ships, and marine surveying and brokerage, and specialising in transporting provisions, spare parts and ships' crews to ships that pass Cape Town on their trading voyages around the world.

By 2013, Offshore Maritime Services owned a work barge and five large utility service vessels, some of which were employed in specific contract work far from Cape Town, including dive support for a coastal operation between northern Angola and Congo and a year-long contract in Beira, Mozambique, supporting tanker operations off that coast.

Leading up to Covid, business was already starting to show cracks. Godfrey was convinced that growth was not possible but realised, after bumping into one of my presentations on building a resilient and profitable business, that for all his experience he was wrong. There was a lot that could be done – but not without help. Signing up with me, as his coach, was a deliberate choice he made to re-plot the course to his success. When I asked him what he wanted to achieve, he replied, "Double my turnover in a year." What came shortly after that was, however, "But we can't really market like most businesses." I raised my eyebrows to gently let him know that I didn't agree and informed him that ALL businesses can and must engage in marketing. Building visibility, relationships, and an ability to compellingly and consistently tell others what you do is critical for success in all businesses. Over time, I convinced Godfrey that marketing is what keeps sales going, money flowing and funds a robust capacity to deliver. All of these are underpinned by consistent messaging, done well, to all stakeholders – especially in hard times. We call it prospecting.

And so Godfrey, by now a seasoned business owner, had to go back to the drawing board and learn new competencies and new ways of doing what he had always done to not only 'future-proof' his business, but to ready the business for the inevitable 'perfect storms' and achieve his stated goal of doubling his turnover.

First up, he and I tackled formalising business systems and processes; crafting succinct job descriptions to replace impossible function lists; capturing performed and useable standard operating procedures (SOPs); and making vital changes and additions to staff and their functions to achieve and support operational goals. I challenged Godfrey to think differently, try new concepts, test proposals against critical review, find ways to successfully introduce highly valuable leads and contacts into his prospecting mix and fall in love with reading, which helped him grow a stronger will to succeed – which he will tell you has been key to him implementing the 5-Ps well.

When the perfect storm of Covid lockdown hit, some of the planning and readying the business to do more sales had been done. OMS was designated as an essential service provider and so was still permitted to proceed out to sea and supply passing shipping with provisions and spare parts, but no staff on foreign ships were allowed to leave their ship, and no fresh crews could join anywhere in the world. Business instantly dropped away by half, with no reduction in overheads possible. Imagine the shock!

But OMS and Godfrey had done the hard yards and were ready and able to pivot, something that became a blessing for him, his family, the sixty-five people OMS employed, their families, their clients, agents, supply chain and service providers. It meant that he and OMS were not only able to pull through, but to do so profitably.

They had the systems that meant they could manage, despite lockdown restrictions. They had a meetings rhythm going and clear lines of responsibility. More importantly, they had also prioritised prospecting, and dating not only prospects but also alliances and talent.

Godfrey held on to the truth that identifying, attracting and securing talent is fundamentally a marketing game. A-players want to work for the sort of business leader who is clear, committed, positive, passionate, resourced, communicative and organised. Remember the Andy Stanley quote: "You have to be the kind of person that the kind of people you are looking for, are looking for" and in this Godfrey excelled.

The other half of business success in hard times is having the cash to pay for it. This entails practised and competent planning, preparation and having a compelling proposition so that you can prospect successfully and close the sale, as outlined in the 5-Ps!

Strategic alliances, other players in the sector, current customers and clients, agents who operate in the field, talent, allied government departments, prospects and, of course, the broader world of shipping, which was caught up in the global chaos, were just some of the players that Godfrey and his team dated well.

Accepting that marketing will always be a long game of relationship-building, Godfrey and the team, with help, created routines of connecting with prospects, remaining visible, calling on, communicating with and providing enjoyable and well-implemented social opportunities to everyone in their spheres of influence.

And it worked.

Their first post-Covid win was for the imprisoned international crews. Godfrey, an experienced mariner, having completed voyages around the world, understood the hardships they faced whilst stuck on board – some of them for the entire two-year period. After lobbying all national government departments and engaging widespread radio support, on October 2020, the Department of Transport issued their statement that international seafarers could join or leave their ships at both Cape Town and Durban ports … and OMS was ready for it! At that point, they effectively tripled their monthly turnover!

The next win was fast-tracking the identification and onboarding of new employees to cope with the round-the-clock workload – both an art and a science to get this right at speed. That this also positively impacted the impoverished areas in South Africa was a double whammy.

Creating career path opportunities for stand-out performers who wouldn't have otherwise had a chance, was real. A young school-leaver, first employed as a support staff trainee, moved to the newly created role of Marketing Officer and, over time, into the role of Commercial Manager. A young shepherd from a rural area achieved a Master Coastal Certificate of Competence in just two years and today is responsible for training OMS's new candidate skippers. A couple of young women, who entered the business as Trainee Seafarers, rose to the level of Senior Operational Managers.

A third win was that they had the cash reserves to enable them to recapitalise and extend their fleet to take advantage of the market opportunities as they emerged. In preparation for even further growth, OMS invested in and currently owns six custom-built, standard-setting, service craft, a fleet of crew buses, the ability to offer helicopter connections, and a couple of dominant branches in South Africa. This has propelled them to a position of market leader in this service sector.

Prospecting, as a priority, also helped in the overdue and welcome formation of an association of players in the industry to ensure industry standards of safety and best practice, create a united front to attract international patronage once again, and re-position South Africa on the international map. OMS was able to play a pivotal role in getting this initiative off the ground and stands to benefit as South Africa finds its worthy place in the international world of maritime services once more.

And finally, their attention to the 5-Ps enabled them to secure the sort of unrivalled customer loyalty that comes with having the resources and relationships to keep on communicating and marketing through tough times, even when it seems no one is listening. The simple efforts and discipline of staying in touch that anyone can learn and implement paid off through the pandemic and, to this day, they are still reaping rewards.

Conclusion

What gets the business flywheel turning in any business, from building momentum to visible consistent results, is when owners are able to keep two plates spinning. The first plate is promoting to sell. Not just promoting... but promoting to *sell*. Start here and you create a market demand for what you make or do that propels action and urgency throughout the business. Base it on a purpose-driven foundation that we outlined in Part One and Part Two's puzzle pieces of 1-ME, 2-BEs, 3-Ts, as well as the 5-Ps, and you get incoming fuel that keeps the business vehicle on the road.

Once this momentum has been established, you can focus on the other plate to spin – your capacity to deliver. You'll have to invest some of the money you've made back into the processes, systems and resources that help you buy back your time. And finally, your people are critical to this plate. The 4-Cs puzzle pieces enable you to deliver on those sales, but they come with a price tag. You'll need money to pay for these growth expenses.

This, in turn, will drive you back to the first plate – promoting to sell. And you'll have to revisit your growth and your gains to make sure you can deliver on this expanded capacity. This, in turn, will mean more sales, which will soon bring you back to needing a scaled-up capacity to deliver which, again, will cost you.

And so "the flywheel" as Jim Collins from *Good to Great*[45] called it, turns. Hesitate, procrastinate or get stuck spinning just one of these plates and the business will fall over. And while this isn't necessarily deadly, it's hard or, at the very least, much harder work to recover each plate once it's down. Ignore the rules of best practice and fail to implement much of what we've covered here, and you'll definitely end up going the long way around, which always creates extra cost, greater vulnerability, and unnecessary delays.

Get it right and the movement between plates is efficient, economical and covers the shortest distance between the two, which conserves energy, effort and resources. What's not to love about that?

And once your flywheel is going, momentum kicks in and the easier lifestyle you went into business to obtain in the first place, becomes possible. Keep this flywheel going and consistent, and profitable success will be yours to enjoy.

You will have built an asset, and a team that gifts you wings and funds the life you want.

Congratulations!

A Final PS Note

Life is an adventure. Even the most fortunate people are confronted with hardship from time to time. It is part of the human experience. And often, that misfortune or struggle can lead us on to bigger and better things. It may need hindsight to come into view, or time for this to be noticed and appreciated, but the silver linings are always there if we choose to look for them.

I have always believed that business and competent entrepreneurial activity are key to some of the world's most pressing problems – how we, as humans, can productively and properly fund our lives well, dignify others with work and generate money to fund overdue societal fixes. SME business can solve things that governments never will. But only if we get better at business.

My greatest joys in life have been in the roles I've played as mum to my daughter and daughter to my mum. A close second is my business and the sort of personal work I've been privileged to do to help so many learn and live what I've enjoyed. It hasn't always been easy. In truth, it's hardly ever been easy, but it has been joyful and given me the life I wanted – on my terms. It's allowed me to travel and teach and help thousands of business owners to realise the potency of business for themselves and take back control over their day-to-day lives and their futures.

What I have found, time and time again, is that there is no cookie-cutter template for business that works all the time for every business, but there are puzzle pieces that absolutely must be in place for success to happen. It's very hard, if not impossible, to have a thriving business without having put these 15 puzzle pieces in place. And it's almost impossible to sustain any sort of resilient life or business success if the PEACE work hasn't been done well and completely.

Whatever life you have and whatever life you want, setting up and building a business can be an amazing way to pay for it and enable you to achieve your goals, while also letting you purposefully deliver value, be of service and help solve problems.

Now, isn't that the very definition of success?

Good luck!

My Top 50
Recommended Reads

Foundational Reads

Start with Why – Simon Sinek
Integrity – Henry Cloud
The Purpose-driven Life – Rick Warren
The E-Myth™ – Michael Gerber
Thinking, Fast and Slow – Daniel Kahneman
The Compound Effect – Darren Hardy
Blink – Malcolm Gladwell
The Hard Thing About Hard Things – Ben Horowitz
The Road Less Stupid – Keith J. Cunningham

Prospecting Reads

Blue Ocean Strategy – W. Chan Kim and Renée Mauborgne
How to Win Friends and Influence People – Dale Carnegie
Instant Advertising – Brad Sugars
Influence: The Psychology of Persuasion – Robert Cialdini
Getting Everything You Can Out of What You've Got – Jay Abrahams
Building a Story Brand – Donald Miller
They Ask You Answer – Marcus Sheridan
Built to Sell – John Warrillow
Pitch Anything – Oren Klaff
Secrets of Closing the Sale – Zig Ziglar
Little Voice Mastery – Blair Singer
To Sell is Human – Daniel Pink

The Little Red Book of Sales – Jeffrey Gitomer
The Greatest Salesman in the World – Og Mandino
The Ultimate Sales Machine – Chet Holmes
Book Yourself Solid – Michael Port
Spin Selling – Neil Rackham
Traffic Secrets – Russell Brunson
Digital Branding – Daniel Rowles
Jab, Jab, Jab, Right Hook – Gary Vuynerchuk

Process & Systems Reads

Found Money – Steve Wilkinghoff
Eat that Frog – Brian Tracey
Clockwork: Design Your Business to Run Itself – Mike Mikhailovich
Getting Things Done – Dave Allen
Mastering the Rockerfeller Habits – Verne Harnish
Great by Choice – Jim Collins
The 7 Habits of Highly Effective People – Stephen Covey
The One Minute Manager – Keith Blanchard

People Reads

Bounce – the Myth of Talent and the Power of Practice – Matthew Syed
5 Dysfunctions of a Team – Patrick Lencioni
Tribes – Seth Godin
Triggers – Creating Behaviours that Last – Mark Reiter and Marshall Goldsmith
Crucial Conversations – Tools for Talking when Stakes are High – Kerry
    Patterson, Joseph Grenny, Al Switzler and Ron McMillan
Tough Choices – Carly Fiorini
Radical Candor – Kim Scott
The Happiness Advantage – Shawn Achor
The Flip Side – Flip Flippen

Promotion Reads

The 4 Hour Work Week – Tim Ferriss
Finish Big – Bo Burlingham
Early Exits – Basil Peters
Property Magic – Simon Zutshi

References

1   Kübler-Ross, E. 1969. *On Death and Dying*. Simon & Schuster/Touchstone).
2   Frankl, V. 2006. *Man's Search for Meaning*. Beacon Press, Boston. (Originally published in 1946 as *Ein Psychologe erlebt das Konzentrationslager*, "A Psychologist Experiences the Concentration Camp".)
3   Csikszentmihalyi, M. 2008. *Flow: The Psychology of Optimal Experience*. HarperCollins.
4   Chabris, C. and Simons, D. 2010. *The Invisible Gorilla: How Our Intuitions Deceive Us*. Harmony Books, New York.
5   Maslow, A. 1943. 'A Theory of Human Motivation.' *Psychological Review*.
6   Cuddy, A. 2012. 'Your body language may shape who you are.' TED Talk.
7   Lyubomirsky, S. 2007. *The How of Happiness*. Penguin, New York.
8   Wallis, C. 2004. 'The New Science of Happiness.' *Time* magazine.
9   Kahneman, D. and Tversky, A. [Study details]
10   Covey, S.R. 1989. *The 7 Habits of Highly Effective People*. Free Press.
11   Garfield, C. 1985. *Peak Performance: Mental Training Techniques of the World's Greatest Athletes*. Grand Central Publishing.
12   Csikszentmihalyi, M. 1992. *Flow: The Psychology of Happiness: The Classic Work on How to Achieve Happiness*. Rider.
13   Kahneman, D. 2011. *Thinking, Fast and Slow*. Penguin, New York.
14   Dunn EW, Norton, M. 2012. 'Don't Indulge. Be Happy.' *New York Times*.
15   Dickens, C. 2007. *The Magic Fishbone: A Holiday Romance From the Pen of Miss Alice Rainbird Aged 7*. Project Gutenberg. First published in 1861 by Dramatic Publishing.
16   Seligman, M. 2002. *Authentic Happiness: Using the New Positive Psychology to Realize Your Potential for Lasting Fulfilment*. Free Press, New York.
17   Mineo, L. 2017. 'Good genes are nice, but joy is better.' *The Harvard Gazette*.
18   Waldinger, R. 2015.'What makes a good life? Life lessons from the longest study on happiness.' TED Talk.
19   Walton, A.G. 2018. 'New Studies Show Just How Bad Social Media Is For Mental Health.' *Forbes*.
20   Colvin, G. 2010. *Talent is Overrated: What Really Separates World-Class Performers from Everybody Else*. Portfolio.
21   Gladwell, M. 2011. *Outliers: The Story of Success*. Back Bay Books (Hachette Book Group).

22 Ericsson, K.A. [Details of study, Academy of Music, Berlin]

23 Levitin, D. [Year]. [Details of study]

24 Losier, M. 2003. *Law of Attraction*. Self-published. Canada.

25 Murry, W.H. 1951. *The Scottish Himalayan Expedition*. J.M. Dent.

26 Gerber, M. 1988. *The E-Myth: Why Most Businesses Don't Work and What to Do About It*. Ballinger Publishing.

27 Harnish, V. 2002. *Mastering the Rockeffeller Habits: What You Must Do to Increase the Value of Your Growing Firm*. Gazelles, Inc.

28 Harnish, V. 2002. *Mastering the Rockeffeller Habits: What You Must Do to Increase the Value of Your Growing Firm*. Gazelles, Inc.

29 Wilkinghoff, S. 2009. *Found Money: Simple Strategies for Uncovering the Hidden Profit and Cash Flow in Your Business*. Wiley.

30 Cialdini, R. [Year]. *Book/Study*. [Publisher/Publication, Place]

31 Sheridan, M. 2017. *They Ask You Answer: A Revolutionary Approach to Inbound Sales, Content Marketing, and Today's Digital Consumer*. Wiley.

32 Cialdini, R., Goldstein, N. and Martin, S. 2007. *Yes! Fifty Secrets from the Science of Persuasion*. Profile Books.

33 Tofler, A. 1984. *Future Shock*. Bantam.

34 Kolmar, C. 2022. 'The Cost of a Bad Hire: How Bad Hires Impact Business.' Zappia. https://www.zippia.com/advice/average-cost-of-a-bad-hire/

35 Harnish, V. 2002. *Mastering the Rockeffeller Habits: What You Must Do to Increase the Value of Your Growing Firm*. Gazelles, Inc.

36 Godin, S. 2008. *Tribes*. Piatkus Books (Hachette Book Group).

37 Kahneman, X. and Tversky, X. 1992. [Book/Study title]. [Publisher/Publication, Place].

38 Mottaz, C.J. 1985. The Relative Importance of Intrinsic and Extrinsic Rewards as Determinants of Work Satisfaction. *The Sociological Quarterly*, 26(3), 365–385. http://dx.doi.org/10.1111/j.1533-8525.1985.tb00233.x

39 Herzberg, F. 1959. *The Motivation to Work*. John Wiley & Sons, New York.

40 Marston, W.M. 1928. Emotions of Normal People. Kegan Paul Trench Trubner And Company, Limited. https://archive.org/details/emotionsofnormal032195mbp/page/n15/mode/2up. Retrieved [Insert date]

41 Pinker, D. [reference]

42 Grazer, B. and Fishman, C. A 2015. *Curious Mind: The Secret to a Bigger life*. Simon & Schuster.

43 Hof, W. [reference]

44 Lok, D. [reference]

45 Collins, JC. 2001. *Good to Great: Why Some Companies Make the Leap and Others Don't*. HarperBusiness.

Kathi Hyde has lived and worked in various countries around the world, achieving an impressive list of firsts. She was lecturing at an internationally recognised university at 21 and making board-level business decisions by 26. At 28 she backpacked solo through Africa and Europe. At 31, she tripled the annual turnover of a Danish multinational operating in East Africa, which gave her a first taste of business possibility  in difficult circumstances. By 35, she'd achieved notable success in the region, addressing obstacles to private sector development as a business owner and on the Chamber of Mines.

Since then, she has had award-winning success on local and international platforms with SME business owners large and small, accompanied by her trademark down-to-earth, practical style; her determination to help others overcome; her substantial knowledge of what makes people tick, and her inimitable sense of humour.

Through her expertise, practical wisdom and impact she has helped her clients overcome setbacks in life and go on to achieve outstanding bottom-line growth, even in impossible times; create more space to enjoy their success and families, and ultimately find the financial freedom to pursue what matters.

Based between Edinburgh (Scotland), Croston (England) and Cape Town (South Africa), Kathi and her husband Neil live with a collie named Joe and an elderly lab Cherry, while tortoiseshell puss-cat Suki stays in Cape Town watching over her beloved daughter, Bryony.

Printed in Great Britain
by Amazon